Finding Me

Finding Me

Viola Davis

EBONY
MAGAZINE PUBLISHING

HARPER LARGE PRINT

An Imprint of HarperCollinsPublishers

Some names have been changed to protect people's privacy.

Thank you to George C. Wolfe for permission to print a monologue from *The Colored Museum* by George C. Wolfe on page 207.

In association with Ebony Magazine Publishing/Lavaille Lavette Books

Unless otherwise noted, all photographs courtesy of the author.

HarperCollins books may be purchased for educational, business, or sales promotional use. For information, please e-mail the Special Markets Department at SPsales@harpercollins.com.

FIRST HARPER LARGE PRINT EDITION

ISBN: 978-0-06-321109-4

Library of Congress Cataloging-in-Publication Data is available upon request.

22 23 24 25 26 LSC 10 9 8 7 6 5 4 3 2

*This book is dedicated to my husband, Julius;
daughter, Genesis;
sisters, Dianne, Deloris, Anita, and Danielle;
mom, Mae Alice; and dad, Dan.*

"*I think human beings must have faith or must look for faith, otherwise our life is empty, empty. To live and not to know why the cranes fly, why children are born, why there are stars in the sky. You must know why you are alive, or else everything is nonsense, just blowing in the wind.*"

—Anton Chekhov

Contents

Chapter 1	Running	1
Chapter 2	My World	14
Chapter 3	Central Falls	38
Chapter 4	128	49
Chapter 5	Minefield	58
Chapter 6	My Calling	73
Chapter 7	The Sisterhood	80
Chapter 8	Secret, Silent, Shame	101
Chapter 9	The Muse	110
Chapter 10	The Starting Block	119
Chapter 11	Being Seen	127
Chapter 12	Taking Flight	138
Chapter 13	The Blooming	158
Chapter 14	Coming Into Me	185
Chapter 15	The Wake-Up	212
Chapter 16	Harnessing Bliss	259
Chapter 17	There She Is	311

Finding Me

Chapter 1
Running

"Cocksucker motherfucker" was my favorite expression and at eight years old, I used it defiantly. I was a spunky, sassy mess and when I spewed that expression, one hand would be on my hip, my middle finger in vast display, and maybe my tongue would be sticking out. If the situation was especially sticky, as backup I would call upon my big sister Anita. She instilled fear in every boy, girl, woman, man, and dog in Central Falls, Rhode Island. She grew her nails to be a better fighter. She was tough, stylish, talented, and well . . . angry. "I'll get my sister Anita to beat yo' ass," I'd say with confidence. But her being three years older than me, she wasn't readily available to protect me.

While Anita was the fashionista fighter who was as loved and adored as she was feared, I was none of those things. I was the ride-or-die friend, competitive but shy. When I won spelling contests, I would flaunt my gold star to everyone I saw. It was my way of reminding you of who the hell I was.

In the third grade, I challenged the fastest boy at Hunt Street School, in Central Falls, to a race at recess. It was the dead of winter and everyone showed up. I had my crew, which was mostly girls, and he had his, which was, well, everybody else. My shoes were two sizes too small and my socks were torn—the part that was supposed to cover my toes. So I took them off and gave them to my friend Rosie who said to me, "Beat his ass!"

I didn't beat him. We tied, which was great for ole underdog me, but humiliating for him. It was bedlam after that. Every kid in the schoolyard started chanting, "Rematch! Rematch!" "C'mon, Chris; you can't let that girl beat you!" I peeked at them in a huddle, laughing, staring at me, whispering, "You can't let that nigga beat you!"

When the teachers heard the commotion and saw my bare feet, I had to stand in the corner. In shame. As if I had done something wrong. Why all the vitriol? I was being bullied constantly. This was one more piece of trauma I was experiencing—my clothes, my hair, my hunger, too—and my home life being the big daddy of them all. The attitude, anger, and competitiveness were my only weapons. My arsenal. And when I tell you I needed every tool of that arsenal every day, I'm not exaggerating.

At the end of each school day, we had to get in line at the back door and wait until the final bell rang. The teacher would open the door, and everyone would dash out to go home. Everyone would get excited because it was the end of the day. Everyone, except me. As much as I could, I would push and shove my classmates, almost clawing my way to the front of the line, not caring in the least if they got pissed at me, because when that bell rang, I had to start running. I had to escape.

A boy in my class who was Cape Verdean, from the Cape Verde Isles off the coast of West Africa, was Black and Portuguese and as Black as I was. But he didn't want to be associated with African Americans, a mindset I later learned was very common among Cape Verdeans in Central Falls. More often than not, they self-identified as Portuguese. They would *kill* you if you called them Black.

So my "Portuguese" classmate and eight or nine white boys in my class made it their daily, end-of-school ritual to chase me like dogs hunting prey. When that end-of-school bell rang, it was off to the races, running literally to save my life. For the gang of boys, it was sadistic-fun time. Every day it was the same madness. The same trauma. Me, taking off like Wilma Rudolph or Flo-Jo, and them tight on my heels.

While chasing me down, they would pick up anything they could find on the side of the road to throw at me: rocks, bricks, tree branches, batteries, pine cones, and anything else their devious eyes spied. But running me down and throwing projectiles at me wasn't enough for them. Their vitriolic screams were aimed at the target of their hate. They threw, "You ugly, Black nigger. You're so fucking ugly. Fuck you!"

Thank God I was fast. I had to run my ass off down Eben Brown Lane, the route I would take because it was a shortcut to get home, an idyllic road that looked like a scene from *The Brady Bunch*. At times, the boys would hide behind houses on that street and I would have to duck and dodge and crisscross. I was being hunted. By the time I got home, I was a snot-dripping, crying mess . . . every day.

One day after a snowstorm the snow was piled so high in the streets anyone could hide behind the giant mounds that seemed to be everywhere. My shoes had huge holes on the bottoms, which meant I couldn't run fast in them because they would make my feet hurt worse than they did already. Because of this, during my daily runs for my life, I would usually take my shoes off, hold them in my hands, and run in bare feet. But with mountains of snow everywhere, I couldn't this time.

As a result, they caught me. And when they did, they held my arms back and took me to their leader, the Cape Verdean boy. I don't mention names because, well . . . their race is way more important in telling this story.

"She's ugly! Black fucking nigger," he said.

My heart was beating so fast. I kept silently praying for someone to come and save me.

And the other voices sounded around me, "What should we do with her?" "Yeah!" "You're, you're, you're fucking ugly!" "You're ugly!" "You're ugly!"

"I don't know why you're saying that to me," I pleaded to the ringleader, the Portuguese boy. "You're Black, too!"

And when I said that, everyone froze and fell deathly silent. For a split second, we were all in a movie, as all the now silent white boys looked at the Portuguese boy, eager to respond to anything he said.

"You're Black, too." I yelled it this time, calling him by name. The gang remained silent. So quiet.

He looked and looked and looked from one white boy to another, frightened and struggling to find a way to hide the truth of what I had just said. The kind of truth that's rooted in a self-hate that we would rather take to our graves. Finally, he screamed in intense anger, "Don't you ever call me fucking Black! I'm not Black! I'm Portuguese!!!" And he punched me in the arm, really hard. He looked down, ashamed at being called out. As if I exposed the ugliest, most painful truth.

"Get outta my face!" Then they threw me in the snow and kicked snow on me. My arm stiffened. It was in pain. I walked home, completely humiliated.

The next day I didn't want to go to school. My mom was doing the laundry in one of those old washing machines where you had to pull the clothes through the wringer.

"What's wrong with you," she asked.

"Mama, those boys want to kill me! They chase me every day after school." After keeping it from her for months, I finally told her about my ongoing daily trauma.

"Vahla"—the southern pronunciation of my name—"don' you run from those bastards anymore. You hear me? Soon as that bell rings you WALK home! They mess with you, you jug 'em."

"Jug" is country for "stab." But if you know what a crochet needle looks like, my mom was actually being ethical. They are not sharp at all! She gave me a crochet needle and told me to keep it in my pocket. It was her shiny blue one.

"Don't come back here crying 'bout those boys or I'll wop yo' ass." She meant it. This was a woman with six kids. She didn't have time to go to school every day and fight our battles. She absolutely needed me to know how to defend myself. Even if she had to threaten me into doing it.

The next day, it took every bone, muscle, and cell in my body to walk after that bell rang. I could hear the voices of the boys behind me. I could feel their rage. The hate. But I walked extra slow. So slow I barely moved. My fingers were wrapped around that shiny blue crochet needle in my pocket. The voices got louder and closer. Finally, I felt one grab my arm violently, and an anger, a finality, an exhaustion came over me. I whispered, "If you don't get your hands off me, I'll jug you." He looked at me terrified, searching my face to see if I meant it. I did. He let me go and the rest of them walked away laughing. The ritual of chasing the nappy-headed Black girl had suddenly lost its luster.

Years later, a conversation I had on the set of *Suicide Squad* with Will Smith was an "aha" moment. Will asked me, "Viola, who are you?"

"What does that mean? I know who I am," I replied with indignant confidence.

He asked again, "No, but who *are* you?"

"What does that mean?" I asked again.

"Look, I'm always going to be that fifteen-year-old boy whose girlfriend broke up with him. That's always going to be me. So, who are you?"

Who am I? I was quiet, and once again that indestructible memory hit me. Then I just blurted it out. "I'm the little girl who would run after school every day in third grade because these boys hated me because I was . . . not pretty. Because I was . . . Black."

Will stared at me as if seeing me for the first time and just nodded. My throat got tight and I could feel the tears welling up. Memories are immortal. They're deathless and precise. They have the power of giving you joy and perspective in hard times. Or, they can strangle you. Define you in a way that's based more in other people's tucked-up perceptions than truth.

There I was, a working actress with steady gigs, Broadway credits, multiple industry awards, and a reputation of bringing professionalism and excellence to any project. Hell, Oprah knew who I was. Yet, sitting there conversing with Will Smith, I was still that little, terrified, third-grade Black girl. And though I was many years and many miles away from Central Falls, Rhode Island, I had never stopped running. My feet just stopped moving.

I had all the brawn in the world but hadn't mastered the courage part. *This* is the memory that defined me.

More than the bed-wetting, poverty, hunger, sexual abuse, and domestic violence. It is a powerful memory because it was the first time my spirit and heart were broken. I defined myself by the fear and rage of those boys. I felt ugly. I felt unwanted, even by God. I wanted so badly to fit into this world, but instead I was being spit out like vomit. Who I was offended them. The memory burrowed itself inside me and metastasized. It didn't help that I was running back to a home where there was no protection. A home that seemed to cement all the horrific things those boys said about me.

At the age of twenty-eight, I woke up to the burning fact that my journey and everything I was doing with my life was about healing that eight-year-old girl. That little third grader Viola who I always felt was left defeated, lying prostrate on the ground. I wanted to go back and scream to the eight-year-old me, "Stop running!"

I wanted to heal her damage, her isolation. That is, until a therapist a few years ago asked me, "Why are you trying to heal her? I think she was pretty tough. She survived."

It hit me like a ton of bricks. I was speechless. What? No poor "little chocolate" girl from Central Falls? She's a survivor?

He leaned forward as if to tell me the biggest secret, or to solve the biggest obstacle of my existence.

"Can you hug her? Can you let her hug YOU?" he asked. "Can you let her be excited about the fifty-three-year-old she is going to become? Can you allow her to squeal with delight at that?"

I sat there with my arms crossed. No way! *I'm* the one who made it out. *I* have the authority. I looked over at the empty space next to me on the couch and saw my younger self so clearly. She sat there waiting . . . to be embraced? To be acknowledged? To be let in.

He leaned toward me, staring at me, tough, stout, insistent, and said, "It's the fifty-three-year-old that needs some help."

Silence is all I could muster by way of response.

"That little girl SURVIVED!!!!!!" he stated emphatically.

I kept my arms crossed. Steely.

He leaned back and waited for those arms to uncross. They never did.

The final stretch to finding me would be allowing that eight-year-old girl in, actively inviting her into every moment of my current existence to experience the joy she so longed for, letting her taste what it means to feel truly alive. The destination is finding a home for her. A place of peace where the past does not envelop the Viola of NOW, where I have ownership of my story.

For my speaking gigs, the title of my presentations

is always the same: "The Journey of a Hero." I learned from writer Joseph Campbell that a hero is someone born into a world where they don't fit in. They are then summoned on a call to an adventure that they are reluctant to take. What is the adventure? A revolutionary transformation of self. The final goal is to find the elixir. The magic potion that is the answer to unlocking HER. Then she comes "home" to this ordinary life transformed and shares her story of survival with others.

That's exactly how I describe my story. As a child, I felt my call was to become an actress. It wasn't. It was bigger than that. It was bigger than my successes. Bigger than expectations from the world. It was way bigger than myself, way bigger than anything I could have ever imagined. It was a full embracing of what God made me to be. Even the parts that had cracks and where the molding wasn't quite right. It was radical acceptance of my existence without apology and with ownership. I saw that young girl so clearly that day in my therapist's office. I could hear her saying, *You are my home. Let me in.*

When she still didn't receive a hug, she got more passionate.

That younger self was sitting there saying, *So, what? You're not going to let me in? I ran my fucking leg of the race! I passed the baton to yo' ass! All those cock-sucker motherfuckas! Shit! I know I was inappropriate, but shit, it got you HERE! Telling those boys to "kiss my Black ass"?!! The crying! The pissin' the bed!!* I still see her sitting, staring, arms to her side with her little 'fro and hand-me-down jeans. Waiting. . . .

My journey was like a war movie, where at the end, the hero has been bruised and bloodied, traumatized from witnessing untold amounts of death and destruction, and so damaged that she cannot go back to being the same woman who went to war.

She may have even seen her death but was somehow resurrected. But to go on THAT journey, I had to be armed with the courage of a lioness.

Man, I'd rather go ten rounds with Mike Tyson than face some inner truths that have lain dormant. Hell, at least with Mike, I can throw the fight. But this inner battle, this inner fight I couldn't throw.

That day in my therapist's office, the goal was clear and repetitive. Individuals on the journey eventually find themselves experiencing a baptism by fire. It's that moment when they are just about to lose their lives, and they miraculously, courageously find the answer that gives their life meaning. And that meaning, that answer, saves them.

In the words of Joseph Campbell, in *The Hero with*

a *Thousand Faces*, "The call to adventure signifies that destiny has summoned the hero. The hero, whether god or goddess, man or woman, the figure in a myth, or the dreamer of a dream, discovers and assimilates his opposites, his own unsuccessful self, either by swallowing it or by being swallowed."

I still see my younger self so clearly from that fateful day in my therapist's office. She stands up, in tears, on a mound of snow. Pissed off, she shouts, "Bitch!!! I'm not going to be swallowed!"

Chapter 2
My World

"Vahla . . . all ya uncles and aunties was in the house eating, dancing, waiting for you to be born."

—MAE ALICE DAVIS

When my mom told me my birth story several years ago, I was quite surprised. It was a healthy, happy memory. "MaMama" (as I call her) has a tendency to spontaneously tell shocking stories: relatives messing around with each other; how she started taking care of her siblings when she was four years old; my father's cheating. Well, buried in the midst of all these fabulously horrid stories, there was a sweet tale—my birth story.

MaMama has two very southern phrases that are a

cause of heavy laughter and a source of great comfort for my siblings and me. One is "Ma" which she calls *us*—her children—as a form of affection. The other is "And stuff like that in tha." She sprinkles this phrase into sentences liberally.

In her South Carolina accent, she said, "Vahla, when you were born and stuff like that in tha, all ya uncles and aunties and stuff like that in tha, everybody was there. They was drinkin' and dancin' and stuff like that in tha, waitin' for you to come. Miss Clara Johnson and stuff like that in tha was late, so ya gran'mama delivered you. Everybody was happy!"

When she first told me, I allowed a long gulf of silence after she finished. I was waiting for the shoe to drop. I was waiting for some unbelievable, traumatic interjection; *something* that interfered with the beauty of it. But the horrible never came. It was a normal, beautiful story of family centered around my arrival in the land of the living. To my shock, my birth story didn't confuse me or induce pain or numbness in the core of my being. It was simply a tale of love and life.

I love that story so much and ask my mom to repeat it often. I mean, a lot. And, every time she retells it, she tops the story off with this wonderful addition: that she ate a sardine, onion, tomato, and mustard sandwich right after she gave birth to me. A disgusting concoction, I know, but she explained, "It was the best sandwich I ever ate." She named me Viola after my great-aunt on my father's side.

On August 11, 1965, in St. Matthews, South Carolina, I was born, the fifth of six children, in my maternal grandmother and grandfather's house on the Singleton Plantation. And yes, it was and still is a plantation. Not a farm. Drive down the long, dusty road leading into the 160 or so acres and you'll come to the big, white, beautiful plantation home. Drive a little farther and there's the tiny, one-room church. An even farther venture will deliver you to the doorsteps of the sharecroppers' houses, outhouses, outdoor showers, and a well.

My maternal grandparents, Mozell and Henry Logan, like the other sharecroppers, had a one-room house with a big fireplace.

Their daughter, MaMama, the oldest of eighteen children, left school after the eighth grade because she got pregnant, but also because she was beaten a lot in school. I mean beaten to where it broke skin and she bled.

My grandmother and my aunt had to go to the school and confront the teacher, who was Black but lighter skinned, and suffering from the all-too-common, intraracial disease of colorism. She was punishing my mom because she was dark-skinned, came from the country, the backwoods, and had nappy hair.

MaMama's family didn't have indoor toilets, showers, or bathrooms. That, mixed with the sheer number of kids, and the desperate poverty, meant she often smelled like piss. Another shame that justified the teacher's fear and anger toward darker-skinned MaMama. Once again, an association of everything that is wrong and negative with skin shade. All I know is, I felt a different level of being heartbroken for my mom when I learned the real driving force behind her decision not to return to school.

My mother pushed on with her life, nonetheless. She was married and had her first child, my brother, John Henry, at age fifteen. She had my sister Dianne when she was eighteen, Anita at nineteen, Deloris at twenty, and me at twenty-two. Years later, at age thirty-four, she had my sister Danielle.

Only eleven of Mozell and Henry Logan's eighteen children survived, MaMama, obviously, being one of them. Several were stillborn, and one my mother constantly talks about died in a fire as a newborn. That baby was named Deloris.

MaMama tells me that she was about four or five years old and had the mammoth responsibility of taking care of her younger siblings. As she tells it, she would take the Binky from her own mouth to put in her brother's mouth. That was how young she was. Like most children at that time, while the adults worked in the fields, the children were left home alone, unattended. Often, they cooked, cleaned, and changed diapers.

She was playing with matches one day in the open fireplace of their wooden shack, and the rug caught fire. It scared MaMama tremendously. She had the presence of mind to grab her younger brother Jimmy and run out of the house. As the house went up in flames, she couldn't reach her younger sister, who was in the back room. When Deloris was found, she was perfectly, beautifully intact, but she had died of smoke inhalation.

"She was a beautiful baby, like a doll," moaned MaMama. Unfortunately, MaMama was blamed for Deloris's death and subsequently beaten by both her father and mother. She says she still has problems to this day with the arm that was beaten.

MaMama tells this story on a loop. Finally, after so many years, I told her, "You know that was not your fault. It was *not* your fault. I'm giving you permission to forgive yourself. Your parents were *wrong* for beating you. It was an accident. You should not have even been in that position."

Painful silence. Then she simply changed the subject. I know MaMama will never forgive herself, even though years later we saw the death certificate that shows MaMama couldn't have been more than three years old, not four or five, when her baby sister died.

I love staring at my mom. I take in every detail of her face, hands, skin. I see all the scars. Some I remember from abuse she endured, and some I don't. The sore left arm. The scar on her right forearm made by my dad ripping her arm open. Scars on her face, legs . . . Scars. I think about the complexity of her childlike heart compared to the ferocious, maternal warrior who would angrily snatch her wig off to kick anybody's ass who even thought about harming her babies.

I think about her bravery in fighting for welfare reform in the 1970s. Getting arrested. Holding us with one arm and waving her fist with the other as we were herded into wagons. Her speaking at Brown University: "I may have had an eighth-grade education and I was nervous, but I spoke." I think of the woman who survived horrific sexual abuse only to marry my dad who was an abuser, yet after many years became a true partner.

All that comes to mind when I look at one of the great loves of my life, my mother, and listen to her retell the same stories.

"That doctor said you were gonna have a water bucket head, a big stomach, and bowlegs," my mom said in between eating bites of rice and drinking her mimosa. She was telling a story of when I was about two years old.

"You was at Memorial Hospital. You was just a baby. They had you all hooked up to machines and all that crust and matter like that in tha around ya eyes and nose. Ya daddy went there to see you and it was the first time I seen him cry like a baby. I knew I had bad milk. The doctor said you weren't going to develop like, you know, normal."

MaMama was visiting my house in Los Angeles telling this story. It was on a day off from shooting *How to Get Away with Murder*. We were in the backyard. I knew the story by heart, but listened anyway.

"He wanted to experiment on you. He said he was gonna break ya legs to see if they grew straight. But I saw how he was looking at me. I ain't dumb. He saw that I was poor and Black. I took you from that hospital. That doctor kept sayin, 'Mrs. Davis, you're making a big mistake!' But I told him he wasn't gonna experiment on my baby. I took you to Miss Cora's house and she made you some lima bean soup, and you ate the whole bowl and drank a big glass of cold water and that was it."

Miss Cora was our distant relative who lived in Prospect Heights, a low-income housing project in Pawtucket, Rhode Island.

"Miss Cora said, 'Ain't nothing wrong with this baby!' And after you ate that soup you hugged Miss Cora's leg and wouldn't let go."

I just listen, always silent. I have a vague memory of this moment hugging Miss Cora's leg, feeling gratefulness, but just that moment.

"I know that doctor's not alive now cuz this was when you were a baby. But I wish he could see you now," she says, as always, with a great burst of joy, smiling, laughing. "You ain't got no bowlegs or big stomach. Ya head is big, but that's what make you a good actor!"

"Vahla, make ya mama another one of these memeesas or . . . you know what I mean." No matter what, I cannot get her to remember "mimosa" so I stopped trying because I sort of enjoy it.

I run to make her another mimosa—more juice than champagne—anxiously getting up the courage to ask a very risqué question. Anything to ply secrets from her. The "water bucket head hospital story" is one of her favorites. I grew up hating it. I let her get it out of the way before I ask her something more challenging. One of the beauties of getting older is really getting to know a parent.

"Uhh . . . Mom . . . did you ever have an affair? Fall in love with someone else? Did you have an affair with Howie?"

Howie was a really nice white guy who lived on the second floor of 128 Washington Street, an apartment building we lived in. Every time my father would beat my mom, she would run to Howie's apartment. He would wash her wounds and let my mom hide out in his apartment until my dad calmed down. Picture the stereotypical '70s hippie. That was Howie. He would play the guitar for us and give us candy. Just regular candy; no hippie "additives."

"No, Vahla. I nevah did nothin' with Howie. He was just a nice guy. Ya daddy always accused me of messin' with him."

I have to say, I was disappointed with that one. I was waiting for not only something salacious but sort of wanted my mom to have some story where she harnessed her joy, desires, or a tiny bit of happiness, even if it was from an affair.

She took another sip. "But I did fall in love with my gynecologist."

I perked up. "OHHH! Really!"

"Vahla, I was pregnant with Danielle and, ya know, he was taking care of me, listening to me. I was so sensitive at that time, and he was so nice."

I waited for more but that was it. She had feelings for a man who cared for her. As stubborn as a bull, as innocent as a child, and loyal even when she has been abandoned. Thank God for mimosas, or as MaMama calls them, "memeesas."

When I was young, I thought, perhaps arrogantly, that I could do better than my mom. I was going to slay dragons. Be stronger and more confident. I wasn't going to run from bad memories. I would be a "hero," an overcomer.

But you know the saying, "Show me a hero and I'll show you a tragedy." As a theater geek, I learned that tragedies always end with the downfall of the hero. Everyone who was influenced by them, who benefits from them, who relies on them is crushed in their downfall. Heroes always cause their own downfall, like Oedipus. I didn't want to cause my own downfall. I didn't want to move through my life and not be accountable for recklessness. I wanted to be aware of my Achilles heel. I believed *awareness* was what would release my blessings. I had no idea the mammoth task I was asking the universe.

In one of my mother's episodes of dropping spontaneous and extremely important facts, without warning or context, she told me that although she has gone by Mary Alice Davis for most of her life, her real name is actually Mae. "M-A-E," she always says, "not M-A-Y." She renamed herself Mary early in life because all the girls in the country were named Mae, and she didn't want to be like everyone else. How badass is that!

The woman I tried so hard not to be was the muse sitting on my shoulder in *How to Get Away with Murder*. She didn't tell me or my sisters about her name change until much later in life. I was thirty-five when I found out. It wasn't a legal change, just a personal one. When she told me, it was absolutely not a confession, but a correction. It was almost as if she was insulted that I said her name wrong. I was sending her money via Western Union, like I always did. "Vahla! Stop writing Mary!! My name ain't Mary! It's Mae. M-A-E! You keep writing my name wrong!"

Silence. "MaMama, what're you talking about? You've always been Mary: Mary Alice Davis."

"Vahla! I've always been Mae. I just never liked that name. Everyone in the country was named Mae."

"I . . . I . . . I'm confused."

"But my ID says 'Mae,' so send it to 'Mae Alice Davis.'"

Silence.

"Vahla?! You heard what ya mama said, didn't you?"

"Uhh. Yeah. Sure, Ma." I just went with it. As confused as I was, I didn't want to ask questions because she didn't seem to be open to it. Plus, she would whoop my ass when I saw her next. I'm not kidding. Two generations removed from slavery, as docile as she appeared at times, she had a brutal right hook. So I didn't bring up that her sister's name was Mary, an interesting sidebar to her name change from "Mae" to "Mary."

As much as I try to chisel into MaMama to get at the core of who she is, I never can. There are decades of suppressed secrets, trauma, lost dreams and hopes. It was easier to live under that veil and put on a mask than to slay them.

Unlike my mother, my father was a simpler man. Dan Davis was born in 1936 in St. Matthews, South Carolina. As far as I know, he had two sisters. For the life of me I can't remember, but he had, I believe, a poor relationship with his stepfather, whose last name was Duckson.

Daddy says his education went as far as fifth grade, but evaluating his penmanship over the years, I would say my father's formal education ended closer to second grade. He may not have been educated, but he was not a dumb man. Illiterate at fifteen, he learned to read because his friend taught him by looking at billboards on the side of the road.

At fifteen, after years of abuse, he ran away from

home to work as a horse groomer at racetracks around the country. He groomed some of the greatest race-horses in history, and yet he hated the work. MaMama woefully says that my father never groomed Secretariat. We still have photos of him in the winner's circle because the groom was nearly always in the picture when a horse won.

I loved going to work with my father when I was younger. I loved being around the horses. Even the smell of the manure, hay, and horse food excited me. Looking at the horses in their stables, and feeding them with my father is a happy memory.

When the owners came and directed my father about how to brush the horses and how to feed them, the atmosphere transformed into something very different. When my father was around those men, it was almost as though he was a slave and they were masters. He would be juggling five tasks at once. The huge syringe with vitamin shots for the horse, the different mixtures of feed, the grooming brushes and hay. They had no understanding of how much they were asking him to do at any given moment. I could feel his frustration, his anger. But what choice did he have?

To make matters worse, grooms were barely paid a living wage. Imagine hauling your family from the South with all the hope in the world that you could do better. Yet all you have, all that you can do is not good enough to keep them alive and functioning. I could tell he was happy that I had witnessed the difficulties of his job. It was a way, I think, for him to validate that what was happening to him was real.

But my father, whom we called "MaDaddy," was more than his work. He was a great storyteller. Dad was also a pretty good guitar and harmonica player. He absolutely loved soul, jazz, and the blues, especially BB King.

Because MaDaddy is gone now, I will never know what demons caused him to run away from his home at fifteen. As much as I love my father, I know those demons haunted him his entire life. They embedded themselves deep within him and boiled into rage and alcoholism. That rage was usually released on payday.

I've always been an introvert, and when I was young, I was extremely shy. At an early age, I became a keen observer of the world around me. I blended into the wall in almost every setting, and I was able to see without saying a thing. What I saw in my father was a man who, alone and single, could've kept his check and spent it all on women and booze. But he wasn't alone. During my childhood my father had five children to feed (minus my sister Danielle who is almost twelve years younger than me). Every penny he worked for had to go to us. Even with the hard labor, enduring the disrespect from white horse owners, it was never enough.

So, he raged.

He had open affairs. The only "other woman" I vividly remember was Patricia. Patricia was a very large woman who lived near Railroad Street in Central Falls. Railroad Street was at the edge of town, which was only a square mile. He would take me over there and always give me a dollar or seventy-five cents in quarters to not tell MaMama where we were going.

"Okay, Daddy," I'd say, excitedly taking the money. I was no more than five or six.

My dad was always very well-dressed, and at various times would have a nice car. The car he had at this time was a convertible. Don't ask me how he was able to afford the car, but I do think of this time period as the "good years," financially speaking.

We would get to Patricia's apartment and she answered the door naked, which absolutely traumatized me. Shut me right down. She in no way attempted to cover up, neither her naked ass nor her ill intentions with my father. Rather, she ran into my father's arms, kissing him and giggling. "Oh, Dan! Is this your baby?" I wanted to say, *Heifer, I'm MaMama's baby! Not yours!* I hated her. My father would just say, "Go downstairs and wait for ya daddy."

Patricia would then close the door in my face, giggling.

I hated going downstairs. They wanted me to play with this little girl who was my age. She had the best toys, but she never wanted to play with me. She never wanted me to touch her toys, and her mom would come out and shoo me away. I ended up just sitting there by myself, wanting my mom more than ever.

My father would emerge after a long time and repeat, "Don't tell ya mama where we been."

As soon as we got home my mom asked, "Where y'all been?"

"We were at Patricia's house! Daddy gave me seventy-five cents to not tell," I blurted.

My daddy would roll his eyes and all hell would break loose.

The affair with Patricia ended when MaMama found out he was at the local bar with her. She told us that she would be right back. She left our apartment and went down to the bar and slapped the piss out of Patricia, who fell right off the barstool. My father was livid and slapped my mom.

Ironically, Patricia wrote my mom a letter explaining what a "no good asshole" my daddy was. She kept the letter under her mattress for a long time and would pull it out to read. It would always make her depressed.

My sisters and I would read it as well. In my fantasy, I always imagined her exploring what the hell to do with this information. I wish that MaMama could have acquired the tools to imagine a life free from that sort of pain. Rejecting everything her family had instilled in her about marriage and never giving up, never leaving your man even if he cheats, putting up with abuse. I imagined that if she had the language and the wherewithal, she would've simply said, "Help me." "Guide me." But even grown with multiple children, she was still that little fifteen-year-old Black girl from the backwoods of South Carolina who got pregnant and married before she could legally drive.

My older sister Dianne retells a story of my mom and dad having a fight outside. My dad was screaming, "Mae Alice! You want me to stay or leave? Tell me? You want me to stay or go?" My sister was sending telepathic messages in her mind, *Please tell him to go! Tell him to go, Mama!* But MaMama just screamed, "I want you to stay!" It was a choice that had resounding repercussions. Abuse elicits so many memories of trauma that embed themselves into behavior that is hard to shake. It could be something that happened forty years ago, but it remains alive, present.

Like I said, Mae Alice has a heart that simply is loyal. It attaches and asks for nothing in exchange. She shows her claws only when those she loves need protection or to protect who she feels belongs to her. She never raises her fist for . . . her. There is a very flimsy barrier between the asshole predators, abusers, and my mom. She is a "self-sacrificer" at the expense of her own joy.

My dad came home from the bar one night and collapsed inside our doorway. My mom screamed, "Y'all go to bed!!"

She helped him to their bed. He had been stabbed in the back. His lower back on the left-hand side. I got up to peek. My mom took his shirt off and used a rag and peroxide to wipe the blood. It was deep and tissue was hanging out. He kept moaning and saying, "Mae Alice, don't call the ambulance. Don't, Mae Alice."

My mom finally just stood over the bed and cried. I remember coming and standing next to her. She put her arms around me and said, "I can't do nothin'. I can't do nothin'!" We just stood there and I remember waiting for him to die. I imagined what our lives would be like without him. I imagined a life with no more drunken rages and the constant abuse of my mom. I secretly felt how much better our lives would be. The next day, he was better. Death wouldn't come until 2006, and man, my prayers at that time were different. Every last breath he took, I took with him.

Coming from St. Matthews, South Carolina, an area influenced by the Gullah culture of the Sea Islands, my father, as well as my mother, grew up believing in "haints," evil spirits or ghosts.

My father made haints present in our lives. We could not sweep over by his feet or he'd become livid, saying it meant he'd go to jail. He said he had already gone to jail for stabbing a guy who pulled his shirt over his head. We couldn't pass by a gravestone without crossing ourselves—performing the "Catholic" sign of the cross—or else the deceased person would not rest in peace. We'd have to spit on our finger, dig it in the dirt, and pass the grave again. We couldn't stare at ourselves in the mirror for very long in the dark, without turning on the light, or we would turn into a monster. If we woke up in the morning drowsy, not yet moving or speaking, my father would run into our room, and ask, "What's wrong? What's wrong?" Before we could answer, he'd say, "The witch is ridin' the broom. It's the haints. I, I, I got it."

He'd get paper or cloth, sprinkle on salt and pepper, and wave it over us to get the witch to ride off. Of course, as we fully woke and started to slowly move around, that was proof to Daddy that he had warded off the haints. Victoriously, he would delve deeper: "What happened? Did ya have a bad thought about a old person who passed by ya?" Deloris or I would mention the hairy, old man down the street whom we thought looked like a monster. Mr. Miacca to be exact.

Mr. Miacca was a fictitious character in a Joseph Jacobs folktale (collected in his *English Fairy Tales*) who ate little boys for supper. Every time this man passed by us, we would whisper to our baby sister, Danielle, "Danielle!! Here he comes. Mister Miacca!" It would send chills up her spine and whatever bad thing she was doing she would stop immediately.

"That's it. That's it!" Daddy would say, again waving the salt-and-peppered paper over us. "Stop fuckin' wit' that man! You understand me? Stop even thinking bad thoughts about him!!"

Because of Daddy, the myth of haints was part of our lives. Haints, which are also mentioned in *To Kill a Mockingbird*, were my parallel growing up to the Furies I later learned about in Greek theater. The Furies are goddesses in Greek tragedies who come from the Underworld to exact vengeance on a person who has done wrong. The purpose of Furies was to make the person accountable for their wrongdoing, even their part in generational curses. Daddy's haint rituals reminded us to hold ourselves accountable. They bridged spaces that helped us learn to navigate life. They were interesting guideposts, of which I was never skeptical, until I was a teen. I bought into haints 100 percent until it didn't make sense to me anymore. As I grew away from my parents, I tried to be my own person, dispelling what I'd been taught.

I had two parents who were running away from bad memories. Both had undiscovered dreams and hopes. Neither had tools to approach the world to find peace or joy. MaMama worked sporadically in factories and was a gambler.

My father was an alcoholic and would disappear for months at a time when we were really young. He always came back, but by the time I was five I never re-member him leaving for any long periods of time. Only later did I realize he was numbing, which is absolutely without question an understandable solution to dealing with a fucked-up world. Then, he would come back, from who knows where, and beat MaMama. Lashing out instead of lashing in.

He was inaccessible to us for most of my childhood. I did not know how to reach him. He was the first man who loved me. Picked me up from school during lunch breaks before we had lunch in school. He would take me to a great mom-and-pop restaurant for wieners, hot dogs with ground meat, onions, and celery salt on top. He would put a quarter in the mechanical horsey machines and let me ride and smile from ear to ear and then drive me back to school. He loved me. That I know. But his love and his demons were fighting for space within, and sometimes the demons won.

One of the many defining memories of my dad is when I was fourteen. We were living at 4 Park Street, a two-story, two-family house. The upper floor had no electricity or heat, but at least it was two stories and we had the whole house. My baby sister, Danielle, was about one and a half years old. I would die for her. She was the most precious gift to all of us.

Well, my mom and dad were fighting. I never knew about what. Most of the time the fights just started because my dad wanted to vent. They were facing each other screaming and my dad picked up a glass. I grabbed my sister Danielle with one arm and put my other arm between my parents willing them to stop. None of my other sisters were home. My older sister Dianne left me a stern warning, "If they start fighting this time try to stop them." Up until this time, we had never tried to stop them for fear it would get worse, because it would. With my arm between them I was gently saying, "Please, Daddy, stop."

It didn't work. "Tell me I won't bust yo' head open, Mae Alice? Tell me I won't?"

Then he just swung his hand and smashed the glass on the side of my mom's head and I saw the glass slice the upper side of her face near her eye and blood just squirted out. A lot of blood. I couldn't anymore. I just couldn't passively stand by as he lifted his hand to swing again. I yelled, "Stop! You just stop right now, Daddy! Give me the glass! Give it to me!" I saw my hand shaking uncontrollably. My heart was in my throat. I was immersed in fear.

He stood staring at my mom, wanting to swing again. My dad never looked at me. He kept his hand gripped on the glass, staring at my mom. His eyes bloodshot wanting so bad to hit her again. I screamed, "Give it to me!" Screaming as if the louder I became the more my fear would be released. And he gave me the glass and walked away. I took the glass and hid it, and my body felt like I had just been beaten up or ran thirty miles.

I had to stand up to my father, the authority figure. The one who should be taking the glass from ME, teaching ME right from wrong. The most frightening figure in my life and the first man we all ever loved. Frightening? Without knowing, I had already been imprinted, stamped by their behavior and all that they were. As much as I wanted my life to be better, the only tools I had to navigate the world were given to me by them. How they talked. How they fought. How my mom made concessions. How they loved and who they loved shaped me. If I didn't bust out of all that, would this exhaustion and depletion be what I would feel after every fight in my life, even the small ones?

That fight marked the beginning of my shift. Looking back on that night when I stood up to my dad and wiped up my mom's blood, I knew my life would be a fight. And I realized this: I had it in me.

Chapter 3
Central Falls

"Central Falls! Central Falls! Brave Courageous and Bold! Long live our name and long live our glory and long may our story be told."

—MOTTO OF CENTRAL FALLS HIGH SCHOOL

Two months after I was born, my parents moved to Central Falls, taking their three youngest kids, Anita, Deloris, and me, and leaving their two oldest, Dianne and John, with my mother's parents. Dianne and John were raised by my grandparents for years until my mom could no longer stand to hear the stories of them being beaten in school. My parents sent for them to come to Central Falls.

Central Falls, Rhode Island, was a square-mile town

with a single claim to fame—one of the most densely populated cities per square mile in the United States. Central Falls also had more bars and churches in its borders than any other city. Central Falls, by 1985, was named the cocaine capital because one of the largest drug stings of all time happened in its streets.

The sweet story, the idyllic story, was that it was once called Chocolateville because of the number of chocolate factories in town. To the naked eye, Central Falls seemed bucolic. There were several parks in Central Falls, but our favorite playground was at Jenks Park because of Cogswell Tower, the site where Native American scouts witnessed the approach of Captain Michael Pierce. This episode was a key part of King Phillip's war, an armed battle from 1675 to 1678 between the Native Americans of New England and New England colonists.

We moved there because two of the biggest racetracks in the country were in Rhode Island. There was the Lincoln Downs in Lincoln, and the Narragansett Racetrack in Narragansett, affectionally called Gansett.

Mom-and-pop shops lined the streets of Central Falls. Sarah's Restaurant had big wooden bench booths with high backs that fascinated me. Sarah's had homemade rice pudding, corn muffins fried with heaps of butter, and the best hamburgers in town. Saint Vincent de Paul (also known as the Salvation Army) located on Washington Street had used clothes, shoes, toys, knick-knacks, and furniture. It was our favorite playground of affordable leftovers.

Across the street from St. Vincent de Paul's was Gabe's Store, or, as we called it, Antar's. We have plenty of loving memories at that store, but complicated ones as well. Loving because the owner, Gabe Antar, who was Syrian, was very kind to our family. It was a wonderful grocery store, stocked with everything you could possibly need. Whenever we were really hurting, he would give us a line of credit so that we could buy food. It was complicated, though, because oftentimes, MaMama and MaDaddy would ask Gabe for monetary loans.

Gabe kept a notebook under the cash register with a tally of what various neighborhood families owed him. Some of my most embarrassing memories are going to the store with a piece of paper, on which my mother had written how much money she needed. Sometimes, the embarrassment was so great that my sister Deloris and I would tear up the paper and refuse to hand him the charity request. Instead, we would just tell my mom that Gabe denied the loan. And sometimes when we asked Gabe, he would, in frustration, throw money at us because my parents had not paid their outstanding debts. This nice man would fly into a rage and scream, "Get out!" We would pick the money off the floor, humiliated, and walk out completely defeated.

When we were really hungry, though, Gabe's was the easiest store to steal food from. Much later in life, I found out that Gabe had lost his son in Vietnam. It probably explained the frustration and sadness in his eyes. It might have also accounted for how kind he was to us as kids, and why he helped us when he saw our need. Our relationship with him was filled with love and appreciation mixed with the shame of having to cling so desperately to his willing kindness, which was all too often a lifesaver. When you're clutching to live, morals go out the window.

We were "po." That's a level lower than poor. I've heard some of my friends say, "We were poor, too, but I just didn't know it until I got older." We were poor and we *knew* it. There was absolutely no disputing it. It was reflected in the apartments we lived in, where we shopped for clothes and furniture—the St. Vincent de Paul—the food stamps that were never enough to fully feed us, and the welfare checks. We were "po." We almost never had a phone. Often, we had no hot water or gas. We had to use a hot plate, which increased the electric bill. The plumbing was shoddy, so the toilets never flushed. Actually, I don't ever remember toilets working in our apartments. I became very skilled at filling up a bucket and pouring it into the toilet to flush it. And with our gas constantly being cut off because of nonpayment, we would either go unwashed or would just wipe ourselves down with cold water. And even the wiping down was a chore because we were often without towels, soap, shampoo. . . . I damn sure didn't know the difference between a washcloth and a bath towel.

One of our first apartments was 128 Washington Street. My sisters and I ominously refer to it as "128." "128" is code for "Hell"! When we first moved in, it was a normal apartment. I was five years old at the time. There was a tailor on the ground level. And on the third floor where we lived was a nice little porch. The building was old, probably built in the '20s or '30s, but it had been kept in fairly good condition. But then the tailor moved out, and very quickly the building became condemned.

The tailor's business was boarded up. Without attention, the wiring became dangerously unstable. There were several fires, and the building soon became infested with rats. In fact, the rats were so bad, they ate the faces off my dolls.

I never, *ever* went into the kitchen. Rats had taken

over the cabinets and the counter. The plaster was constantly falling off the wall, revealing the wooden boards holding the house together.

We had to go to the laundromat to wash clothes. But having no money, five kids, and freezing cold weather meant that most of the time laundry would go unwashed for weeks. That, compounded with the bedwetting, made for a home with a horrific smell. Closets and space underneath the beds would be stuffed with shoes, dust, miscellaneous items. We were afraid of even cleaning for fear rats would be lurking underneath all the "rubbish." On the first day of the month food stamps would come and we would make a huge grocery run at BIG G market. In less than two weeks, the food would be gone.

A short time after we moved in, I remember Mayor Bessette came to the apartment and made a big speech in our living room, saying he was giving us the apartment for free. We didn't have to pay any rent. That was because the building was condemned. In a year, the city planned to tear it down to build a school. Mayor Bessette sent someone to the apartment who knocked a hole through one of the walls that led to the apartment next door, creating a makeshift doorway. That apartment next door never had any heat or electricity. Never. Even in the short spans that our apartment had heat and electricity, the one next door never did. But we had that space.

We used it for bedrooms, running extension cords from the apartment that had electricity. Months later, I went to Mayor Bessette's house to sing Christmas carols. It was on the other side of town, the part where the rich folk lived, or the people who had a little bit of money. His house seemed to have forty-foot ceilings, a fireplace, a huge staircase, and a Christmas tree that was the largest I'd ever seen in my life. The heat from the house just whooshed out at us, we who were shivering in the freezing cold.

"128" might as well be the code name for "the dungeon" for my sisters and me, although our time there was also speckled with good memories. My oldest sister, Dianne, had remained in South Carolina with my grandparents. She was growing up in segregated schools where the education was substandard, and dark-skinned students were frequently beaten with switches until they were bloody simply for refusing to be born "high yellow" or "Red Bone."

Two years after we moved to Central Falls, my mom and dad finally said, "We got to raise our own kids," and saved enough money to move my sister Dianne and my brother, John, to Central Falls with us. Dianne was nine when she entered Broadstreet School, the same school where I was in kindergarten. It went from kindergarten to sixth grade. MaMama took her to enroll in fourth grade.

After testing, her reading and math skills were marked so substandard she couldn't be placed in the fourth grade. Mr. Fortin, the fourth-grade teacher, who always wore a nice suit and black-rimmed glasses and slicked back his hair, said the school would keep her in the third grade. Dianne remembers saying to Mr. Fortin, "If you work with me every day after school, I promise I'll show you I can be in fourth grade."

Mr. Fortin said, "I'll do it." And he kept his word. Every day after school she stayed, and he would sit right there with her. Dianne told us, "Because I'm the oldest, everything that I learn, I'll teach you guys when I get home so you'll be ahead."

We bought a secondhand school desk from the St. Vincent de Paul. The chair was attached to the desk and had little beams on it. They really bought it for me. I would sit in it while Dianne taught us what she learned in school. I was mischievous in the crappiest way in school because I was bored. I'd say, "I already know this. My sister Dianne already taught me the multiplication tables." Bored, I wanted to have a conversation, I wanted to play. "I already know how to write in cursive. My sister Dianne taught me."

Dianne had another gift. She was a fantastic story-teller, like our dad, and could transport you to another reality simply with the power of her words. We would all sit down and clap, "Dianne. Tell us a story. Tell us a story." She would stand in front of us and captivate us. A lot of her stories were anecdotes about her life down south, what that was like. Others were fables she made up, similar to ones told down south, fables of haints, witches, and old folklore. We totally believed.

The story I remember her telling us the most was, "One night, we heard something in the woods behind ma granmama's house," Dianne started. We all were sitting on the floor in the kitchen at 128. She would always stand. "I could hear it in the trees. I went out there to see what it was because everyone was scared. It was so dark, you couldn't see your hands in front of your face. I didn't even know what was in the woods." That part always scared me.

"I heard a knocking and looked up, down and saw drops of blood everywhere! I went farther and saw Uncle Arnold." Uncle Arnold was our closest uncle. "His legs were way over there! His arms were even farther away. His body was in the middle and his head was not even attached to his neck. I was in shock! I started screaming and then put my hands on my hips and looked at his head and I said, 'Arnold! Pull yourself together!'" When we heard the punch line, we would fall out laughing our asses off. I would always scream, "Again, Dianne! Tell it again!"

When I met Dianne for the first time, it was a rare occasion when we had hot water. I was maybe five years old. Dianne was nine when she walked into our lives in Central Falls. I remember her so clearly: she wore a nice coat; she had money; she smelled nice. I was taking a bath and allegedly fussing about getting dressed when I heard Dianne say, "Where's my baby sister?"

She came into the bathroom. I looked at her and she stared at me. It was love. In my child brain, part of the love was her offer to buy me candy from Gabe's store. As an adult, though, I recognize there was something more important that made me love her.

She looked around at the disheveled apartment. "Viola, you don't want to live like this when you get older, do you?" she asked in a whisper. She didn't want my mom to hear.

"No, Dianne."

"You need to have a really clear idea of how you're going to make it out if you don't want to be poor for the rest of your life. You have to decide what you want to be. Then you have to work really hard," she whispered.

I remember thinking, *I just want candy*. I couldn't understand the abstract. I was too young. But something I didn't have the words for, yet could feel, shifted inside me. "What do I want to be?" The first seed had been planted.

Was there a way out?

Achieving, becoming "somebody," became my idea of being alive. I felt that achievement could detox the bad shit. It would detox the poverty. It would detox the fact that I felt less-than, being the only Black family in Central Falls. I could be reborn a successful person. I wanted to achieve more than what my mother had.

From age five, because of Dianne, re-creation and reinvention and redefinition became my mission, although I could not have articulated it. She simply was my supernatural ally. Much later, after college, Juilliard, Broadway stages; after first being nominated for awards—Emmy, Oscar, Tony—I could finally actually articulate what that big moment was, prompted by my sister that day. It was the catalyst or agent that provoked a larger question: "Aren't I somebody NOW?" What do I have to do to be worthy? That moment, that revelation, was the true beginning to my call to adventure.

Chapter 4
128

"He who has a 'why' to live for can bear
with almost any 'how.'"

—Friedrich Nietzsche

When I was six, my three older sisters, my brother—although my brother was almost never around—and I loved going to school. School was our haven. It was right next door and we were big on school, especially my sister Dianne. She absolutely loved school. She never wanted to miss a day.

It was the dead of winter and we had no heat. Next, the electricity was cut off. And then we had no phone. It just kept escalating. When you have no heat, no gas, you have no hot water. . . . It was subzero weather.

Freezing. Absolutely freezing. And the pipes froze, so there was no running water. We couldn't even flush the toilet. To make matters worse, we were all extreme bed wetters. Not going to school was unheard of for us, but that day we all stayed home. I remember sitting in the living room all day in subzero weather, all huddled together, pissy, freezing, watching my mom.

Mama was lost. Just lost. Didn't know what to do. No running water. Pipes frozen. No heat. No phone. We clutched together, all shivering, and somewhere around midday my sister Dianne stood up and announced, "I'm going to school." She spat on her hand. She wiped all the mucus out of her eyes, and she asked, "How do I look?"

MaMama said, "You look good, ma," using her southern term. "You look beautiful, ma."

"Okay. All right, I'm going to school." And she went.

The rest of us were still there shivering when MaMama finally said, "We're going to have to go and try to get some heat assistance."

We layered on every item of clothing we could find. Even on the best days, we never had the right size shoes or clothes. A lot of times, we couldn't even find socks. We almost never had clothes that were new. Every once in a while, we would go to Zayre's, a clothing store like J.C. Penney back in the day, and get something on layaway.

For the most part, we went to St. Vincent de Paul. We loved going there because it was an adventure sorting through everybody else's used stuff. Everything seemed to have a story: books, old toys, roller skates, Skippy's sneakers, even fur coats and furniture.

That frigid day, we put on whatever we had and started out into the cold. The heating assistance offices were in downtown Pawtucket, one town over. Mom, Deloris, Anita, and I walked in freezing, subzero weather. I was still the youngest at that time, and I would cry in a minute—I was a total crybaby. As we started walking, I howled in tears. When we walked by the school on our way, the principal of the school, Mrs. Prosser, saw us. She was a great woman, tall and thin, with bright red hair. She always looked so regal to me and was both powerful and kind. She saw *me*.

Mrs. Prosser would call me to her office, and whenever she did, I would think, *Oh my God. What did I do?* because I was really a troublemaker. Even when I hadn't done anything wrong, I would wait for the shoe to drop. But often she would call me to her office and shower me with bags of hand-me-downs that belonged to her daughter, really cute clothes and little purses. I would wear them to school and just stand in the schoolyard during recess and pose in the clothes she had gifted me as if to say, *Look at me!* It was like I was demanding or begging for attention, positive attention, not wanting anyone to touch my perfectly put together outfit.

Mrs. Prosser knew our situation. When she saw us, she yelled from the window, "Mrs. Davis, Mrs. Davis." MaMama stopped. We were huddled together, shivering when the principal ran out. She was so desperate to get to us that Mrs. Prosser didn't even have a coat on. "Mrs. Davis, your kids aren't in school. What's going on?"

"We don't have no heat, no electricity. We ain't got nothing. And the pipes froze. There's no running water. They can't even wash up. We can't do nothing."

"Oh, Mrs. Davis, I'm so sorry. I'm so sorry." Tears welled in her eyes as she looked at us and she touched my face. "I'm so sorry. I wish there was something we could do."

"We're going to downtown Pawtucket to see if I can get someone to help us to pay the bills."

"Okay. Well, just let us know if there's anything we can do. I'm so sorry. I just wanted to know why your kids weren't in school."

That period of my life was filled with shame. The feeling you get in the pit of your stomach when you have stage fright or humiliation, that was the shame of 128. Shame completely eviscerates you, destroys any sense of pride you may have in yourself.

One day in class I had to use the bathroom real bad and I just kept my hand raised but the teacher never acknowledged me. I couldn't hold it anymore so I peed in my seat. It dripped on the floor and flooded my seat. My teacher got me a dry pair of pants from the nurse's office, put my wet clothes in a paper bag, and sent me home. But the most humiliating part of this was coming back the next day to find my desk in a back corner of the classroom with the same big puddle of urine still in my seat. It stayed there until it slowly dried up. What? My six-year-old piss was too disgusting for even the janitor to clean.

I was embarrassed a lot, and 128 only heightened that sense of humiliation. Our apartment building caught fire so many times. The first time it caught fire, I was in first grade. All the kids in school peered out their classroom windows at the red fire truck in front of the building right next door to school. We watched firefighters reel out the hose pipe and spray streams of water in the building, smoke billowing out.

I heard an orchestra of voices:

"Oh my God!"
"There's a fire!"
"Who lives there?"
"That's Viola's house."

The teacher, Ms. Picard, stared at me. "Viola, is that your house?"

I'm in my schoolroom with my first-grade classmates, who already looked down at me for being Black, now looking out at my home burning. "Yeah," I answered, watching as firefighters ran inside of my building with hoses. I did not know if it was our apartment that caught fire. It was a perfect metaphor for the devastation I felt in my heart. Because the source of my deepest shame was now a source of horrified entertainment for people who had exiled me from the day they met me.

When I went home that day, the entire apartment was in disarray. It *was* our apartment that had caught fire. The fire damage was extensive, but the water damage was worse. The very water that the firefighters had sprayed into our house to save it also destroyed it. The linoleum was warped, bloated and curved like waves across the floor. Looking at the remains of our apartment, I thought not even the firefighters had respect for the place we called home. I knew it was shit. But it was *my* shit. It was my home.

So many of the fires were uneventful. I was awakened in the middle of the night, led down a dark and smoky stairway, and stood for a long time, sleepy, with my hair wrapped up. The source of the fire would be found and order was restored, so we went upstairs and back to bed.

Then there were times when Millie, our next-door neighbor, would come banging on the door, "Dan! Dan! Get ya kids outta the house! The house is on fire!"

Millie was Black and she had a daughter named Kim and a son, Reggie, who had been in Vietnam. Kim was a fast friend. She and my sister Anita were especially close, until they weren't. Millie was one of those cigarette-smoking, hard-core, cuss-you-out-in-a-minute, light-skinned Black women. She was also the town crier.

"Dan! Get your kids out! This fuckin' house is on fire! You can't go down the stairs; there's too much smoke!"

My father yelled and woke us all up. Black smoke was coming up the stairs and we were all on the third floor.

"Y'all go to the fire escape!" My father pushed us to the porch and everyone frantically started climbing down. Now, we were all experienced fire escape climbers. We were experienced climbers in general. We climbed the fire escape when we were locked out of the house. We climbed fences to pick apples, peaches, and pears from neighbors' yards without permission. But climbing under duress when you are convinced you're going to die is a different story.

Well, the fire trucks were there and the firefighters

had already taken their hoses out. People lined the street, just looking and gasping. My family jumped off the fire escape one after another like the Incredibles. Only one, lone family member was left behind on the last landing. Me.

I just stood there crying my eyes out. "Mama!"

My mom, dad, and siblings were all screaming, "Viola! Jump! Just jump!" My mom was in an absolute panic. She started crying hysterically, "Baby! Jump to ya mama!"

I squatted down with my arms outstretched trying to reach her because I was terrified to jump. It was just too high. I imagined flames behind me, ready to engulf me at any minute, like Dumbo when he had to jump off that wire, but I just didn't have those big ears that could help me fly. But, as sure as I'm Black, I saw my mom fly.

She took about five big steps back, ran, and just at the right moment, leapt in the air like Michael Jordan, grabbed my arm, and pulled me down. We both fell on the concrete together. She screamed in pain! My father picked her up and we just held on to each other, tight. My sisters just slapped me on the head. "Stupid. You shoulda jumped! It wasn't that high. Mom almost got hurt." I just watched my mom limping and saw my sisters and brother looking shell-shocked, lost, waiting for the fire department to clear us to go back into that hellhole. It was just a roof over our heads. Nothing about it was home.

The truth is no one cares. No one looking at the fire was aware of my little "dumb show" and there were no flames. We stayed at 128 for another two years. And yes, it remained a firetrap. But in my mind, no one cares about the conditions in which the unwanted live. You're invisible, a blame factor that allows the more advantaged to be let off the hook from your misery.

At 128, the fires simply got more frequent. The rats multiplied. The first landing stairway had holes leading straight to the basement. A family of eight kidnapped children and two female guardians moved in on the second floor and many bloodied fights, scars, and stitches were a part of our day-to-day life.

Still, in the midst of the life shitstorm, there was one teeny, tiny light. A guide. A whisper. A voice.

That one question from my Dianne. *"What do you want to be?"*

Chapter 5
Minefield

"Ya Honor, these kids been messin' with my children for a long time now! I had to do somethin'."

—MAE ALICE DAVIS

128 continued to deteriorate. People continued to move in. It wasn't until our last few months there that we were the only ones left in that death trap. But, at this point, in came the Thompsons.

You know, when you're poor, you live in an alternate reality. It's not that we have problems different from everyone else, but we don't have the resources to mask them. We've been stripped clean of social protocol. There's an understanding that everyone is trying to survive and who is going to get in the way of that? The Thompsons were a perfect example.

They were a family of eight kids, mostly girls. Their parents or guardians were two women we called bull-frogs. Why? They wore glasses that made their eyes bulge out and they both had underbites. They had these huge bottom teeth that came over their top lip. They were also meaner than mean. They would always scream at the kids and beat the shit out of them. Once again, no one cared. My father would beat us and beat the hell out of my mom, so we were in the same company. But the kids, who were all around our age or older, were especially violent. The boys would start fires in the basement. The girls waited in a group for one of us to come out of school to terrorize us. We all went to different schools at the time, so we all arrived home alone.

If I saw them lurking in the yard, I simply would hide out until they went inside. The "Bullfrogs" would carry a belt around and herd them inside like animals. We would hear their screams from outside.

One day getting out of school, they saw me from yards away. The two boys whispered to each other and pointed. They got on their bikes and started pedaling fast toward me and I ran. They caught up real fast. I was seven and so terrified I couldn't speak. I ran and screamed! I knew they planned to run over me.

As soon as they got *über*close and it was obvious I wasn't going to outrun them, I screamed. They had me cornered. I lost it. I grabbed the front wheel of one of their bikes and started screaming and going crazy! I lifted the bike off the ground and just pulled, trying everything in my power to shake this bastard off his bike!

"Stop! Stop!" He and his brother were screaming.

"Leave me the fuck alone or I'll kill you," I shouted like a madwoman.

They finally turned back around and left me alone, plotting for their next torturous shenanigans. And there would be many. My sister Anita smashed a brick on a car and made herself drool to get the five girls off her one day. She literally acted crazy. A technique my father taught her. Deloris was slapped a couple of times by them.

One day, my mom was done. Four Thompsons girls were blocking my sister Deloris's path to get inside the apartment building. They finally hit her and she ran upstairs. My mom went into an alternate reality. In other words, she lost her mind. She came running down the stairs to the door of the building. I ran behind her. I absolutely loved to witness any kind of fight outside of our apartment. It was better than prime-time television.

My mom raised her fist. "Y'all need to stop messin' with my children! You understand me? Keep it up and I'll beat yo' ass myself!"

I was beyond impressed. My mom turned around after she made her point to come back upstairs. I looked at them as if to say, *My mama told you!*

Well, as my mom turned to walk up, the meanest of the mean girls, Lisa, said, "You bald-headed Black bitch."

The best comparison I can make to what happened next is that boulder coming after Indiana Jones in *Raiders of the Lost Ark*. If he didn't run, it most definitely would've flattened his ass. Well, my mom was that boulder. She leapt down the one flight of stairs she was on and said, "What did you call me?" But it really wasn't a question because she proceeded to slap Lisa so hard her entire body raised up off the ground and she fell flat on the dirty floor of our apartment building entryway. Her sisters were frozen. She didn't stop there. While Lisa was on the ground, my mom pointed her finger and finished her historic "cuss out."

"Don't you ever call me any names! I'll slap the piss out of you again! You understand me! And leave my children alone!"

She turned around and walked up the remaining stairs to our apartment cussing the whole time. "C'mon, Vahla!"

I was impressed and looked back at Lisa crying on the ground. "That's right! My mom beat yo' ass!" Then all hell broke loose.

The Bullfrogs were informed and decided to press charges. We were all terrified. We were sure my mom would go to jail. Words were exchanged. There was a lot of back-and-forth, cussing, fists raised. The strangest part of all of it was that the Bullfrog family would disappear for weeks, even months at a time and then suddenly appear in their car and stay for a while before disappearing again. And one of them always had a wad of cash in an apron pocket.

Every day my dad would pace back and forth and chain-smoke. "You done it now, Mae Alice. Oh man! The judge may send you to jail or give you a fine."

My mom would only say, "I'm gon' tell the man the truth." She was still hot. Still mad.

The day came when my mom finally went to court. My dad went with her. It's funny that there were moments within all the fighting, horrific abuse, and alcoholism that they had real moments as a united front, a team. But also in the presence of authority, my dad took the passive back seat and my mom dominated.

My dad prepared MaMama. "Mae Alice! What evah the judge say, you listen to. Don't say nothin'. Don't talk back. Don't do nothin'. I been through this Mae Alice. I know," he whispered nervously.

"Dan! I know how to talk!"

"But Mae Alice, you gotta say 'yes ya honor, no ya honor.' I'm tellin' you."

He should've kept talking to her. Because apparently when the judge called on them, my mom went off.

"Ya honor! These muthafucking kids keep messin' with my children! Every time my children come home from school, they outside blocking they way in, hitting them, trying to beat them up! I got tired of it! And yeah, I slapped the shit outta her cuz she called me a bald-headed Black bitch! And yeah, I call they so-call 'parents' bullfrogs cuz that's what they are. They eggin' they kids on."

My dad kept tugging my mom's arm, saying softly, "Mae Alice! You can't say that."

"Dan, stop tuggin' on my arm! I'm trying to talk to the man! I'm tellin' him the truth about these common bastards."

The judge interrupted her. "But Mrs. Davis. Mrs. Davis! You cannot hit other people's children. It's illegal."

"Ya honor, I'm tryin' to tell you, I had enough! They

somethin' wrong with those people. I had to protect my children!"

My father kept trying to both shush her and show his exasperation. "Mae Alice. Sit down! Be quiet, Mae Alice!"

"Dan! Stop trying to shush me! I'm tryin' to tell the man what the situashin' is."

As unlikely as it may seem, the judge understood. MaMama was and always has been a charmer, even when she's out of control. He let her go. And for the next several weeks, epic jabs were traded between our families. From our third-floor porch, we would see them across the street in a parking lot. The two Bullfrogs would shout, "You do it again, you see what you get."

"I ain't gon' get nothing. But I'll slap the piss out of them again if they call me a bald-headed Black bitch," my mom yelled back, laughing. "I knocked her little ass down."

"Don't you touch my kids," the Bullfrogs responded.

They'd yell and yell, trading jabs. It built up resentment and made us more afraid to be cornered outside. However, something else was happening. As the adults were yelling, the kids, all of us, were subdued. It's as if we were saying it was too much. They knew that they had crossed the line and we just wanted it to stop.

But the vitriol of our "protectors" was overriding our renewed feelings of wanting to, dare I say, bond? Be friends?

The catalyst of friendship would come days later. We were in the backyard playing softball. The Thompson kids suddenly came out and Lisa picked up the bat. She started circling the yard ominously. The others were behind her silently egging her on. My sister Deloris ran upstairs to get my parents. Only, my dad came downstairs. The Closer. The big dog. The one who cannot be named. Lord Voldemort. The HNIC. There was no stopping him and there was no buildup. He came out like a category 5 storm.

He grabbed the baseball bat. "Stop this muthafucking shit right now! You want to mess with me, muthafuckers?" He began waving the bat at them, beating the side of the house, the ground, the air. I believe even the Bullfrogs came out.

"Come at me, you Bullfrog muthafuckers! Mess with my kids one more time and I'll beat all you muthafuckers! You hear me?" Then he dropped the bat and went inside the house.

There was dead silence. No one moved. My father, when he got mad, was a man of his word. He would keep various "toys" by his bed throughout our childhood. A pitchfork, a machete, an ax. And he used every last one of them. He chased Porky with the pitchfork; Porky was one of his friends who was about five feet tall, dressed like Elvis, and had a car with no backs to the seats. It was just a bunch of tattered foam. He came to the house demanding money for fixing my dad's car. My dad showed him the pitchfork instead. I've never seen a man run with so much terror. My dad chased him by foot with his pitchfork and Porky was in his car. Dad came back home, started boiling a pot of water, and sat by the window waiting for him to come back. As for the ax and the machete? Well, those events would come much later.

Dad's confrontation with the Thompsons and the baseball bat was effective. After that, believe it or not, we became friends. Good friends. There were smiles, protectiveness, laughs. We were all just figuring out how to love and connect. We were just ensnared in the trap of abuse. The constantly being beaten down so much makes you begin to feel that you're wrong. Not that you did wrong, but you *were* wrong. It makes you so angry at your abuser, the one that you're too afraid to confront, so you confront the easiest target. Those you can. Until your heart gets tired. No one ever, up until that point, talked to us, asked us what our dreams were, asked us how we were feeling. It was on us to figure it out.

There is an emotional abandonment that comes with poverty and being Black. The weight of generational trauma and having to fight for your basic needs doesn't leave room for anything else. You just believe you're the leftovers.

Many years later, my mom saw Lisa, the meanest of the mean ones, and Lisa apologized. She told my mom, "Mrs. Davis, I'm so sorry for how I acted back in the day, but I missed my mom. They had taken me from her. They took all of us and were committing welfare fraud. That's why we had two different homes. All those girls were not my sisters, and the boys weren't my brothers. Plus, those women were sexually and physically abusing us. They even accused you of burning John's arm. We all knew that was a lie. I'm sorry, Mrs. Davis."

Then came James, Bobby, and Frank. They were my best friends next door. They had a mom and dad who called them in for dinner and lunch. Their father, Tommy, even built them a little partitioned play area behind the house. They were rough-and-tumble boys, but kind, funny, and I felt, well, that I had some power over them. They'd listen to me. I was nine or ten at the time but the wise Seer who would bring information from my older brother and sisters.

Tommy was a man with a temper. The boys' mother

had cerebral palsy and the father constantly abused her. I didn't know it at first because I was too busy admiring the fact that they had food and dinnertime, and a nice apartment. Also, I was too busy sanitizing the character flaws of people in general. There was just a basic understanding that they (everyone else) were better. They were victims of unfortunate circumstances and needed love and healing. I, however, was just born bad.

Everyone knew that Tommy abused his wife. The worst part of it is, my sisters and I found him sneaking out of his apartment around 9 p.m. at night to fool around with his next-door neighbor, Rhonda. We would see it because we always pushed our curfew by a few minutes and started snooping around like Sherlock Holmes. We all wanted to be secret detectives and, voilà, we uncovered the best-kept secret.

Tommy and Rhonda would sit on the stairway leading to her apartment and hold hands and kiss. We would watch, hidden, and then at an opportune time would jump out and scream, "Cheater!"

It pissed him off so bad. He would chase after us.

Now, we also had the world's best pet at that time, our dog, Coley. Coley was a collie. My father brought him for us from the racetrack. He was a trained dog, very smart, and he absolutely loved us.

He was so loyal that my mom took him to City Hall

with her one day. She finished her business but went out the back door instead of the front door where she came in. She kept calling Coley and wondered where he was. He was gone. She was in a panic so we all combed the city. We found him hours later at the front door of City Hall where my mom went in. He was whimpering and still waiting for her to come out.

One day, I got the epic idea of seeing the ghost of a girl who had died at Cogswell Tower. Cogswell Tower was in Jenks Park, our favorite after Washington Street Park closed down. During the summer we were involved in recreational competitions. At night, Cogswell Tower was as ominous as they come. It looked like a tower of terror. I had heard a very blurry story of a girl who committed suicide there. She morphed into an unsettled spirit whose only purpose was to roam the tower minaciously.

I told James, Bobby, and Frank the story. Like always, I had their attention and they were as fascinated as me. That night, I told them that I would help them sneak out of their apartment and we would walk to the park. Well, as soon as it got dark, around 8:30 p.m. or so, I went to their first-floor apartment and knocked on their bedroom window. I slowly helped all of them climb out. We were pumped, but scared and tired. "We're going to see a ghost! But soon as we see her, we should run," I instructed my crew. We started off walking toward the park. James, the youngest, was absolutely exhausted and I could tell that all they wanted was to go back home. We were in over our heads.

"Bobby! James! Frank!" A booming voice shouted behind us.

Holy shit! It was their father. He was carrying a belt and running. He started whipping them. "What the hell do you think you're doing? Get back home! What're you doing with my kids?" His last shouted words were directed at me.

I said, "They wanted to come."

"You can't play with them anymore! Find some other friends." They walked off, the boys wailing and crying. I felt like shit and was a little jealous that their father came running out with a belt to find them. No one came running looking for me.

The next day Tommy, livid, approached my father and told him what happened. He ranted. He screamed, "She's a bad influence on my kids! I don't want her around them!"

My father kept saying it was a mistake, but Tommy started directing his anger at my dad for not controlling me. He was inches away from my dad. It occurred to me that these were two men who had similar anger issues. Finally, my dad grabbed his neck, "You white muthafucker! Don't ever get in my face talking 'bout my children being a bad influence. You messin' around on your wife, and yo' kids are just as bad!"

He was choking him. Then he just pushed him away and told him to never get in his face again. Tommy walked off gasping for air, terrified, and humiliated.

The next day, Coley got real sick. He stopped eating and drinking water. He had foam around his mouth and matter in his eyes. Our friends, the Weigners, lived up the street and their father was what we called a "Dog-catcher." He basically worked at an animal shelter. He came over and determined that Coley had been given rat poisoning. There was nothing we could do but put him to sleep. He was in so much pain that dementia had set in.

The last time we saw him, we all said good-bye. He was in the kitchen and was wagging his tail. He loved us so much. I clutched my mom hysterically. We were devastated. The loss of any pet is hard, but it's especially hard when they serve a larger purpose that is fulfilling the deficit of loyalty and love.

Tommy poisoned the dog. Or at least, that's what my father suspected. He said he saw Tommy in the yard.

Central Falls was my home, but it was also a minefield. It was a small town where you were constantly trying to dodge little and big explosions that could level you while trying to occupy space in it to be somebody. It was an emotional war zone made worse by the war zone at home. I didn't know what boundaries were. I was constantly doing messed-up shit to be seen, exercising any semblance of power and authority I had to feel alive. I wanted to squeeze out any level of joy and laughs I could. But the worst part is, deep inside there was a demon, and another part of me that was wrestling with the "alive" me. She, the demon, kept whispering, "You're not good." But the other part, the fighter, the survivor, screamed back a resounding, "No!"

Chapter 6
My Calling

*"It was like a hand reached for mine
and I finally saw my way out."*

Our television set at 128 did not work, but it had *another* television set that did work sitting on it, one that relied on an aluminum-foil-wrapped antenna. Connected to an extension cord from one of the few working outlets, the TV sat in the next-door apartment. One evening while watching TV, a new world opened up before my very eyes. A woman who looked just like MaMama came on television one night, and something *magical* happened.

Suddenly, I saw *her*. I saw her. It was Miss Cicely Tyson in *The Autobiography of Miss Jane Pittman*.

She had a long neck and was beautiful, dark-skinned, glistening with sweat, high cheekbones, thick, full lips, and a clean, short Afro.

My heart stopped beating. The shame, pain, fear, confusion, all these negative feelings I had about my life and my situation were blasted through a brand-new doorway. It was like a hand reached for mine and I finally saw my way out. The beauty of that moment was that my sisters saw an exit too.

I experienced the true power of artistry. At that moment, I found my calling. How Miss Tyson transformed from 18 to 110 years old was supernatural. I wanted to be supernatural. I wanted my life to mean something, and this was it. I finally found it.

It wasn't long after, I had my first performance—a skit, with my sisters in a contest at Jenks Park, sponsored by the Central Falls Parks and Recreation Department. It was a big deal. The whole city was buzzing. All the white kids who went to Theresa Landry's School of Dance for tap dance, acrobatic lessons, and so forth— some of whom very freely called us nigger, nigger, nigger all the time—were favored to win. But anybody in Central Falls could create a skit and whoever won got a profile in the paper and a prize. My sisters and I decided *we* were going to win that damn contest.

Dianne, being the academic high achiever and oldest

sister, took the lead and told us: "I studied this. We need a producer. We need a director. We need a writer. We need actors. And we need a wardrobe budget." Dianne became the producer. I was a writer/actor, and Anita was an actor as well. Deloris was a bit of everything and took on director, actor, and coproducer.

We decided to create our own original skit called "The Life Saver Show" based on Monty Hall's *Let's Make a Deal*. MaMama was addicted to game shows. In our game show, contestants would come on and share their story about saving another person's life. Whoever had the best lifesaving story would win the contest. Deloris played a Monty Hall–type talk-show host character. I played the Ooh-Wee Kid—that's Ted Lange from the television show *That's My Mama*. Dianne was Fred Sanford from *Sanford and Son*. Anita was Aunt Esther from the same show. We wrote our skit over the span of two and a half weeks, and we started early.

We had a wardrobe budget of $2.50 that we put together by finding loose change, and for things we couldn't afford to buy, we raided my mom and dad's closet. They said, "You can take whatever is in our closet and use it." We took the fur coat she got from St. Vincent de Paul, her straw purse, hat, wig. We got a suit of my father's, which Deloris and Dianne wore, although it was totally oversized. The rest we bought from St. Vincent de Paul with the $2.50.

Our rehearsals were *intense*. We approached the skit like it was Shakespeare. If a line didn't work, Dianne would stop the rehearsal and tell me "It isn't landing." Then, I would go into the closet to focus and come up with something better. To put it in context, this closet was filled with junk and rats, but I braved it for rewrites.

Finally, the day came. We had researched the skit to an inch of our lives. I had massive stage fright. Massive. I could barely perform in private with my sisters. My throat would constrict. My stomach would be in knots. I would just . . . freeze. But my sisters threatened me not to flake out or else. That's how important this was. It seemed like the entirety of Central Falls was gathered in Jenks Park that day. Reporters and photographers from the *Pawtucket Times* were there. Kids and their parents were sitting on the grass and on the huge rock that was smack-dab in the middle of the park. Some spectators even brought folding chairs.

When it finally started, and the group of kids who were favored to win were introduced, the *whole* park screamed in excitement. When they finished, it was to thunderous applause, with the knowledge that they had found their winning group. I remember my sisters and I looking at one another, pumping each other with confidence.

And then they all sat back down and Dianne said, "Okay, you know we got to do it like we practiced. We're up."

We did our little chant, which consisted of "We're gonna win! We're gonna win!"

Dianne looked at me and saw my fear. "We're not freezing today, Viola. Right?" I nodded reluctantly. The butterflies in my stomach were overwhelming, but so was the desire to not destroy what we created.

When they introduced us, there was clapping but nothing near the ovation for the previous group. That group stood near the stage with their arms crossed. We were the last group of the day. We started off by all singing our own rendition of the jingle from *The Tonight Show*. Deloris came on first and said, "Welcome everybody to 'The Life Saver Show.' I'm your host, Monty Hall. And I'm here to tell you that we have a show where everyone is asked to share your lifesaving stories. We've got the ultimate $1 million prize for each of you. Wait a minute. Wait a minute."

There was an interruption.

The interruption was me. I came on as the Ooh-Wee Kid and mimicked Ted Lange, the town gossip as best as I could: "Ooh-Wee. I got it. I got it. I'm here

to report it." Then nine-year-old me said, "Fred Sanford is coming on the show. He's coming on the show.
And he, and he's about to mess things up. You've got to
watch out for him."

Dianne as Fred Sanford came on and shared his
story that he saved a bunch of lives when he saw a
group of people fall off a bridge and jumped into the
water to rescue them. Anita as Aunt Esther came out
and Fred said, "Aunt Esther, I should put your face in
some dough and make some gorilla cookies," and he
and Aunt Esther started fighting, the way they did on
the TV show.

Fred finally ends his lifesaving story by saying, "I
jumped into the water to save Aunt Esther."

Aunt Esther, played by Anita, was so moved she
said, "You went in to save me, Fred?" To which he replied, "No, I went in to save the fish because you so
damn ugly."

They began to fight even more, and Fred tore off
Aunt Esther's wig, revealing her bald head underneath.
The skit ended with a standing ovation. But nostalgia is
powerful. The memory of the winning. The applause.
The acceptance is my takeaway. But my lack of self-love
and my complete inability to open up to anyone about
my one driving fear—"My father is going to beat my
mom to death one day"—couldn't be voiced. The ado-

ration is as powerful as that curtain was in *The Wizard of Oz*. It hid a lie that gave me temporary asylum. That's what winning was . . . an instant protection and smoke screen to hide the fact that I was simply scared all the time. I felt like an "outsider" all the time.

We won! We got first place and I'll never forget the faces of the chosen girls from Theresa Landry's School of Dance when they watched us do our happy dance, too. "We won. We won."

Some gift certificates, maybe to McDonald's or a place like that, is all I think we won, along with a softball set. One of those plastic sets with the softball and a hard, plastic, red bat. We weren't interested in the softball set. We just wanted to win. We wanted to be somebody. We wanted to be SOMEBODY.

Chapter 7
The Sisterhood

"A happy family is but an earlier heaven."
—George Bernard Shaw

My sisters became my platoon. We were all in a war, fighting for significance. Each of us was a soldier fighting for our value, our worth. We were all in it together; we all needed one another. None of us could fight individually. I know I didn't have enough strength. We were fighting a war with seen and unseen enemies. Regardless, our commitment was to the whole. It was a together-or-nothing ethos. Eventually, we would separate and some would be left on the battleground intact but missing something. But, as children, we were in it together: Dianne, the oldest; Anita, one year behind her; Deloris, two years younger; and me, three years her junior. We all wanted out and our bonds of sisterhood helped make a way. Dianne was the brains. Anita the brawn. Deloris was the mastermind. Me? I was the one who could either drag the whole team down or up miraculously in the final hour.

We were transformed by Miss Tyson. Then, winning the drama skit contest shifted our lives because our sister platoon had seen a physical manifestation of winning our war.

The bat from the softball set, the red bat we won, became the rat catcher, a tool in our arsenal.

Rats always come out of nowhere. You could be sitting in front of the TV, watching your show, and all of a sudden, a rat jumps on the couch. Or one comes scurrying out of a hole in the wall and in a flash is underneath the couch.

Whenever we saw a rat, we told Anita, "I saw a rat!" Once she saw the rat, she got the prize we won—that red bat—out. We would all stand behind her, clutching her. Dianne said, "It went under . . . It went under there. Get it. Get it. Get it." We were all really quiet, waiting for it to slow down. We saw its tail, visible under the couch. Anita waited. She, who, by the way, became an all-star softball player, timed it perfectly. Bam! She actually knocked the tail off the rat. She didn't kill the rat. She just knocked its tail off.

The prize bat came in handy again when Mama was napping in her bedroom, her mouth open, in the middle of the day one weekend. Unafraid of our black cat Boots, the biggest freakin' rat we had ever seen was on her pillowcase, slowly inching toward her.

We snuck out and told Anita, "There's a rat. It's about to kill Mom—bite Mama's neck!"

Anita got the bat and once again, we were behind her, holding on to her, as the rat stealthily inched toward Mama's open mouth. Why we just didn't yell, "Mama! Wake up!" to make the rat jump off the bed and run, I don't know. Boots leapt onto the pillow, viciously "Meowed," and the rat darted into the closet and hid among the crowded clothes.

Mama awoke startled. "The rat is somewhere in the middle of the clothes," we screamed. Was it in between the coats or hidden in the dresses? We were trying to figure it out, peeking to see its tail from behind Anita who wielded the red bat. "I think it's right here," she said. "Make sure you get it, Anita, because he's somewhere in the middle of these clothes," we chimed. Anita aimed perfectly. She timed it, just like she later hit softballs. And as hard as she could, she brought that red bat down and flattened the rat like a pancake.

The great memory of winning that contest—my acting debut, that started me on my journey toward becoming an actress—is accompanied by recollections of that red, plastic bat and its handiness as a rat killer. Rats are a huge part of that memory of winning. I'm terrified of rats to this day.

Our growing-up years were speckled with good moments. Happiness for me was Valentine's Day. My father knew how to celebrate Valentine's Day and other major holidays. He bought lots of chocolate, and believe it or not, for Easter he bought Easter eggs and gave us cards. Christmas, especially when we were younger, was festive and we would always put up a tree. Once I got to be about eleven or twelve, there weren't many gifts. But still, we had a Christmas tree and my dad was the happy drunk when he would play his guitar.

I was seven or eight when my dad got us a pool table. It was a full-size pool table. My dad bought it because he liked playing pool at the bar. I loved playing pool. After a while, that pool table was jacked up, and we never had another one. But sometimes we would go to the bar—back in the day when parents could take kids to the bar—and play darts and pool and be treated to Sprite and potato chips.

These happy moments would soon be followed by trauma—the rage of my dad's alcoholic binges, violence, poverty, hunger, and isolation. In my child's mind, I was the problem. I would retreat to the bathroom, put something against the door so no one would come in, and I'd sit for an inordinate amount of time staring at my fingers and hands and try to erase everything in my mind. I wished I could elevate out of my body. Leave it.

One time, when I was about nine years old, I succeeded. I left it; my body that is, in a manner of speaking. I floated up to the ceiling, looking down at myself, observing my hair, my legs, and my face. Then I faced myself, staring directly into—me. Wow! I loved it. It was a magical, secret power, only I didn't see myself as magical or powerful. I just felt free. It was my way of disappearing. It was my high. I couldn't always control this out-of-body sense, but when I could, it was beyond fabulous. The power to leave my body, to be relieved of Viola for a while, was an ever-present image that followed me for decades.

I never liked how it ended, though. These out-of-body experiences would always seem to stop abruptly. I would come crashing down, like in movies where someone has telekinetic powers and would lift an item but couldn't concentrate anymore, so the item would come crashing down. I was out of my body and suddenly, back in it. I tried to compartmentalize, to dodge those heavy emotions, until I couldn't. The power was temporary.

Even now, me and Deloris have dreams about "128." It created the backdrop for bonds of sisterhood. "128" was a womb of sisterhood. At night, we sisters would huddle on a top bunk for warmth, horrified at the sounds of rodents eating pigeons on the roof, eating our toys, squealing, when we felt the weight of their bodies as they jumped on our bed searching for something to eat. We would wrap bedsheets around our necks to protect ourselves from bites.

Going to the bathroom at night in the midst of this was not an option. Cutting on the lights and watching them scurry was not an option because there were no lights in the part of the apartment where we slept. The bathroom was a faraway place on the other side of the apartment, but it may as well have been on the other side of the world. If you didn't go before bed, you could forget making that journey at night. So, we just peed.

We dreamed away our problems. When Dad was drunk or there was turmoil, my sister Deloris and I would disappear into the bedroom and become "Jaja" and "Jagi," rich, white Beverly Hills matrons, with big jewels and little Chihuahuas. We would play this game for hours. "Ooh my, Jaja," Jagi would say, "I bought this fabulous house and my husband bought me this beautiful diamond ring." We played with such detail that it became transcendent.

We played with the backdrop noise of our mom being beaten and screaming in pain. But we believed we were in that world, until eventually, Deloris would break the spell, saying, "You're not Jaja. You're poor. You're on welfare. You don't have diamonds." We'd fight and the game of pretend would be over—until the next time there was family tumult. It was how we escaped. We transformed into people we felt were "better." People who existed in a world we only dreamed of; women who were not us. We played for fun and out of desperation. Jaja and Jagi were our pretend protection.

The majority of my most joyful memories were from my relationship with my sisters. We dreamed together so fiercely. We started a band called the Hot Shots. We were trying to be the Jackson 5. We never wrote a song or played an instrument. We had no money to take lessons. But what we lacked in ability, we made up for in drive and imagination. Deloris was on drums. Dianne was the lead singer. I played the tambourine and Anita was on guitar. We could pretend and escape into our imagination.

We were fascinated by fireworks. One day we purchased firecrackers. Having the money to do so was a big deal. We bought them from one of the corner stores. For reasons I don't remember, we decided to light a firecracker in the kitchen of 128 and throw it out the window. I was in charge of holding the firecracker. I froze, or as they say in the vernacular, I "nutted up."

My sisters screamed at me to throw it but I couldn't move. It exploded in my hands!! My hands went numb, completely! Visualize a Looney Tunes cartoon where I totally lose my hearing and smoke comes out my nose and ears. Like Wile E. Coyote, I stood with the exploded firecracker in my hand. My mouth gaped open. I saw my sisters mouthing the words, because I couldn't hear: "Viola, are you okay?" "Stupid! I told you to throw it." Then my ass started to cry. "I'm deaf! Oh my GOD!"

My hearing came back.

My sisters and I continued to navigate our world. We continued to figure it out on our own in the absence of parents. Our parents were just trying to keep us alive the only way they knew how. They controlled what they could and injected ritual, joy, hope in little ways. For example, we were gifted new clothes at least once a year on Easter. Despite pissed beds, almost never having clean clothes, rats jumping on our bed at night, broken furniture, food insecurity, shoddy plumbing, no phone, we all got a brand-new outfit. The potency and power of tradition is deep.

My mom would break out the hot combs—a metal

curling iron and straightening comb that she would put on the stovetop fire. With Blue Magic pomade, she would proceed to straighten and curl our hair for Easter. It was a sadistic ritual as I saw it. She would slap and yell at us "Keep ya ass still or I'll burn ya" if we squirmed. When that hot straightening comb hit that greased piece of hair, sizzled, and fell on your ear or face, you had to squirm. Sometimes she'd get to talking and leave the comb and curling iron on the fire too long. Those hotter than hot irons would burn the hair black.

"Keep ya ass *still*!!"

In the end we looked really cute in our maxi dresses and new shoes, but, man, did we look greasy. We didn't care! We loved it. My parents gave us candy, some money, and we would stand in the yard waiting for anyone to pass by so they could see how cute we looked. Finally, Dianne came up with the idea of going to church. She said that's what they did down south. The only churches in Central Falls were Catholic. We got up the courage to go since most people we knew in Central Falls were Catholic.

We went into Holy Trinity Church and sat in the back. From the moment we stepped into the church all eyes were on us. I thought everyone was mesmerized by how cute we looked. We pretended or tried to learn the songs and different responses. Then, prompted by

Dianne, we went up for Communion. "Just say Amen after he puts the bread in your mouth."

I was excited about getting the little piece of bread. When time came to take the bread of Christ, the priest leaned down and whispered, "Are you Catholic?" Dianne, with her mouth still open, ready, shook her head truthfully, "No." He motioned for us to leave. I then realized why we had been so closely observed.

After that, we took our Easter money to Leroy Theatre to watch a double feature and eat either hot dogs or large bags of M&M's. Seventy-five cents for a double feature and 35 cents for a big bag of M&M's.

The other holiday was Halloween. We would be the first ones out trick-or-treating and the last ones home. The goal was to get as much candy as we could. We would fill one bag and go out with another one. We never really had costumes so we would just put my mom's makeup on our nose, forehead, cheeks, and that would be it. There was no money for anything else.

One year we made it a point of going out before it got dark. We ran out with our pillowcases and paper bags. It was the best idea because we were the only kids out. We saw no one else! Absolutely no one. We were going to get the best candy because we were the first. We knocked on our first door. It was a father and a mother with about three kids. We screamed, "Trick or treat!"

The man looked completely startled and burst out laughing, "Halloween is tomorrow! You all came out on the wrong day!" His wife and kids came to the door and proceeded to laugh hysterically at us. We ran away fast and didn't stop until we got home.

Some battles we won—survived together and emerged with laughter and perspective, and some brutal ones—sexual abuse—we lost.

Sexual abuse back in the day didn't have a name. The abusers were called "dirty old men" and the abused were called "fast" or "heifers." It was shrouded in silence and invisible trauma and shame. It is hard to process how pervasive it was. What made us sitting ducks was our lack of supervision and lack of knowledge. It was a different time.

The abuse spanned from random old men on the street telling us, especially me because I was the youngest, how adorable we were. Then came, "I'll give you a quarter if you give me a kiss." I wanted the quarter. I would take it, give the old man with a cane a kiss on the cheek. He would linger there. Staring. Waiting for something more. I would look around suspiciously until something in me told me to run.

A birthday party at a friend's house was crowded with hard-drinking, beer-swilling types. The house had a back porch that led onto the rooftop of their garage. It was a great space to play as kids, which is what we did that day. One of the men at the party would pretend to chase us between drinks. We would run and laugh. He chased us until he just about cornered us, but all the kids managed to duck, dodge around him. Except me. I froze and he grabbed me!

All the kids were pointing, laughing at the fact I was caught. He grabbed and said, "You are so cute and pretty. . . .". Then he proceeded to lift my skirt, pull my underwear aside exposing my butt cheek, and begin to rub making sexual noises. The children screamed in horror and ran. I squirmed and punched my way out of his arms and ran. The other kids began to tease me, "Ha! Ha! You got caught! That was nasty!" I was absolutely devastated. Making matters worse and even more confusing, I was the one being humiliated, not the man who felt me up in front of everyone. I was just eight but felt dirty, spoiled. Even more insidiously painful, I was ashamed at how I felt, not just what happened. Think about that for a minute—ashamed at myself for feeling violated by a grown-ass, perverted violator. I was by myself at that party. Alone. Left to fend and navigate the shark-infested waters by myself.

We were left with older boys, neighbors who would "babysit" us and unzip their pants while playing horsey with us. My three sisters and I (Danielle wasn't born yet) were often left unsupervised with my brother in our apartment—sexual curiosity would cross the line. He would chase us. We would lose. And eventually other inappropriate behavior occurred that had a profound effect. I compartmentalized much of this at the time. I stored it in a place in my psyche that felt safely hidden. By hiding it I could actually pretend it didn't happen. But it did!

Once again more secrets. Layers upon layers of deep, dark ones. Trauma, shit, piss, and mortar mixed with memories that have been filtered, edited for survival, and entangled with generational secrets. Somewhere buried underneath all that waste lives me, the me fighting to breathe, the me wanting so badly to feel alive.

But this is the *journey*! The only weapon I have to blast through it all is forgiveness. It's giving up all hope of a different past.

My mom is now seventy-eight and her memory is slowly starting to fade. As I watch her now, I am desperately trying to hold on to every bit of time we have left together. I'm trying to take all the secrets and barriers off the table, any barriers we could possibly have between us.

One day over some green tea and toast, we sat and talked about past memories and my childhood in Central Falls. As we talked, a knot in my stomach bubbled up and showed itself. It's that familiar feeling I get before I do something risky or uncomfortable, like when I'm in social environments where I feel I don't fit in. But this particular time, I pushed forward anyway. I dug down deep. I harnessed my anger, my hurt, and I told her about a painful memory.

"Deloris, Anita, Dianne, and I were sexually abused," I told her as I uttered my brother's name in that same breath. "He chased us in the apartment. He was aggressive. We were scared. We were so young, Mom. There was penetration with Anita and Dianne. Me and Deloris were touched."

There was silence. She didn't move. It's ironic that she was sitting in my beautiful kitchen of marble and porcelain, with the subzero refrigerator and high ceilings, and it meant absolutely fucking nothing compared to the largeness of the truth of what was happening. Success pales in comparison to healing. Not just the truth of the abuse but the decision to love, to forgive . . . what I knew the reaction would be . . . which was silence.

Silence.

Heavy silence. The silence that's steeped in shock, hurt, guilt, recognition of her own abuse. The silent desperation of trying to negotiate the complexity of being a mother. The only sign that something had shifted in her was her uneaten toast.

There were other kinds of incidents we experienced as a sisterhood.

We were trying to make sugar candy on the stove while my parents were out, either at the local bar, though my mom never drank, or my mom was at bingo and my dad at work. Sugar candy was a country tradition that my sister Dianne taught us. You pour an insanely inappropriate amount of grease in an iron pan and pour enough sugar to give an entire school full of children diabetes in it and just stir over a high flame. It would caramelize.

You then turn the heat off and let it cool and harden into sugar candy. We would try anything involving food. We were always, always hungry. One time we let the grease cook too long and it popped out and splattered all over Anita's face. She screamed! We screamed! Dianne got a greasy rag and wiped. A layer of skin came off. She grabbed her coat and ran out to get my mom. Anita ended up in the emergency room and had big blisters on her face.

Our silent competition about who wet the bed the most and who would end up stopping first.

My brother playing Bruce Lee threw a butcher knife

at my sister Anita. Miraculously, it missed her organs, and embedded itself in her leg instead.

My parents started fighting while my mom was doing Dianne's hair. My father got so mad and out of control he threw a glass at my mom, which hit Dianne in the head, splitting her head open. Blood gushed out.

When I look back at what I've seen, my only thoughts are that it's amazing how much a human body can endure.

There are not enough pages to mention the fights, the constantly being awakened in the middle of the night or coming home after school to my dad's rages and praying he wouldn't lose so much control that he would kill my mom. Sometimes her head or arm would be split open. She would have a swollen face, split lip. I was always afraid when he picked anything up like a piece of wood because he would hit her as hard as he could and keep beating. Sometimes all night. There were so many times that we would see droplets of blood leading to our apartment and we just knew what was happening. It was chaos, violence, anger, and poverty mixed with shame.

One night, my father came home profoundly drunk. He kept saying, "Mae Alice, I'm dying. I'm not gon' live past the night! Wake up the children!"

My mom, crying, woke us all up. We were exhausted

and just sat in their room trying not to fall asleep. My dad was on the floor, wasted and periodically throwing up clear liquid. My mom was holding his head, crying.

"Y'all! Ya daddy's dying," he moaned. "I ain't gon' be here much longer. I want to say bye to all of y'all."

I started crying. I was the "crybaby." My sisters were stoic. My dad began to say good-bye to each of us.

"Deloris; you smart. You gon' do good but you gotta stop stealing ya sisters' shit and sellin' it at school. Don't think I don't know watch ya doin."

Deloris then started crying. A little.

"Dianne, you take care of ya sisters."

"Vahla; you my baby. You know ya daddy loves you, but yo' ass need to stop pissin' in the bed and stinking up the house!"

"Nita; I don't know what the hell to do with you. You piss in the bed, steal, fight people . . . AAAAAhhhh!" He convulsed, threw up, and went cold. Stopped moving.

I wailed, "Daddy! No! Don't die, Daddy!"

Then he woke right back up. "I love y'all."

My mom looked at us and said, "Y'all go back to bed."

There were continual battles. After every one of them there was a looming reality. How will we overcome this one? The only hope was that these ever-present battles would be little traumas, not a big trauma. In the early '70s, my sister Anita came face-to-face with a big one.

It started out as a normal, uneventful summer day, and my family and our next-door neighbors, the Owenses, were all sitting on the porch talking. Now, this was at 128. The Owenses had the apartment that we eventually would occupy once they moved out. They were a large family just like ours. We were very close and would just play together all the time. As the adults enjoyed the calm of the porch, we kids were running inside the house, periodically ducking our heads outside. While we young'uns frolicked without a care in the world, Mrs. Owens and my mom suddenly blurted, "Look at the monster! OMG! What is he doing?" Of course, we ran outside to see.

"Look! He ran into the backyard," we exclaimed with excitement, absolutely unaware of where this seemingly innocent ride would later take us.

As we ran to see the monster in the backyard, our parents screamed behind us, "Don't you go near that man."

We saw him: a man in the middle of the backyard with no shoes on, jeans that were torn at the leg, and a shirt that was haphazardly buttoned. He just stood, rocking back and forth, back and forth, and groaning. His eyes didn't register us at all even though he was looking straight at us. Our parents weren't joking. If he wasn't a monster, he would certainly do until a real one came along.

We screamed at him, "Look at us! Wooo-hooo! Look, monster! We're here!" We were terrified, but playing it off brilliantly, in our minds, with our rude taunts. Suddenly, a stray cat we had unofficially adopted came walking over to this man. We screamed, "Cat!" We hadn't named the damn cat yet. "Cat! Get away from him!"

We screamed at the top of our lungs hoping to startle the cat enough for it to run away. We certainly didn't have the guts to run near the monster and get it. So, we just kept screaming, at the cat and to the man not to pick up our kind-of pet.

Suddenly, the rocking entity that looked every bit the part of horror movie villain picked the cat up by the back of its neck. Our screams got louder. If he heard us, we couldn't tell because he didn't respond to us. Instead, he looked at the cat, stroked it almost lovingly, and then calmly broke its neck.

Blood oozed out of the dead feline's mouth. Its head hung, although it seemed like it was still trying to live. The man held the bloody cat up, let its blood drip down his face, and licked it. He flung the cat down and smeared the blood on his face ritualistically, like war paint.

We were absolutely still. Not believing what we were seeing. Traumatized.

Suddenly, like a switch turned on, he finally registered us, his childish tormentors, growled, and charged at us full speed. We ran inside our apartment building like hunted animals, clawing over each other, scrambling, crying. We made it up the stairs. When we looked around, out of breath, crying, we discovered Anita wasn't there.

We called the police. My dad ran around the city looking for her. We cried. Meanwhile, unbeknownst to us, Anita was being hunted. She later told us as we, her sisters and friends, ran to the apartment, she went in another direction. And soon, the monster saw her and began his hunt. Anita shared how she was running, hiding behind trees, the huge rock at Jenks Park. She tried being quiet to not give away her positions, but he was hunting her, as if he was in a war. And everywhere she hid served only as a temporary safe haven, until he again spotted her and continued the chase.

While my sister was literally running for her life, we had no idea where she was. The cops came to our home, but they didn't know either. Then we saw her running down Washington Street from Jenks Park. She was out of breath, crying hysterically. She ran into the market across the street from our house, the bloodied "monster" right behind her.

The butcher from the Colombian market came out with a machete and screamed, "You stop!" Miraculously, this real life *Friday the 13th* Jason stopped. Frozen. Limp. He then put his head down as if someone took a battery out of him.

We watched the cops put a straitjacket on him and put him on a gurney and into a padded wagon. We later found out that he had just come back from Vietnam where he spent months in the woods eating all kinds of rodents . . . and cats. His PTSD was so bad that his wife had thrown him out of the house that day.

Anita was always the brawn in the family. The survivor. The fighter. But even some of the mightiest of warriors have wounds that leave them debilitated. This incident threatened to leave Anita feeling depleted. The blood on the floor that belonged to my mom or blood on the streets from the damaged souls that we encountered needed mounds of salve. And we didn't have the knowledge or tools to grasp that. We just . . . didn't.

Chapter 8
Secret, Silent, Shame

"The invisibility of the one-two punch that
is Blackness and poverty is brutal."

School was our salvation. We coped by excelling academically. We loved learning. We didn't want to end up in the same situation as our parents, worrying where the next meal was coming from.

School was also our haven. We stayed late, participating in sports, music, drama, and student government. My sisters and I became overachievers, even in areas that didn't interest us.

Deloris and Dianne made the Rhode Island and National Honor Society. They blazed a path for me. But, at school, I was always so sleepy, hungry, and ashamed. I would arrive to school at 8 a.m. and by 8:30 I was falling asleep. For many years I had problems sleeping through the night; I never slept through the night. At best, I slept periodically, warily, because it was during the middle of the night that a lot of my parents' fights happened.

If I got two hours of full sleep, I was lucky. We'd be awakened by a scream, a screech. The only hope, the only blessing, was the fight that didn't last long. But sometimes their conflicts would last all night or night after night, for days. If it lasted all night, we did not sleep. Imagine your father beating your mom with a two-by-four piece of wood, slamming it on her back, the screams for help, the screams of anger and rage. That trauma would keep me up at night and make me fall asleep in class.

I wet the bed until I was fourteen. I'd often go to school smelling. Having no hot water sure didn't help. Try washing up with ice cold water and rarely any soap in the dead of winter. We chose between laundry detergent, soap, or dishwashing liquid. Usually, we substituted one for the other based on our needs. Hauling bags of laundry a mile or two in freezing temperatures, with ice and snow, was no picnic. And having the quarters for laundry was a luxury.

So, usually the night before, we washed our clothes

by hand in cold water and soap and hung them to dry. We would hang wet clothes over doors or a chair because a clothesline would be exposed to snow, rain, and/or freezing cold air that would make the clothes turn to ice. The next day, they were almost never dry, but we had no choice. We would put on wet clothes and they would dry as we went through our day. I reeked of urine.

My sister Deloris and I went to Cowden Street School when I was in fourth grade and she in fifth. Deloris absolutely loved school. She was that student who came home excited if she had a test coming up. She was also a voracious reader. Before she entered sixth grade she was consuming books like *Wuthering Heights* and those by Agatha Christie. And unlike me, she never got in trouble in school as she was very respectful of teachers.

Well, one day Deloris came home excited about a science test. It's all she would talk about for a week. At this point, she wanted to be an archaeologist. On the day of her big science test, something different was happening in class for me. My teacher, who I loved, kept staring at me. Whenever I moved closer to her to answer a question, she would step back. Then I saw her talking to the teacher next door. Only a door separated the classes, so they would talk in the doorway. On this day, they whispered and looked at me.

Finally, when we got in a circle to read, I ran to sit next to her and she leaned back with a distressed look on her face. She then gestured for me and whispered in my ear, "You need to tell your mother to get some soap and water and wash you! The odor is horrible!" Then she shooed me away as if I had vomited on her. I was numb.

A few minutes later I was called to the nurse's office. When I walked in, I saw Deloris. The nurse hadn't arrived yet. Deloris was sitting in a chair in front of the nurse's desk and she was catatonic. She obviously was called in for the same reason. I whispered, "Deloris! Oh my God can you believe . . ." But I never finished because she told me to shut up and she put her head down again.

The nurse came in and gave a whole lecture of the complaints from teachers about our hygiene. She asked how we washed up. We said nothing. We were trained in the art of keeping secrets and we never, ever shared with anyone what went on in our home. Ever! She then proceeded to tell us how you should never wear the same underwear twice; how to wash up; how to use soap and what areas to wash first. Then we went home.

Many decades later I brought up that day to Deloris and she told me her memories of that day. She said she had taken her science test and gotten an A. She was beyond excited and took her paper back to her desk.

She was being incessantly bullied by a girl named Maxine. Maxine looked at my sister's test and went up to the teacher and said, "Miss, Deloris cheated." And without missing a beat the teacher called Deloris up to her desk, took her test from her, and put a big, red F on it. She was devastated!! But she said this was a teacher who simply never liked her because she always got straight As. She was the same teacher who told me in second grade that Black people could not read or write at all when they were slaves.

I told Deloris I was sorry that happened to her and we didn't help her. She said, "That's okay, Viola. That was the day I decided to be a teacher. It devastated me so much that I didn't want another kid to go through what I went through."

Deloris has been a brilliant teacher for the past thirty-five years. It's funny that with the complaints about hygiene, no one ever asked us about our home environment. No one asked us if we were okay or if anything was wrong. No one talked to us. There was a lack of intentional investment in us little Black girls. A few people would drop what they called useful affirmations like, "Work hard," "Stay in school and do good," "Be great," "Behave and don't get in trouble." There was an expectation of perfectionism without the knowledge of emotional well-being. What it left in me was confusion. How do I get to the mountaintop without legs? But we constantly push it with kids now and when you're a poor kid growing up with trauma, no one is equipping you with tools to do "better," to "make a life."

It's funny that I loved my fourth-grade teacher so much and wanted her to love me with the same intensity. As traumatizing as it was to be told I smelled, it was worse feeling the shame. It was so overwhelming that I went home and did everything the nurse said. I washed my underwear, clothes, scrubbed my "privacy" and underarms. It gave me such a sense of pride to go back to school the next day, clean. I sat in class with a huge smile and waited to be acknowledged for the change. But . . . I wasn't. None of the teachers who complained ever really noticed us at all after that. You're expected to be clean not celebrated. The invisibility of the one-two punch that is Blackness and poverty is brutal. Mix that with being hungry all the damn time and it becomes combustible.

If you're hungry, you can't focus—you have no energy. School lunch was our stable, assured meal. The food stamps our family received the first of each month paid for a grocery run. But the food soon ran out. When it was gone, my sisters and I mooched off the families of friends and dumpster-dived, rummaging through garbage for food. I would befriend kids whose mothers cooked three meals a day and go to their homes when I could. One time a friend came over to our house and when she opened the refrigerator and saw there was nothing in it, asked, "Are you guys moving?"

I shoplifted food. I was nine the last time I stole food from a store. That day I was caught slipping a brownie down the front of my pants, but I never got it out of the store, because the owner screamed at me, looking at me like I was nothing. "Get out! Go away and never come back!" The shame forced me to stop.

The experience of going to bed hungry is something that neither my sisters nor I will ever forget.

I messed up all the time. I hid my feelings—my anger and pain—or I lashed out and got into fights. Detention every day. Back talk with teachers. I pushed a teacher once. I wanted attention really bad. I didn't know the butterflies that were ever present in the pit of my gut were actually massive anxiety. I felt I just didn't fit in. I was a whirling dervish of complexity and emotions. The true me was so trapped inside, like that demon inside of Regan in the movie *The Exorcist*. When Regan is tied to the bed to keep from harming herself and her body is racked by scars from this powerful demon, her mom's secretary comes barging in the room and as clear as day, slowly but deliberately, the words "HELP ME" form on her belly. The sweet, kind, authentic, precocious Regan fighting to be released is still alive. Well . . . that's what I felt like. Imprisoned and possessed by outside forces that were way more powerful than me.

No one wanted to drink from the bubbla' after me. Bubbla' or bubbler was the Rhode Island term for water fountain. My classmates would always wait for the teacher to turn her head and whisper, "Yuck!! I'm not drinking after that nigga. You're dirty." This would both shut me down and anger me. One day I tried to rip the pretty, yellow dress off Maria, a Portuguese girl who used the word *nigga* with impunity. My teacher punished me. I tried to explain, but she said there was no explanation. This was a teacher I loved, for whom I stayed after school once and volunteered to clean the chalkboard. She was young and pretty. I felt she liked me. This, unfortunately, was an illusion. I created a phantom to survive.

We watched an American history filmstrip that day that had a blurb about slavery with pictures of Black people in slave quarters down south. Everyone laughed when the images came up and the voice-over said, "Black people or slaves at this time were illiterate. That means they couldn't read or write." The kids laughed and whispered, "You niggas can't do anything."

I stayed after class to ask my teacher one question. Despite being a "troublemaker," despite pushing her once by accident, I was terrified as I waited until everyone was gone and quietly cleaned the entire chalkboard. She thanked me, and as I was leaving, I got up the courage to ask, "Miss, it's not true, is it? Black people could read and write? They could, couldn't they?"

She shook her head sadly and said, "No. I'm sorry, honey. They couldn't."

I left with my head down. She never explained to me or to the class that it was illegal during slavery to teach the enslaved to read and write. It was a way to keep them subjugated.

I was looking for something or someone to define me. To infuse in me self-love, acceptance. To show me how to live. To show me I was all right.

I held on to what I had, all that I had, the team effort with my older sisters. That preserved me. We were a girl-posse, fighting, clawing our way out of the invisibility of poverty and a world where we didn't fit in. The world was our enemy. We were survivors. Until another squad member was introduced. She needed protection that we had no weaponry for.

Chapter 9
The Muse

"Y'all meet ya baby sister."

—MAE ALICE DAVIS

When I was eleven, another girl was added to our family—Danielle. We didn't have a phone, so when my mom went to the hospital in labor the night before Danielle was born, they said they would call the fire department once the baby was born. The next morning, my father made us wake up early and clean the house from top to bottom. It was his way of contributing and working out his nerves. We swept, wiped. Finally, a young man came running up the hill, out of breath with a piece of paper. It read, "Congratulations! A 7 lb, 6 oz baby was born this morning."

We were so excited. We screamed and jumped up and down. It was a moment tattooed in my mind as pure, unbridled joy. My father told us to get dressed and we started our long walk to the hospital. It took us hours because we had no money for bus fare. But man, we were fueled by excitement. We walked single file, on the side of the road at times, on the sidewalk at other times. We finally made it to the hospital after a two-hour trek, walked into the room, and saw my mom. She was lying down with a blanket over our baby. I remember her words precisely, "Y'all meet ya baby sister!" She pulled the blanket away and revealed the most beautiful baby. Chocolate brown with the biggest Afro. We cried, melted with love.

I was the baby of the family before this time, but now I had a role of big sister. A type of transformation began to take place. At the time, I had no words to describe the shift to loving someone more than myself, seeing beyond myself. Words cannot explain our closeness. We did absolutely everything together. I never wanted to leave her. Ever. It was as if life was injected into our lives. I changed diapers, put her to sleep, babysat, gave her medicine when she was sick. And held her tight when my parents fought. She was our cub and we accepted her into the pride.

I was eleven and had already had my period for a

year but was by no means grown. I had attitude for days. When I was at home, that attitude stopped cold. I was too terrified of my father. But at school, I was out of control. Always talking out and back. My teachers sought every day to find ways to keep me still and quiet. I would get white and pink disciplinary slips. Pink was the worst. You get three pink slips, then you're suspended. I had three white and two pink. I would forge my dad's signature or get my sister to do it. It was a good thing we didn't have a phone or that would've been my ass.

I was unsettled. I was an awkward, angry, hurt, traumatized kid. I couldn't articulate what I was feeling and nobody asked. I didn't believe anybody cared. I was saturated in shame. There was so much we didn't have, or couldn't do, so much anger and violence that threatened the love. I was trying to be better. I focused on not wetting the bed. There were days I woke up dry but still days that even after going to the bathroom beforehand, I woke up soaked to my neck.

My baby sister was a cure at this point. Not for the bed-wetting, but she was day-to-day joy because she loved me. She saw me.

One day, Deloris and I were coming back from school. We neared the house and saw huge drops of blood on the pavement. Deloris whispered under her breath, "Oh my God." We got to our front steps and saw more blood and the front window on the door broken. We walked in and Anita and Dianne looked shell-shocked. Dianne was holding Danielle whose front shirt was saturated with blood. I almost screamed but Dianne said, "She's asleep. MaDaddy is out looking for mom. He said he's going to kill her. He busted her head open and she grabbed Danielle to leave and Daddy grabbed her back. We stopped them . . ."

The blood on Danielle was my mom's.

We were terrified. Finally, my dad came back. Pissed. The night before, I tried to stop him from beating MaMama. He was still angry at me about that. "Get y'all asses out to help me look for ya mama. Soon as we find her, I'm gonna kill her." Me and Deloris went out to help him look. He kept yelling at me to walk faster. Finally, he veered off to the right and told us to go to the left. Deloris was looking one way. I was looking another. I heard Deloris cry, "Viola! Oh my God, look." I looked to the left and there was my mom, in the Rexall Drugstore window. Her face was totally bloodied. Her eyes were swollen shut. She had on a dirty turtleneck and pants. She was standing next to the ice cream freezer motioning for us to come in. Deloris ran away to get my dad. I went in. People started gathering around and I heard the ambulance siren.

My mom was crying. "Vahla. Ya daddy's gonna kill me. I couldn't take it anymore."

The clerk at the store who was married to our science teacher was leading the paramedics in and kept asking me, "What happened to her? What happened to your mom?" I couldn't speak. I looked to my mom to tell me what to say. What do I say? Do I expose our dirty secret? The paramedics tried to get my mom to the back room. My mom looked like a frightened animal or child. She didn't want to go back there alone and with her arms outstretched she screamed, "Vahla! Come with me! Don't leave me." I just stood there and couldn't move. All I saw was the paramedics mouthing, *What happened to her?*

I walked out of that drugstore. People I knew from school were among those gathered outside. "Viola! Was that your mom? What happened?" I couldn't tell them that my mom is more than what you're seeing. The pity and the judgment saturated their faces. I wanted to scream out. *This is my mom!!! My MOM!!! She's scared . . . . but she is a survivor!!! She's somebody!!! I LOVE her!* But nothing came out of my mouth. I froze under the traumatic weight of the scrutiny and the judgment. Once again, I had no internal weaponry. It wouldn't occur to me until much later that this moment was not just about shame, value, or protection. It was about inheritance. . . . I was given her blood, her eyes, her survival skills, her pain. My world was a constant train of imprinting.

Because of the "war zone" that was our home, I always felt that I had to stay home to protect Danielle. The fights were brutal, with little attention paid to a baby in the line of fire when punches or knives were thrown. Mostly, we, her big sisters, just loved her. That was the best protection we could provide.

After being the youngest for so long, Danielle's birth gave me a sense of responsibility. It was as if Flo-Jo passed me the baton when I hadn't been practicing. I now had the last leg of the race to run, the clock ticking, on a journey where every other runner has 0 percent body fat and mine is at 40 percent. My shoes are untied. I can't see because I've got dry eye. But I still have to run my leg of the race. My practice run was being a primary-schooler who was sent home, soaked with piss. Piss-soaked, I must now run holding my baby sister.

I didn't have words to explain our poverty, dysfunction, trauma to Danielle, but I could hold her. I could love her; and that's it. I didn't have the tools to protect. I didn't know that I needed protection and guidance just as much as Danielle. I didn't know, nor could I admit, that I was broken.

Danielle was eight years old the summer between my first and second years of college. A weekend, in the middle of the day, while I was working at Brooks Drugs on Dexter Street around the block from our apartment, someone ran in and said, "Oh my God! Viola. You've got to come. Something's happened to your little sister." I ran outside and the cops were there, with my mom screaming at the top of her lungs. MaMama had on my brother's sneakers and stood there crying, just shaking one fist in the air at this man who was sitting in the back of the cop car, handcuffed. With the other hand, she was holding my baby sister close to her.

Danielle had been roller-skating and still had her skates on. She was crying in my mom's arms. "That dirty bastard hurt my baby," MaMama said. "Dirty motherfucker."

Later, I found out that an older Portuguese man would frequent the corner store on Dexter Street and molest little girls who came in. Supposedly, he came to the store to buy cigarettes. However, he would hang out at the store and walk up and down the aisles offering to give young girls money if they allowed him to touch them.

Danielle and one of her young friends roller-skated to this store, which was maybe a minute from our house, to get some candy. They were in the candy aisle when the old man approached Danielle, speaking in Portuguese, trying to offer her money. She didn't know what he was saying. When he touched her "privacy," she freaked out and she and her friend skated out of there fast.

Her friend said, "You've got to tell your mom. You've got to tell your mom."

Danielle told my mother and MaMama put on the first shoes she saw, ran down to Dexter Street, and yelled, "You, motherfucking son of a bitch, touched my daughter! There's a man in this store who touched my daughter. I'm going to call the police."

The guys who owned the store tried to calm my mom down by saying, "Ma'am, he does that to all the little girls. It's not a big deal." My mom said, "It *is* a big deal, you motherfuckers," and then ran out of the store, into the middle of the street, flagged down the police, and identified the old man. "That's the man. This is what he did with my daughter. I'm pressing charges." That's the point where I was summoned. The cops had arrested him, MaMama was cursing him, holding crying Danielle.

He didn't speak English. The only thing the court system did was fine him. My sister got $9 a month for the next few months from the man who molested her. Nine dollars a month. That was the fine. No charges were ever pressed.

Danielle was our baby. Your first instinct when you love a child is to protect her from the pain of the world . . . and life. The most excruciating revelation is when you realize you can't. To be human is not to be God. What that man was allowed to do is destroy souls.

It was hard to pick up the pieces after that. She had the mammoth task of healing. To this day, almost forty years later, she is still figuring out how to do that. Only thing I could do was love her . . . and I did and do. She is a reflection of me.

Chapter 10
The Starting Block

*"I ain't never found no place for me to fit.
Seem like all I do is start over. It ain't nothing
to find no starting place in the world. You just start
from where you find yourself."*

—AUGUST WILSON

I wanted to be a great actor like Miss Tyson. I wanted to talk like an actor and train like an actor. The process and artistry of piecing together a human being completely different from you was the equivalent of being otherworldly. It also has the power to heal the broken. All that was inside me that I couldn't work out in my life, I could channel it all in my work and no one would be the wiser. And if I was good at it, I could make a life. It was perfect. . . . All of it was a perfect alchemy for healing, acceptance, and worthiness. Then Ron Stetson, a young actor and coach, came into my life when I was fourteen.

Ron Stetson was my acting coach in the federally funded program Upward Bound. For six weeks in the summer, I would live on a college campus and take classes. Usually there were forty-eight students from various communities in Rhode Island and from many different backgrounds.

Our classes started at 8 a.m. and ended around 5 p.m. The summer program was meant to mirror college so that we could learn how to make that transition from high school to college: the classes, living with people from different backgrounds, being on your own. We were all first-generation, higher-education-bound students. Our cohort was a mixed bag of college-bound kids, each with their own crosses to bear. Some had huge language barriers, others challenging family environments, and still others with absolutely horrific stories of political abuse and genocide from their respective countries.

I loved Upward Bound. It gave me a jolt of perspective and grace about my family situation. Someone who spent four years living in a jungle or watching a parent get their head blown off by militia made my problems seem small. I know they weren't, but it introduced me to the painful truth that everyone is going through something.

The evenings were free time until 8 p.m. or 8:30 p.m. So after dinner they gave us a choice of an extra-curricular activity. Drama was one of them.

In came Ron, who to me was the coolest, most handsome, unique, dynamic individual I had ever met. He drove a beat-up car that had no door on the passenger side. Way cool. He put a sheet of plastic in its place so you wouldn't fall out or get wet from the rain. He wore flip-flops, tank tops, and jeans. He was not only cool, he was different. He had different views of the world, people, race. He spoke his mind. In fact, all the counselors and teachers there did. They blew a hole in my world and opened up a new space that I could occupy.

Ron gave me two huge gifts that changed my life. The first happened during our first day in acting class. He asked all fourteen of us how many wanted to be actors.

We all raised our hands.

"You know you have to work fucking hard every fucking day," he said.

A fourth of the hands went down, but, I thought, *Wow, that is awesome.*

"Every day," he repeated.

More hands down.

"You can go on an audition every fricking day for six weeks and never, ever, get a job. You know that, right?"

More hands down.

My hand remained raised, as if reaching for the sky.

"And you're gonna get rejected time and time and time again," Ron continued.

I was the only one now who had my hand up.

He kept going at me. "You're gonna get egg on your face. You're gonna fail. Your family is not going to understand what you do and neither will most people."

I kept my hand up, staring at him. When you haven't had enough to eat, when your electricity and heat are cut off, you're not afraid when someone says life is going to be hard. The fear factor was minimized for me. I already knew fear. My dreams were bigger than the fear.

He stared at me. "Okay, let's get back to class."

The second gift Ron gave happened at our wrap party at his house. My sister Deloris, who was also in the class, was talking to me about some boy. I don't remember what exactly she was saying to me but somewhere in there was a reference to us not being pretty.

He said, "Wait! You both don't think you're pretty? Why?"

We looked at each other completely embarrassed and

laughed. I said, "Ron! No one in Central Falls thinks we're pretty. We've never had boyfriends. We've never kissed anyone." There was a very uncomfortable shift in the air.

"What?"

"Ron, most of the people in Central Falls are white and they just . . . we . . ." Deloris and I were at a loss for words.

"You both are fucking beautiful! I always thought that. You don't see it?"

The air in the room shifted again. Or was it the air in our lungs? It's that life-changing thing that happens when you're seen, valued, and adored. Adoration for girls validates our femininity. When you are a dark-skin girl, no one simply adores you. They laugh with you, tell you their secrets, treat you like one of the boys . . . but there's no care given to you, no devotion given to you. The absence of that becomes an erasure.

I learned so much from Ron that first summer of my drama training. He said, "Theater awakens the imagination." Ah, imagination. The mind's ability to create ideas and images. That's what was injected in me when Ron stated with so much conviction, "You're beautiful." It opened up another space in my world where I actually could be anyone or anything I wanted to be. I could define my world in that space and piggyback to my world, stronger.

Like Wonder Woman spinning and transforming into this superhuman being that could bust through lies and beat down two-hundred-pound men. He gave me the first ingredient I needed to be an artist, the power to create. The power of alchemy, that magical process of transformation and creation to believe at any given time I could be the somebody I always wanted to be.

He also gave all of us something even more special: a sacred space where we could all share without shame or fear. A space where we could share our deepest, darkest secrets and they would be received with love and empathy. He encouraged us not to hold it in, and man oh man, did he love it when we did anything bold, odd, unique. He would just exclaim loudly, "Fuckin' look at that!"

I became an actor because it's a healing wellspring.

Upward Bound was a melting pot of races. What we shared, besides all being desperately poor, was a passion to be the first generation in our families to get an education and be high achievers. In the evenings, when we were allowed to connect, the stories were bone-chilling. We were the Blacks, Whites, Cambodians, Laotians, Hmong, Vietnamese (then labeled "the Boat People"), Angolan, African Portuguese, Dominicans,

Puerto Ricans. The Southeast Asians would primarily have stories of their entire family being slaughtered and escaping to the jungle only to have to live there for months, sometimes years, before finding a refugee camp, where some contracted malaria.

Most had language barriers or severe health concerns, but all were exceptional students. All had a willingness to share. It was the first place I knew where João, Phy, Vanna, Maria, Peaches, and Susie were on the same playing field. Suddenly, my stories of hardships seemed small, an awareness I felt God was orchestrating. I wanted my story to be small. I wanted it to shrink like a tumor down to a manageable size.

Drama provided an escape. The emotional release acting allowed gave me great joy. Perfect joy. When I was acting, I felt everything—every last receptor in my body was *alive*, 100 percent *alive*, and I was not hiding anything. I felt free to talk about all kinds of different shit when I was in a group with other actors. That's why the most troubled students would always be put in drama class. Everybody vomits! Everybody is allowed to disclose their trauma, share their stories of horrific sexual and/or physical abuse, unmask really quirky humor, reveal their deepest, darkest secrets, everything. People listen with empathy, 100 percent on board, supportive.

But . . . but . . . then you have to go out into the world as you. You move through your life trying to retain the life force you had on that stage and in that class. Whoopi Goldberg, as the medium in the movie *Ghost*, had a talent to channel all these souls. Some were good and some weren't. But regardless, she then had to come back to herself and her life. As an actor, you become a soul searcher. A thief. After the curtain call, you are left with you.

When I went to Upward Bound, I hadn't wet the bed in over a year. I was so proud. But then, out of the blue, my first night of our six weeks on a college campus, I woke up and I was wet, shocked, ashamed, and said, "No one can come in this room." I didn't have a roommate, but there were suitemates, twelve little rooms in the suite. My room was probably 150, 200 square feet. I had gone to my room and proudly set it up with whatever I had, which was next to nothing. That was the last time I wet the bed. It pissed me off. I thought I had more control.

My lesson from Upward Bound was you have to open your mouth and own your friggin' story. That terrified me more than rats.

Chapter 11
Being Seen

*"May you live long enough to know
why you were born."*

—CHEROKEE BIRTH BLESSING

From ninth grade until I finished high school we lived on Park Street, then Parker Street because we were evicted from the house on Park Street. Parker Street was an attic apartment, tiny, with slanted ceilings and only two bedrooms. My sister Anita had gone to college and got her own apartment. Dianne was long gone. She'd gone to Howard University when we were on Park Street and made her home in Washington, DC. So it was only me, and my sisters Deloris and Danielle, with my mom and dad. My brother, John, was never around.

We were cut off welfare, because they found out that my father was still living with us and he was making a salary. It was not a living wage, but it was a salary. Back in the day, they'd just cut you off. When we were evicted, we got shopping carts, put in everything that fit, and wheeled over to Parker Street to the tiny attic apartment on the third floor. If I had to carry a shopping cart of belongings up three winding flights of stairs now, I'd not make it. It was that abrupt; we had to get out. I was in the tenth grade when we were forced to make that move.

Aside from not paying rent, this is how the eviction happened. My mom and dad got into a brutal, bloody fight with Carlos, the landlord. The fight may have been about the rent. Carlos was Portuguese with a very heavy accent, and it was obvious this was the last straw. He wanted to move a family member into the house and was tired of my parents not paying rent. They would always make promises then get so behind, he was done. My dad was convinced Carlos was racist. When my dad felt any hint of being seen as less than, he let loose. I understood the man just wanted them to pay the rent.

Carlos came by with his wife demanding their money. My dad began to argue with him after he said we had to get out. The argument escalated. My dad had come home that day with a new toy, a machete. He had it wrapped in a towel, newly sharpened. Carlos saw the machete and started screaming that my dad was planning to attack him. He tried to grab it from my dad who subsequently tried to grab it back. Carlos's wife freaked out and tried to grab it as well. Add MaMama; not wanting to be left out, she started grabbing too.

It became a game of tug-of-war with screaming, crying, cussing. Everyone yelling different commands in Portuguese and English. "Let go!" "No! You let go!" "You're trying to kill me!" "No, I wasn't! I was bringing it in the house, muthafuckah!" It ended with Carlos getting sliced under his arm. My dad's hand, I think, was also sliced and we were, well, evicted. So relieved was Carlos that we were leaving, it's probably the reason he never pressed charges.

At this point, I was trying to leave the last vestiges of my bad behavior behind and was *über*focused on achieving as much as I could. Once again, I hadn't made the connection that my behavior matched the chaos at home. I was a powder keg of secrets. I kept them in because it allowed me to get through my day. I couldn't let what I was feeling out.

Any chance I had to be a part of something where I could make a mark, I joined in. Teachers at Central Falls Jr. Sr. High School and counselors were my lifeline.

Mr. Aissis, Mr. Yates, Mr. Perkins, Jeff Kenyon, Mariam Boyajian.

Mr. Aissis, who was a doppelgänger to Gene Wilder, only smaller, was my science teacher in ninth grade. He was also the musical director and Glee Club instructor. I drove him crazy. I was just bad. I talked too much. I was the classic theater kid who needed a creative outlet and couldn't find one, so I created it for myself, inappropriately, in class. In other words, I acted out. Literally.

He was always screaming at me. In ninth grade, he threw me out of his class and they put me in another science class. There was no one in that science class I knew, so it shut me right the fuck up. I didn't have anyone to act out with.

A few years later, he came into one of my classes, and said, "Viola, I have something for you."

"What is it?"

He said, "I went to a dentist appointment today, and as I was in the waiting room, I see this pamphlet, Viola." And it was a pamphlet for Arts Recognition and Talent Search, a national competition in Miami, Florida, in five disciplines: drama, visual arts, dance, music, and writing. Each had its own format. Thirty kids in each category were to be chosen for an all-expenses-paid trip to Miami. It was only for kids entering their senior year of high school. "You can enter in drama," he said.

"What do you get?" I asked.

He looked through the pamphlet. "Scholarship money, I think."

"I can't do that." A national competition? The pamphlet was thick and contained a laundry list full of things you had to do simply to apply. As he stood there, I read it out loud, believing with every word I uttered, the utter absurdity of it. I had to put together a tape of a classical monologue and a contemporary monologue. I had to fill out a huge application form with an essay. And then, of course, there was an application fee. "I can't do that," I repeated.

"Well, think about it," he said. "When I looked at it, I thought about you. I thought about you, Viola."

The throwing me out of class was all because he saw me. He saw what was in me.

I kept staring at the pamphlet. Eventually, I shared the pamphlet and its impossible opportunity with my Upward Bound counselor, Jeff Kenyon. You could call Upward Bound counselors by their first name. You could call Jeff in the middle of the day and say, "Hey Jeff! I'm having an anxiety attack and I'm in the middle of science class. Can you help me out?" and he would be there. He was always there.

He was the first person who took me and my sister Deloris to a political party gathering so that we understood what political campaigning was all about. He was the first person to take us to the Rhode Island Black Heritage Society so we could learn about abolitionist ex-slaves who could read and write and were instrumental in freeing others from bondage. As white as he was, Jeff taught us a lot about Black history. He heard me and my sister talk one day in his car and picked up on our ignorance about our own history. That was it. That was all the impetus he needed to spring into action. He would pick us up in the middle of the week, take us to get some food, talk to us to see how we were doing.

"What's going on?" he asked that week.

"Well, my science teacher . . ." and I told him the story, ending with "But I can't do it."

He was silent. I could see him suppressing anger. He said, "Let me see the pamphlet." He looked through it and then asked, "Why can't you do it?"

"Because, Jeff, I don't have a VHS tape."

"How much are VHS tapes?"

"Well, I don't know. But they are probably . . ."

"I'll get you the VHS tape."

Silence.

"Yeah, thanks, but I don't have the $15 application fee."

"Viola, I will get you a $15 waiver for the application fee."

Silence.

"Well, Jeff, I have to film myself doing two monologues. Where am I going to film it?"

"Viola, there's a TV station on the campus of Rhode Island College. I know the people in the TV station. You can film the monologues in the TV station."

After a long pause, he said, "You've run out of excuses."

And he was right. It was now time for me to, as I've heard Black people say so many times, "shit or get off the pot." So, I shit.

I got my monologues together. I went up to Rhode Island College where Deloris was a student. She was so excited. I kept changing clothes, most of which belonged to Deloris, in her room, searching for the right look. I went to the TV station. I filmed my classical and contemporary monologues. I filled out my application. I sent it all in. Free from the chains of my excuses, I was handling my business and exercising my agency, instead of sitting around doing nothing. And claiming that agency was a win in and of itself.

Thousands applied in the competition for drama alone, and only thirty would be chosen. I didn't believe I had a chance, but I was proud that I did it; that I did the hard, arduous work of applying.

I remember walking home from school one day with

my friend Kim Hall as we had done on countless occasions. On this particular day, as we neared my home, I looked ahead in the distance and all of the sudden I saw MaMama running toward us. Not casually jogging, but sprinting top speed, like her life depended on it. Now, you have to understand, MaMama is real country. As she was Olympic-sprinting in our direction, I noticed that she did so wearing my brother's shoes. I don't know why she had my brother's shoes on. Probably, she couldn't find hers. But as she drew closer and closer to us, we could see clearly that she was going nuts, waving this piece of paper in her hand, sprinting, yelling. It was a Western Union note, something foreign to those younger than Generation Xers like myself. Think of it like a text, but in physical rather than instant, electronic form. MaMama didn't even take time to catch her breath before revealing the contents of message.

"You have been chosen to come to Miami, Florida, for the Arts Recognition and Talent Search competition."

I was frozen. Silent. Frozen like I had been as my sisters yelled at me to throw that firecracker out the window. Frozen like when my entire family begged me to jump down from what we thought was our burning apartment. Frozen like when I sat silently all those many times while being lectured by teachers, nurses, and principals about my bad hygiene. But this was a good kind of frozen; a spectacular, glorious kind of frozen. Dumbfounded by the sheer unbelievability of the news my mom was sharing with me. Stupefied by the idea that the work I invested in a crazy dream actually paid off. Astonished that individuals I had never met actually saw me and deemed me worthy to participate in this prestigious competition.

I could not for the life of me see myself as one of the chosen few, but of the twelve hundred applications, I was one of the thirty. I got an all-expenses paid trip to Miami. I was in.

I don't recall exactly what I said to my mother when I broke out of my stupor, but whatever it was, it was accompanied by a lot of screaming, laughter, and tears. I was such a crybaby.

That summer going into the twelfth grade was the first time I flew on an airplane. I felt really out of place in Miami. That trip was one of the biggest things that had ever happened to me. My two monologues were from *Everyman* and *Runaways*, which had a lot of great monologues about feeling abandoned. I forget which particular one I performed. It could have been "Footsteps" or it could have been the last monologue in the play. They were all delicious in the sense that they provided actors a smorgasbord of feelings and emotions to tap into and share with audiences. And now I had the opportunity to share all those feelings, so many of which came out of my own experiences, with the best of the best gathering in Miami.

That being said, I felt so out of place around the best talent in the country. We stayed at the brand-new Hyatt Regency Hotel in Miami. News outlets were there that week, even *Good Morning America*. Great actors, dancers, musicians, visual artists from the toniest performing arts school arrived in full regalia. I came with a $30 dress from a store in downtown Pawtucket and a $2 suit from St. Vincent de Paul. I was overwhelmed and utterly not prepared artistically. Neither was I prepared socially. These kids were in their bodies, confident or at least good pretenders, and rowdy. I was none of those things. And on top of that, I was intensely shy. I felt alone. Looking back, I see I had more social anxiety than shyness. I felt that who I really was, was not worthy of a reveal. I was terrified every time she had to come out.

My roommate was a girl from Pennsylvania who talked about winning, who she thought was great, who wasn't. She wanted it! Whatever "it" was. She would torture herself after every daily audition. I didn't understand. I was just trying to survive.

I did great with my monologues. Afterward, it seemed that everyone wanted to "know" me. Everyone loves a winner. When I had to do my improvisations, which I loved, I froze. There were five-minute, three-minute, and one-minute improvs. After I froze, there was a collective silence that settled over me and the rest of the group.

It was a week of five-course meals, boat trips, television crews, media attention . . . In spite of the momentary lapse during the improvs, my talent was being recognized. However, my talents and the recognition that came with it were far more evolved than me, Viola. I didn't feel worthy. All the symbols that could give me status, I never had. Now, one was within reach.

I was named a Promising Young Artist and was lauded at City Hall once I got home. It was a big deal in Central Falls even though I didn't win any scholarship money.

If I created a fable of my life, a fantasy, I see myself finally meeting God, gushing, crying, thanking the Almighty for the accolades, a fabulous husband, beautiful daughter, my journey from nothing to Hollywood, awards, travel. I can clearly see the Lord's face, staring at me, taking me in and saying, "You never thanked me for creating you as YOU."

Chapter 12
Taking Flight

*"If you want to identify me, ask me not where
I live, or what I like to eat, or how I comb my hair,
but ask me what I am living for, in detail, ask me
what I think is keeping me from living fully for
the thing I want to live for."*

—Thomas Merton

Eventually, I received a full ride to college with the Preparatory Enrollment Program scholarship. PEP, as we called it, was the sister program of Upward Bound. I started in a familiar place, Rhode Island College, and space, housing in the same all-girls dormitory—Browne Hall—where I'd spent summers in high school and visited my sister Deloris during the school year. I went into college at seventeen, and like a lot of kids, I wasn't mature, but I definitely thought I was.

I was so excited to leave home. I worked for it and earned it. And once I arrived, I unpacked, settled in, and proceeded to fall into a deep, deep depression, probably the deepest depression I've ever experienced. I haven't had one like that since. Not that deep. I was depressed about being away from my little sister, Danielle, but that separation alone didn't fully explain its depths.

Since age fourteen I had saturated my life with acting, becoming an artist. But when I found myself in college, I still could not give myself permission to do the thing that I loved. My mind was like a railway station where two trains were leaving at the same time. One train was my academic career life; it was on track to graduate from high school, go to college to get my bachelor of arts degree, and become an artist. But the other train leaving the station tracked back to the place of trauma I came from, a place where I was bruised, did not believe in myself, had no sense of self. I could not understand self-love. I never felt like I was enough.

I went to college asking myself, as many artists do: *How am I going to make money? How am I going to support myself?* When I didn't see a clear path, I thought, *I'm not going back home. It's just not going to work as an artist. I have to be something else. Acting is just something I'm going to do on the side.* So I took a lot of English courses, which I loved, and decided I was going to be a teacher. Something inside me, however, must have had different ideas, because I fell deep and hard into a major sadness.

It was a depression about trading in my dream.

My dorm, Browne Hall, was all female. It had suites of twelve rooms, and each had a single bed, a desk, and a little closet. The building had a front door and a back door. Whenever someone was at the front door, whoever was manning the front desk would call you and say, "You have a visitor." I was settling into my new life, and despite the weight of the depression, happy to be surviving away from home. I had my room, showers, food, heat.

One night during that first year, I got a phone call from my sister Anita who was crying, "We're at your back door." I came out to find Anita in tears and almost eight months pregnant with my first niece, Brianna. MaMama was with her, also crying, bloodied in the face, bruised. My little sister, Danielle, reeked of urine.

It returned me to the trauma I'd grown up in, that had catapulted me out of my body. My father had again attacked my mom, and they had to get out of the house.

So they drove up to Rhode Island College in Anita's beat-up car because they had no place else to go.

"You guys, you can't stay. I can't have anyone in my room." I panicked. I had no idea what to do. "I'll get thrown out of the dorm."

"Then we have to go back home," Anita said. "He's out of his mind crazy. He may kill Mom."

I couldn't move. Again, I was frozen. Yet I managed to respond. "I don't have any money. I don't know what to do?"

MaMama was crying, terrified. "Why don't you just keep Danielle here for the night?"

Danielle was crying. It was awful. So I took Danielle. I barely had money to do my laundry downstairs in the dorm, but I took my sister anyway, tried to wash her clothes, let her take a shower. My best intentions did not match my resources. She'd sleep with me in my single bed. She slept on one end, I slept on the other. I barely had money for weekend meals when the dining hall was closed, but I somehow fed her. That's all I could do. I was trying to find my way, get my foothold, and also throw a rope to my family.

It was trying to save someone else when I was drowning. One of my regrets is the trauma Danielle had to endure, and my lack of ability in the moment to do anything about it beyond the temporary Band-Aid of that night. Now that I have a big bank account, resources, I wish I could reach back to that time period. If I could, I would travel back in time and take my sister away from all that, right then and there.

She called me at least fifteen times a day. My suitemate would say, "Viola! It's your baby sister." She would almost always be crying, saying, "Come get me, Vahlee." I always had to say, "Danielle, I can't come. I'm far away by bus." She would then begin openly weeping or I would hear my dad's drunken rages in the background while she wailed, "Please come get me."

Sometimes, especially on the weekends, Deloris and I would go home to be with her, pool our money to buy Heavenly Hash ice cream, fixings for a Greek salad and pasta shells with red Prego sauce. Danielle would be so happy. She would run out to us like Celie did in *The Color Purple* when she saw her sister Nettie. That reaction when you miss someone so much, and finally they're right in front of you. We would eat and watch *Fantasy Island* or *The Love Boat*.

Tattoo, the character played by Hervé Villechaize, would run up to this lighthouse when he saw the plane coming toward the island and would ring the bell shouting, "Da plane. Da plane!" Danielle loved that part so much she would say in between bites of pasta, "He's going to say 'Da Plane! Da plane.'" We would tease her and say, "No, he's not. Who told you that?" She would say, "Watch, you'll see." He would say it and our jaws would drop. We would look at her in amazement and she would cross her arms as if to say, *I told you*. That was our ritual. We went home because we absolutely loved our baby sister and she loved us so much. Then on Monday, we went back to school.

My older sister Dianne experienced every accolade imaginable during her journey: National Honors Society, Rhode Island Honor Society, All-State basketball. In addition, she was a great actress and singer. She could do it all. Successful Black women almost normalize overachieving. That was definitely Dianne.

She started out in acting at Rhode Island College before transferring to Howard University. At Howard she still wanted to become an actress until she found out how hard it was. "I want health insurance," she told me.

Even though my mom and dad didn't go to college—didn't finish high school—Dianne had driven it into us that **We. Were. Going. To. College**. She instilled in us that if we did not have a college degree, if we did not find something to do, if we did not focus, if we did not have drive, we were going to be like our parents. I felt if I did not go to college, if I did not get a degree, if I was not excellent, then my parents' reality would become my own. There was no gray area. Either you achieved or you failed.

I love them dearly, but I didn't want to live a life of poverty, alcoholism, and abuse. I thought I had only two choices: either succeed or absolutely sink. No in-between. I had no understanding that I possessed the tools to dig my way out if I somehow made a mistake. I had no understanding that there would be hard times and then joy would come, or sometimes the shoe would fall, but failing wasn't permanent. None of that emotionally healthy thinking was instilled in me. I only understood secrets, suppression, succeeding at all costs, overachieving. You make it or you don't. You either sink or you swim.

I don't know specifically how I came into my truth, but I'm pretty sure other caring people had a lot to do with it: counselors in the Upward Bound program and my sister Deloris who constantly asked me, "Why aren't you acting?" Until finally, one day in my second year, I said, "You know what, I'm just going to do it." That was when much of the depression fell away. The cure was courage. The courage to dare, risking failure. I decided I was going to be a theater major and I was going to be an actor.

I made a lot of friends in college. My suitemates were my crew: Jodi, Chris, Jane, and especially Terri Noya because we lived in the same town, Central Falls. Noya was Portuguese and came from poverty like me. Cheryl the RA, resident assistant, had cerebral palsy, but you almost wouldn't know it, even though she walked with an apparatus, because she was so beautifully tough.

They were a motley crew of forward-thinking girls God-ordained to be protective of me. I felt like they all believed in me. We loved one another. We were there for one another when parents died, getting married, having children. One of our suitemates got pregnant while we were still in school and had to drop out, but we rallied around her.

We had good times, but that first year was a rough transition. I drank three times my first year, and every single one of those times I got caught. I'd go out with friends and drink or whatever, but it wasn't my jam and I should've known it. It's like our parents would say when we were younger, "A hard head makes a soft ass." That means some lessons you have to learn the hard way.

The drunkest I got my entire life was in college. Some of my suitemates and I went off campus to the east side near Brown University and did shots of te-quila and shots of beer at Spats. Before I knew it, I was crawling out of there. I went back to my dorm, threw up, and had a hangover for a week. I don't know what my jam was, but it wasn't drinking, and I certainly wasn't dating or having sex. The moments of fun for me were when the girls in our suite sat in the common room and talked . . . about everything.

College was an interesting experience of not fitting in with the white kids and not fitting in with the Black kids. Harambee was the school's Black Student Coalition. Even though I knew a lot of the Black folk, went to the Ebony Fashion Fair and all of that, I didn't fit in with them because I was from Central Falls and those Black kids were from South Providence or Providence or Middletown, areas where there were more Black people. It was as if I didn't have my Black Card.

I was dark-skinned, didn't dress worth a damn, and had no "swag." None. Hell, I was coming from a square-mile city that was predominantly white when I was growing up, but now had more Hispanics. I didn't even know I had to have a certain behavior to have a sense of belonging with my own race.

Yet my "card" was too Black to get with the white kids. I was lost in that in-between space.

Mine was a journey getting through college, even after surviving that freshman-year depression. I was on my own. There was a food program during the week but not during the weekends. There it is: food again. There was something about the inability to get food that made me feel that I was slipping back into my fucked-up childhood. I always felt like I was foraging for it from Friday evening to Monday morning.

Imagine what it's like when you don't have a weekend meal plan? Worse off, you don't have a family who can send you a care package or a home where you can drop in for a kitchen/laundry-room raid. Imagine you don't have one of those little refrigerators in your room packed with food to carry you through those days when the cafeteria is closed. The result: the hunger pains of poverty.

To combat that, I always had a lot of jobs. I worked as an RA and counselor in the Preparatory Enrollment Program during the summer. I always worked. Senior year I had four jobs while in school full-time. I worked in the college library. I worked at the Rhode Island College front desk. I continued working at Brooks Drugs in Central Falls. And I had one other on-campus job.

Working at Brooks Drugs required me to leave campus, get on the bus, and schlep to Central Falls. Envision you have to work full-time but don't have a car, so you have to take three or four buses one way in subzero weather to get to a damn job that's four or five towns away from campus, in order to make enough money to eat on the weekend. Then you've got to take three or four buses back to your dorm room so you can make your Monday morning classes. You've got to graduate; you still have to study. You feel like you're on a treadmill.

To this day, I don't like taking the bus. I lived in New York City for thirteen years and took the train all the time, never the bus. During college, I walked in cold, freezing weather, at the very least, a mile and a half to the bus stop off campus. Either that or I'd have to wait for the bus to come to Rhode Island College, and that bus schedule was unreliable. Most times I just walked to the first bus stop in freezing cold weather.

It was especially heinous when it was dark because I had to walk through the back entrance of the college, over the sports field, then up to Smith Avenue where there were very few streetlights, and wait for the bus. That bus would take me to downtown Providence. Then I would wait again at a major bus stop for the bus to take me from downtown Providence to downtown Pawtucket. Usually I didn't have the money for the last leg of the trip, or sometimes when I had the money, I would miss the bus from Pawtucket to Central Falls because, well, it was unreliable. It was a scheduling nightmare. I would walk a mile or two from downtown Pawtucket to Brooks Drugs in Central Falls. After work, I would go back to my parents' apartment, sleep on the floor, and go back to school the next morning or take someone else's shift.

Working hard is great when it's motivated by passion and love and enthusiasm. But working hard when it's motivated by deprivation is not pleasant.

A lot of college for me was great laughter and connection with suitemates and other friendships I began to make, mixed with isolation and fucking pain. I still felt like I had to hide my deepest truths to fit in. I recreated myself as this "other." I imagined myself as this fabulous, overachieving, funny, quirky theater geek from Central Falls. Every once in a while, I sat with the Black students in our area in the cafeteria, but most of the time, I sat with my tribe, my suitemates, or by myself.

Rhode Island College was less than 1 percent "other" back in the day. "Other" meaning any student of color: Hispanic, Asian, Black, Middle Eastern. The rest were white. There were probably close to nine thousand students. I was a lost girl trying to find my way.

It didn't help that back then, Rhode Island College (RIC) had fraternities and sororities that were rowdy and all white. Kappa Epsilon was one. I mention this because some of those members were blatantly racists. Many years after my college days, I read where some researchers trace the founding of the Ku Klux Klan to the Kappa Alpha fraternity. In hindsight, some of those RIC Kappa Epsilon members must have been kissing cousins with the brotherhood, emphasis on "hood," of Kappa Alpha because their acts of blatant racism were a constant narrative perpetuated by its members. I think they believed that whites all gained college admission based on merit while Black and Brown students were all beneficiaries of affirmative action.

There was no cognitive understanding of the real complexity of race at the school or in its admissions process. How do you excel when you're Southeast Asian, highly intelligent, hardworking but spent two years in a Cambodian jungle, two years in a refugee camp, and watched your family being massacred before coming to the country? Without the Preparatory Enrollment Program, there would have been zero students of color because we were starting with major deficits. Most destructive was the view that we weren't worthy. It is the foundation built into the DNA of America, and when you couple it with personal challenges like poverty, violence, trauma, and compromised communities, it can become a death knell. Years later, Frank Sanchez was appointed president and totally transformed the demographics of the school.

I focused on acting classes: character study, voice and articulation, creative classes, dramatic criticism, the history of theater—every aspect of theater. The other academic classes, not so much. I had felt the huge malaise until deciding that acting was the path I was going to take. It's what made me happy. It's what brought me joy. But there was no way in from Rhode Island to being a working actor. None. How do you even get a job? How do you get an audition or an agent? I was getting closer to starting my life and needed to figure it out.

The area in life that is parallel to work, to academics, is home. Your emotional center is rooted there. For me, the result was being late for class a lot, not being as prepared as I could be. I was always catching up, always a little disorganized. I lacked organizational skills, even in my room. I didn't know how to dress or present myself. I had the persona of being real because I didn't know what or who else to be. But being real and being transparent are two totally different things. Being real is wearing fifteen-dollar shoes and being proud to wear them. Being transparent is saying, "I'm always anxious. I never feel like I fit in. I need help." I wasn't transparent.

I didn't feel like I was in my body. People probably felt I was because I never spoke about my father's alcoholism or growing up poor and hungry. I kept big secrets. I felt like I was the big secret. A huge part of me, my pathology, was a big secret. What I presented to the world was a little Black girl overachiever from Central Falls. And I was.

I immersed myself in theater once I decided that was what I wanted. I woke up one day and said, "Just jump, Viola." I auditioned and got two roles in Main Stage Productions, *Hot L Baltimore* by Lanford Wilson and *Romeo and Juliet.* I was the prostitute April in *Hot L* and the nurse in *Romeo and Juliet.* For my portrayal of April, I was nominated for an Irene Ryan Award, the top acting award in college. I also created a one-woman show that I performed for years. It had seventeen different characters. Every character from Celie in *The Color Purple* to Pilate in Toni Morrison's *Song of Solomon* to St. Joan. I even performed an improvisation piece where I created a comic piece based on words the audience just spontaneously threw at me.

The one-woman show was my senior thesis project, and the purpose was to show that I had range, that I could transform just like my white counterparts. At the time, I felt it was a show that was a true coming-out event. But in hindsight, the objective of it was fucked-up. How do you create a show to prove you're worthy?

There's a bartering, desperation factor attached to that. *Let me prove to you that I have talent* instead of just, being. Forget about the dark-skinned girl who just walked into the audition room. Let me use my training and technique to make you "forget" that I'm Black. The extent of that obstacle is way more burdensome than the obstacles placed in front of my white counterparts. White students just had to show up and be good. There was no transforming to make you believe that this Rhode Islander could actually be Russian in a play by a Russian playwright. They simply had to be, well, white. This obstacle would be the four-hundred-pound gorilla that would constantly inhabit the various rooms I entered throughout my life.

Rhode Island College was known for its great musical productions, but I was never part of that. In fact, if you asked many of the theater students there during that time, they have very little memory of me. I did find mentors in Bill Hutchinson, Elaine Perry, and David Burr. I did mostly Black Box Productions, Readers Theatre, and off-campus Summer Theatre.

If there is another pet peeve as a theater major there in the '80s, it's this: Educational theater should be just that. College should not operate like a Broadway or regional theater whose main goal is profit. Educational theater is for the training and preparation of the student actor. Its purpose is to give them the tools to be able to operate on a professional level. It's why we pay tuition. There are and were theater majors who have never done a main stage production. How do you learn if you don't do?

I graduated after five years because it took me a long time to decide on my major. I had to take some courses to catch up. I stayed on campus the whole time.

My last year, I went on national student exchange to California Polytechnic University in Pomona. I went because I wanted to get out of Rhode Island, out of the cold winters. I just wanted a different scene. The greatest surprise of my life is that in one semester, I flourished. I performed in *Mrs. Warren's Profession*, a George Bernard Shaw play. I was a part of an improv group. I took a life-changing public speaking class. I did very well academically and made wonderful friends. It was the first time I got a weave, which was a big deal back in the day. At the time, I felt cute; real cute. I kept that damn weave in until string was hanging down my shoulder.

I loved the theater program at Cal Poly. I totally fit in with all the theater geeks. I had a great roommate, Eva Rajna, a tall, wonderful, Jewish woman from Hungary whose father owned a bakery in Sunnyvale, California. The nicest family. He would send her boxes of pastries, which we would devour. I could eat enormous amounts of food back in the day.

I was still painfully shy, uncomfortable, and awkwardly introverted outside of theater. I avoided conversations, avoided dating, still no boyfriend and no sex. It took a lot for me to trust people. To really allow anyone in. My posse was always small because of that.

I came back to Rhode Island College for my final semester, renewed. Going three thousand miles away and throwing myself into the belly of the beast that was California forced me to dig deep to survive. I made the Dean's List for the fourth time.

A month before graduation, I auditioned for grad programs for theater students. They're called URTA, University Resident Theatre Association, Auditions. Even though they're called URTA Auditions, no one ever got any work in regional theaters after these auditions. It's another example of the brutality and nebulous aspects of the business of acting. However, schools courted me for their master's programs in theater. Once again, I was a mess of contradiction. I was, on one hand, brave, courageous, able to be independent and out on my own. And at the same time, I was emotionally conflicted, not comfortable in my authenticity, in my own skin.

As brave, courageous, independent Viola, I took the train into New York City for my audition without any instruction or research. I just went and auditioned and it was a great audition. No matter how nervous I was, I could use it as fuel to really attack my monologues, which were Celie from *The Color Purple* and Martine from the Molière play *The Learned Ladies*.

It was the Celie monologue that always got me in. It would later get me into Juilliard and into a lot of Readers Theatre competitions in New England. I thought it apropos that Celie was so incomplete, not fully formed. If not for the love from her sister and Shug Avery, she would've never seen her value.

When I was onstage, I could ingest the applause, audience member tears and words saying *they were so moved* and *they never saw a performance like that before*. It gave me temporary self-love from the outside. But it would soon wear off because self-love from the outside, by definition, really isn't self-love. So I quickly went back to my ordinary world where I felt awkward. I could handle my quirkiness, pain, shyness when I could put it all in my character. It would be accepted in a way that made me feel even more awkward and not accepted in my real life.

I graduated with a degree in theater in 1988. The whole family came down for my graduation from Rhode Island College—my four sisters and my brother, mom, dad, and even my grandmother, Mozell Logan, came from South Carolina. They sat in the bleachers and screamed like banshees when I got my diploma. My grandma kept saying, "I'm so proud of you, baby. Your grandma love you so much." She was small and dark-skinned. I remember thinking, *Why am I staring at her so much?* Something about her drew me toward her and tattooed itself in my memory. It was her voice. It was deep, clear, melodious. I wanted to freeze this moment in my memory. It was her voice that stood out to me. She had the voice that most actors would die to have. They spend thousands of dollars to tap into it. It was regal. It was commanding. It took me by surprise. It sounded just like . . . ME!

Chapter 13
The Blooming

*"Jump, and you will find out how
to unfold your wings as you fall."*

—RAY BRADBURY

When I graduated from Rhode Island College,
a voice somewhere far in the recesses of my
psyche, which was always true, honest, and in hindsight, beautifully cognizant, that I didn't have the
courage to always listen to, but when I did, it served me
perfectly, steered me to apply to a six-week summer
program at Circle in the Square Theatre in New York
City. I got accepted after the URTA Audition in New
York.

I got a full-tuition grant to the six-week program,

but I needed money to live in New York City for those six weeks. A great woman ran the Rhode Island State Council on the Arts at the time, Iona Dobbins. She was dedicated to artists and the arts. I cried in her office begging for money. She listened to my sob story, gave me a napkin, and said, "I'm going to get you the money." And she did. She got me a $1,200 grant.

That incentivized me to earn the rest of the money I needed to go to New York and study at this great theater.

That summer, a month before the program started, I worked in a horrible factory. To actors who say, "Oh, I don't care, I'm not going to compromise myself artistically, even if I have to live in poverty," I say, "You've never lived in poverty. If you've ever been poor, as a child or adult, it's no joke."

I worked in factories where those in unemployment offices were sent. You signed up to work in whatever place needed laborers that day. At six o'clock in the morning, you crowded into a van and were driven to a factory. In Central Falls, I knew people who worked in factories—people I grew up with, undocumented immigrants who came with no job skills whatsoever. Even my mother worked in factories.

I worked at a factory where you just made boxes. That's all you did. You made boxes. All. Day. Long.

I worked at another factory and then started working at P-PAC, which is the Providence Performing Arts Center, doing telemarketing work, which is horrific. People scream at you through phones: "Stop fucking calling me on the phone! I don't want you calling me. Ba-ba-ba-ba." It was great training for an actress because it's the height of humiliation, the height of rejection. I had a technique where I would always ask for the man in the house if the woman answered. I would use my sexiest voice. Almost always, the woman would ask, "Who may I ask is calling?" or "Who is this?" Then I had them. I could keep them on the phone. That was all I had in my bag of tricks.

My life was topsy-turvy that summer as I earned enough money to supplement the Rhode Island State Council on the Arts grant so I could go to New York and just enjoy my time doing the work as an actor at Circle in the Square Theatre.

Once I got to New York, I also got a job passing out flyers in Times Square for *Tamara: The Living Play*. It was almost like dinner theater. You walked into a building on Fifth Avenue, where you stood and watched the play—a murder mystery—unfolding in the room, right there. Then each character veered off to a different room, and you had to choose which character to follow. At the end, the mystery culminated in the same room where it started. During intermission, you were served dinner.

A friend, who'd also been a student at Rhode Island College, was the head of publicity. "Viola, I will pay you $20 an hour in cash," she said, "if you pass out flyers about the play in Times Square." So that became one of my jobs during the six-week program at Circle in the Square. I only passed the flyers out and didn't have an acting role because I was just out of school, didn't have an agent, and newly arrived in New York from Podunk Rhode Island. I certainly wasn't a professional yet.

I thrived at Circle in the Square. I loved, loved, loved New York! I lived in a loft apartment in Gramercy Park with two women I knew from Rhode Island College, Donna and Mary. New York kick-started the part of me that was always friggin' scared. It catapulted me out of my comfort zone. New York was just a different vibe. The crowds, the smell, the noise, the buildings, the life. Men whistling at you as you walked to the subway. In one day, I learned how to ride the train. I just did it. I sampled restaurants and delis owned by people from all over the world.

I received my best acting training, ever. I've had a lot of wonderful acting teachers. Ron Stetson, Dr. Hutchinson, Rob Dimmick, Elaine Perry, David Burr. But Alan Langdon, in that six-week program at Circle in the Square Theatre that summer of '88, was the absolute greatest I've ever had. I came to life under the tutelage of teachers there, like Jacqueline Brooks. Great actors like Philip Seymour Hoffman, Felicity Huffman, Kevin Bacon were students. It was no-holds-barred, courageous scene study, acting study, voice, movement, everything. It was comprehensive, a training program where you couldn't emotionally hide.

Alan himself was, well, a strange man. He was mysterious. Looking back, I think he was just quiet. As artists, we're so used to the flamboyant personalities, and we're almost offended when someone is not that way. Alan's flamboyance was in his intense quiet observation.

There were close to thirty kids in my group, and more than a hundred students in total, and you would pair off to do scenes. Everyone was coming from a different part of the country and staying in apartments in different parts of the city. We would go to each other's apartment or, sometimes, practice a scene on a stoop. We would come in, perform the scene, and Alan would just stare. Then he would get up and stand in the back of the room and then sit again. It was as if he was silently watching a football game and internally getting anxious because his team was close to winning. The

scene would end and there was always deafening silence. He would either ask a series of questions or do
something to wake you up.

One actor—Emily—who had a very, very soft voice
and always looked nervous was a part of the group that
summer. Emily always looked scared. She was enor-
mously sweet and accommodating, almost too much so.
She was a part of the program not because she wanted
to be an actor but wanted to find herself. Or heal? From
what I didn't know. An actor brings their story with
them in the work—past, present, fears, mess, humor,
trauma.

Emily decided to do a scene from the play *Agnes
of God* by John Pielmeier. The story is about a young
nun who becomes pregnant inside the convent. She
insisted she had no intercourse and says God impreg-
nated her. There's absolutely no evidence of anyone
on the grounds of the monastery or in her room. At
a certain point, she begins to bleed from her hands, a
stigmata. It becomes apparent that the baby may be a
case of immaculate conception. The Mother Superior
calls in a court-appointed psychiatrist to make an as-
sessment. But the conflict in the scene Emily chose is
between the insistent logic of the psychiatrist and the
passionate insistence of the young nun whose faith in
God is fervent.

The scene started with the actor playing the psychiatrist who had pinned Agnes, Emily, to the wall, screaming, "Agnes, whose baby is it? Tell me! Tell me?" She's supposed to shout back, "It's God's!" Emily whispered, "It's God's," barely audible.

I cringed knowing Alan would dig down deep to see what was blocking her.

There was the usual silence after the scene. Alan looked at Emily and finally said, "Where's your voice?" Emily was shaking at this point. She said she didn't know. Alan insisted, "You must know. Who took your voice?"

Emily and I were really close that summer. We were both painfully shy and awkward, and people like that usually find and cling to each other. We talked about life all the time and she just kept saying she wanted to get better. Better from what I didn't know. But even I wanted to know where she lost her voice, and why she always looked scared, jittery.

Showing intense emotion, she finally said softly, "My father would hold me down on the bed when I was nine and beat and rape me. He would cover my mouth."

The whole class fell silent.

My heart raced.

Alan asked if she wanted to do the scene again. She wanted to. She was braving something and it wasn't acting. This class was a tool to unlock a deep pain, to save that little nine-year-old girl. Her scream was the sound of an animal that's about to be slaughtered by a pack of wolves and is calling on every strength left in its body to fight, to live. It was also a sound of loss. "It's GOD'S! THIS BABY BELONGS TO GOD!" She fell to the ground in a heap. Alan held her. We were all in various stages of shock and tears.

Me? I was jealous. All my scenes were emotional, well explored, I thought. But this was next level. I was broken and my brokenness brought me here, to acting, to New York, to wanting to heal and live and feel alive!

Stanislavski, Sanford Meisner, Stella Adler, all teachers from the famed Actors Studio, said to study *life*. It's those moments that you study in life that get injected into your work. You're creating human beings. You're not just creating a different walk, a different manner of speech, and a different emotional life. Circle in the Square pulled that home for me and they did it with love. Alan Langdon is still teaching at Circle in the Square Theatre.

After the six-week summer program, they ask one student to join their theater. They asked me. I declined, saying, "Circle in the Square is a great training program, but I want a program where I can get a job afterward." I wanted a training program where I knew that as soon as I finished, I would be working as an actor, that I would have an agent. Without an agent, you don't get jobs. I wanted to be able to say that I trained as an actor, now I'm working as an actor. I wanted to be assured I'd have a paycheck to cover my bills, put food on the table. I didn't want to go back to Central Falls.

I asked Mark, another good friend of mine who was in the program at the time, "What program can I get into where at the end of it we're auditioning for people who can actually get you a job?"

"Well, those would be Juilliard, Yale, and NYU, Viola. Those are the programs, and maybe SUNY Purchase, where they have auditions in the fourth year," he replied. "They called them league auditions back in the day because there was a league of thirteen schools. But now only these four invite agents and casting directors from all over, for your fourth-year auditions."

Toward the end of my gap year, I applied to Juilliard, one of the four Mark named. I would have applied to all three schools, but I only had money for one application fee.

People have asked if I got connected at Circle in the Square, if I developed a network from being there. I suppose there was an acting network in New York, but I've realized there is no true network, no rhyme or reason or textbook way of getting into this business, except finally getting a job that leads to the next job and the next.

I decided my next move was to get training at one of the programs Mark told me about, but I had missed my boat to be accepted and enrolled for the coming year in any of them. I decided to take a gap year. I knew I needed to grow up. Circle in the Square Theatre is smack-dab in the middle of Manhattan. I was taking the subway on my own. I was living in an apartment in Gramercy Pack with two friends from Rhode Island College. I never had sex, never had a boyfriend, never lived on my own. Never traveled overseas. I just wanted to grow up. I wanted to experience life. I wanted my life to be as expansive as I felt my mind was, my imagination was.

I remember praying. I was a nonchurchgoing person. But I had started praying when I was younger before bed every night in order to sleep, to calm my anxiety. I prayed harder when my father was beating MaMama, especially when it got bloody or brutal. I prayed when he slit her arm open. I prayed when he stabbed her in her leg or in the neck with a pencil. It's all I could think to do. Now, at twenty-one, I prayed that my life would manifest in a way that made me worthy to become a professional actress, travel out of the country, and get a boyfriend.

In that year off, I became a professional actress. My first professional production was in Providence, Rhode Island, at Trinity Repertory Company in August Wilson's *Joe Turner's Come and Gone*. After I came back from those six weeks training at Circle in the Square Theatre in New York, I acted at Trinity Rep for a year. The artistic director was Adrian Hall. I had auditioned for him, knew him. He had seen my work. He retired during my gap year, but we did maybe three plays together. After he retired, director Susan Lawson, whose shitty apartment in New York I would later sublease when I went to Juilliard, took over for him.

I juggled a day job and a night job. I returned to work at Providence Performing Arts Center as a telemarketer during the day. The Trinity Rep performances were at night, so I had my days free. The acting training of humiliation/rejection at the Performing Arts Center by day; then actually performing professionally in a play at night.

Danielle, who was by then eleven, and I became even closer during my gap year. Although I had a roommate at the time, sometimes she would sleep over. Or I would sleep at my mom's house on the floor with her, because MaMama and MaDaddy's apartment was so small. That's why I got my own apartment in Pawtucket. My roommate was a very nice friend of a friend and the apartment was beautiful. The landlord, however, was a raging racist. I haven't met anyone like her since. She was Brazilian. Aghast when I moved in, she thought I was a prostitute because she saw me waiting for a bus.

When my roommate, who was the only one she would talk to, said I was an actress, she didn't know what that meant. She said I wasn't allowed to have visitors, even my little sister, because Black kids destroy property. She said she was terrified of being raped and killed by me or any Black man I invited over. She kept a baseball bat near her door. Many years later, after I moved to Los Angeles, I came home to visit, and during a trip to the mall, I saw a woman selling jewelry at a pop-up shop. It was her. "Where are you from?" I asked and she replied, "Brazil, sweetheart." She proceeded to be extraordinarily kind. I put her on the list of racists who like Blacks from a distance.

By then I understood that housing redlining was a part of our culture—North and South—affected by Jim Crow. Whether you have an education or not, the ugliness of racism comes down like a hammer. It enveloped my life when I was eight and at twenty-three, I was still bullied by it. When you have little to no money, there's no way to combat it. Where could I live? My sister Deloris was living with her boyfriend-soon-to-be-husband in a one-bedroom apartment. My sister Dianne lived in Maryland, and my sister Anita had two children and was having her own challenges.

I wish I had had the power, resources at that time to tell that racist woman to shove her apartment up her ass but MY ass would've been on my parents' floor. That was like being sentenced to live out my childhood again. I was still running.

In *Joe Turner's Come and Gone* there's a role for an eleven-year-old girl—Zonia. Danielle auditioned for it and got the role. This was in a professional production directed by Israel Hicks, who was probably one of the greatest theater directors in the business. Terrific actors came in from New York. It was a great production. Danielle thrived in it and got great reviews from the *Boston Globe*, the *Providence Journal*, and several other newspapers. She was also getting straight As in school.

After school, she would take the bus from Central Falls to downtown Providence for rehearsals and once we were in production, she would take the bus to make it to the theater on time. Man, we were still running for buses all the time. I could easily make Danielle run by egging her on, "Danielle! The fastest runner in Central

Falls." At night, after the play and we were exhausted, I would take her back home on the bus and stay with her at my mom's house, because it was too late to walk to my own apartment, which was close to Mom's.

A lot of the fighting between my parents had subsided by this point although the alcoholism was still rampant.

While rehearsing *Joe Turner's Come and Gone* at Trinity Rep, two big events happened. I auditioned for Juilliard and I met David, the man in my life for the next seven years. David was in the play.

David played Jeremy and I played the role of Molly. He was a professional actor who came from Boston. To me, it was like meeting a Black Marlon Brando. He was a great actor. I saw him. He came to me. I thought I was completely, absolutely, without question in love. He was my first boyfriend.

David was older and blacker than Black. He had immersed himself in Black history and Black consciousness and Black literature. His favorite type of music was jazz. He was also a film enthusiast. He would start watching films early in the morning and wouldn't stop until the next day. His harmonica or mouth harp skills were spectacular. It all made me feel so, so . . . grown. We would go out after the play to the bar next door. We bonded over Long Island Iced Tea. I liked Long

Island Iced Tea because the drink actually tasted like iced tea. I would only have one. I was a twenty-three-year-old big girl now and a professional actress, using the lingo, doing what professional actors do, hanging out with experienced actors.

Once a play is running, you have your days free. That's when I traveled to NYC to audition for Juilliard.

I wanted to be able to audition. An actor doesn't just show up and say, "I want the job." An agent is a conduit, the connection between talent and work. Not all agents are created equal. Some agents can't get you an audition for one line on a TV show. My goal was to attend Juilliard and graduate with a top-notch agent.

I got my ass on that train in Providence to NYC, thinking I would knock out the audition and make it back for my 7:30 p.m. call for *Joe Turner's Come and Gone* at Trinity Rep. In theater, 7:30 p.m. is your half-hour call. That means you have to be at the theater at 7:30 p.m. That's when the stage manager does a roll call. That's like marking your timesheet. You have to be in your dressing room at 7:30 p.m.

I had no idea that when you audition to get in Juilliard, the auditions take place over three days. I found that out much later after trading admissions stories with classmates. I didn't even know Juilliard was a four-year program. Yale is three years. NYU is three years. I was simply intent on going to a school where I could get more training and then an agent . . . and I wanted to get better.

Ignorant of the three-day audition regime, when I received my audition slot, I allocated one day, thinking, *Well, I'll just go up for the day and tell them, "You're going to tell me now whether I'm in or I'm out. Because I have to get back. I have to get back on the train."* It took four and a half hours to get there, four and a half hours back, and a half hour from Penn Station to Juilliard, which is Midtown Manhattan, at Sixty-Sixth Street and Broadway. I had just forty-five minutes to devote to the audition.

I was pretty confident that I was going to get into Juilliard because I didn't know better. I felt I had power in my acting. I had a feeling I was good. The longer I had been in theater settings, the more confident I became. And New York City was very easy for me to navigate, even coming from Central Falls, Rhode Island.

The day I went to my Juilliard audition, the clock was ticking. I got on the first train smoking and arrived early. I weighed about 165 pounds and was nervous, sitting in a room with dozens of skinny actors who had been in magnet schools since they were two years old, dance classes since they were toddlers, all warming up, doing their ballet techniques. I sat there, waiting my turn. I had no sense of what to wear so I had on poufy jeans, a huge red sweater, and a headwrap that had wide silver, purple, and gold sparkles. I was too inexperienced to understand that any of that could be a distraction from my performance.

My two audition pieces were lines of Celie in *The Color Purple* and something from *The Learned Lady* by Molière. You needed a contemporary and a classical piece. Usually, three and a half minutes at the most. That's a true monologue. Sometimes you get a little longer. But that's usually the standard. I was confident in my pieces.

At Juilliard you audition for three or four main teachers and if you're good enough, you go on to the next level and do your audition again. Then you go to the next level, and you audition again until the entire faculty has seen you. Then there are interviews. Applicants stayed in hotels, allowing time for all of that. I only had forty-five minutes and no idea how unorthodox that was. I did my monologues, then said "Thank you" and returned to the room filled with actors who looked like they had been in training for this moment since they were two years old.

The atmosphere is staunch, authoritative hierarchy; the faculty are the boss and absolutely strict about classical training; you speak when you're spoken to. I put my hair rag back on and said, "I just thought you should know, I've got forty-five minutes. I'm doing a play in Providence. My half-hour call is at 7:30. It's a four-and-a-half-hour train ride. You have to tell me whether I'm in or out." I can't believe I said that.

They looked shocked, as if I pimp-slapped them. But they said, "Okay. Just stand by."

I sat in that room, feeling out of place. Everybody's doing their vocal training at the same time. Screaming, yelling, yelping. Doing their yoga moves. All that shit. I'm trying to sit quietly in the corner and look into the hallway as the teachers and the head of the school picked up their chairs. Later, I learned they carried their chairs into the biggest training room at Juilliard, room 103. I heard whispers, "What's going on? What's going on?" Then someone called me. The teachers had fast-tracked me. Instead of waiting three days, I was asked to do my audition again for all the teachers of all the departments in one room.

When they called me in—"Okay. Viola, in five minutes"—I knew I had undivided attention in that damn room with everybody. I did my audition for all of them. They interviewed me. The head of the department, who, by the way, was an asshole. Great director. Great interpreter of Shakespeare. . . . But an asshole.

Michael Langham, director of Stratford Festival in Canada for many years, said, "There are things you have to work on. But we see your gift as an actor, your emotional wealth."

"Thank you. Thank you. Thank you. Thank you. Thank you. Thank you," I said. Looking back, I see I wanted to say, *Hurry the fuck up, and just let me know if I got in, because I have to get on that train. I gotta go.* But I knew I had gotten in. I ran for the train and made it back on time.

Getting into a school is usually a wonderful story that's the equivalent of falling in love or being on the honeymoon. There's a difference between falling in love and actually being in the marriage. By the time I received the acceptance letter, I already knew I had gotten in. By the time I got to Juilliard, I was already in the marriage. That magic and excitement of the audition was back-burnered, a long-forgotten dream. I wish I could've held on to the fact that my audition was badass.

Back in Providence, David loved Danielle. He loved kids in general. He already had one from a prior relationship. During breaks in rehearsal, we would all get the most magnificent sandwiches from Mark's Deli. After the performance at night, I would take Danielle home and walk back to my apartment. Because

Danielle was underage, eleven, another actress would play the role of Zonia four performances a week. They would switch. On the nights Danielle didn't perform, I would stay with David.

As much as I would love to romanticize that part of my life, I can't. I was so unfinished. I asked God for a boyfriend, professional acting status, and the experience of traveling overseas. But I didn't ask for wisdom. I didn't ask for self-love. And it showed.

I was with a man who never loved me. My objective the entire seven years was earning his love. I would internally pray, convincing myself that THIS would be the day he'd profess that he couldn't live without me. THIS would be the day he'd just look at me and tell me I'm beautiful. I practically gave him VIP access to relationships with other women. I felt lucky to have him. That's how damaged I was. He never remembered my birthday, my favorite foods, Christmas, Valentine's Day. I was into the outward marks of achievement rather than the inner sense of home with a man, a sense of belonging to oneself.

He wasn't a great boyfriend but I didn't demand anything from him. I didn't create any boundaries. I didn't teach him how to treat me, so I wasn't the best girlfriend. I used to be secretly jealous of people who were even in bad relationships. I would hear women say, "Yeah, he was begging me to take him back after he cheated on me. He was crying, going on and on about how much he loved me and wanted me, so I took him back." My thought was, *He cried and said he wanted you and loved you?* I never heard that in seven years. But it was not David. It was me.

Before I met David that gap year, I met someone else on the way to work. He became: "My First Boyfriend Who I Never Talk About." His name was Carl and he was a wayward soul. Our connection started with him telling me I was beautiful at the bus stop and me smiling. I never knew where he was, what he was doing, where he worked, nothing. I remember very little about him because he didn't stick around long. I slept with him four times. I'm ashamed because I have puritanical values that I was not admitting to. I'm ashamed also because the last time I was with him, I went to his house to tell him, "We're done." He wanted to have sex and I most definitely didn't. I was on my period. We struggled. He kept pulling my pants down. I thought about punching him, but I didn't. Maybe that would've been an acknowledgment that what was happening was rape. So I gave in and afterward left, ashamed. That's how I felt, but what I showed was a young woman in control. I compartmentalized the trauma and filtered it so that it would lie to me and keep me safe. Another dirty secret, another shame lashing.

Why didn't I punch his ass in the face?! Why didn't I fight the same way six-year-old Viola did when the boy next door tried to kiss and touch me in his house? Six-year-old me punched him as hard as I could. No apology. Hell! He kicked me hard afterward but I got back up, with tears, to kick his ass again!! Somehow along the way, I guess I felt she was wrong. That in my journey to "the top," to being more "evolved," I left the street fighter behind. I left my claws.

David was an out-of-town actor. Equity rules dictated that the theater had to provide him his own apartment for the duration of the play. I had another place to stay, to lay my head. I tapped into another part of my soul that identified me—my Blackness. David was bold and unapologetic about it. He once saw a poll on the PBS show *Tony Brown's Journal* that said that 80 percent of whites felt Blacks were unpatriotic. It pissed him off so that he studied every war America has ever fought and researched African American involvement in them. Every single war we fought in. Even during Jim Crow when we were not nearly given the same rights as our white counterparts. That was patriotism! If that didn't speak volumes about our love and commitment to this country, nothing did. He also studied music, Black history.

Just before I went to Juilliard, David went to LA to do the Shakespeare play *Measure for Measure* at The Old Globe theater in La Jolla. Then he moved back to Rhode Island to become a company member at Trinity Rep. During my years at Juilliard, every time I went home on the weekend or during holidays, I would stay with him in his apartment.

David was an actor who worked a lot. I was the newbie actor, then acting student. In that gap year, I was also working as a telemarketer at P-PAC, Providence Performing Arts Center, selling tickets over the phone, while doing play after play after play at Trinity Rep. I was finally a working actor, not making bank, but enough to get by, to live. Rhode Island didn't have a high cost of living. I didn't have a car, but I had my own apartment—with a roommate. I could buy food. I could do all that I needed to get by. I was an overly busy working actor.

But I didn't want to stay in Rhode Island. I wanted to grow, to travel. Toward the end of my gap year, I resigned from Trinity Rep and flew to Edinburgh, Scotland, where I performed three plays in the Fringe Festival. One of my mentors, Dr. Bill Hutchinson,

My daddy at our Parker Street house.

My dad and my baby sister, Danielle. They spent so much time together when she was little.

My mom and dad at the racetrack after a win. The groom of the horse was always in a photograph. My dad wanted my mom beside him this night.

I seriously don't know if this is ninth grade or senior year. I just love my smile. At the time, I couldn't even look at pictures of myself.

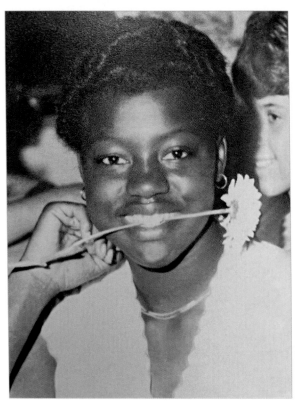

Me at my ninth-grade Freshman Frolic.
I went with Bill Martel who was a senior.
I had a big crush on him. My mom curled my
hair with one of those iron curlers. I had the
BEST time, but my hair smelled like smoke.

Viola Davis
35 Parker Street
NICKNAME: *Vi*
FAVORITE SAYING: *"When I'm rich and famous . . ."*
FUTURE AMBITION: Professional Actress
ACTIVITIES: Drama 9, 10, 11, 12; Chorus 9, 10, 11, 12; Cross Country 9; Model
Legislature 11, 12; Girl's State 11; Yearbook Staff 12; school newspaper 11, 12; art
club 9, 11, 12; 1983 Homecoming Court.
FAVORITES: Jennifer Holiday . . . Sylvester Stallone . . . theatre . . . dance . . .
reading . . . writing . . . acting . . . ice cream . . . pizza . . . Fame . . . all food in
general .

Viola Davis

I'm mortified by the description of me in my high school yearbook. My only
defense is that I was young. But . . . I manifested being a professional actress.

All of my siblings together for my Rhode Island College graduation.
They were all so happy for me, and I felt proud.

My first headshot after graduating
from Juilliard. I took this picture on the
same day I found out I was pregnant.

My first Broadway production, *Seven Guitars*.
Here I am in a scene with the terrific Keith David.

Me and the great Julie Kavner in *God's Heart* by Craig Lucas
at the Mitzi E. Newhouse Theater at Lincoln Center.
I played a woman dying from breast cancer. I went
through the entire dying process onstage.

Me playing Ruth Younger in *A Raisin in the Sun* by Lorraine Hansberry. Awesome cast! Kimberly Elise, Ruben Santiago-Hudson, and Gloria Foster. It was at the Williamstown Theatre Festival.

This was the first of our three ceremonies. It was at our condo in The Valley. We invited only fifteen people. It was perfect!!

About a month into dating Julius. We were at Steven Bochco's house. Steven was the creator of the show *City of Angels*, where we met.

Me and my beautiful mommy at my vow renewal. We had a wonderful time!!!

Me being prepped for the Emmys—the night I won.

Another win—me and my Genesis
at her baby shower.

My dad with my nephews
Derek and Warren.
He loved his grandkids.

Me and Miss Tyson. I secretly used every opportunity to hold and kiss her.

MITCHELL HAASETH

The last table read of *How to Get Away with Murder*. We were all in tears afterward.

The cast of *Ma Rainey's Black Bottom* in Pittsburgh. My last pic with Chadwick.

filled out the application for us to enter. I went to Boston to get my first passport and was amazed at how my dreams were manifesting. It's the largest theater festival in the world.

Emily Baker, whom I met at a six-week acting program at Circle in the Square, loaned me the money to participate. She had written a play about her experience with her dad abusing her that she wanted me to perform. The other play I did was a comedy written by a theater teacher from Rhode Island College. I played Socrates's wife who went into therapy because her husband never talked to her. He would just think all the time. The third was a play by another RIC teacher/director. I played the snake in a reinterpretation of Adam and Eve. I flew British Airways and stayed in an apartment on Sir Arthur Conan Doyle Drive in Edinburgh.

We would walk to the theater from there, a long walk. During the day we would visit the Mary Queen of Scots Castle, explore the city, eat fish and chips with malt vinegar. At night, we performed or saw other performances. A performance from the Traverse Theatre in Scotland was about men in a South African prison. They were naked the whole time. Sometimes simulating sex. At one point they go to the bathroom in a bucket and later in the play, throw the contents at each other. There was either real poop on that stage or it was made of clay. I had to force myself to believe it was made of clay. No way could they time that out.

It was riveting, and the surprise was the elderly people in the audience who were completely into it. I saw a production of *Salome* by the famous auteur director Steven Berkoff. My favorite was the Festival de Spana out of Barcelona. It was a pagan fireworks extravaganza on the grounds of an all-boys school. The school looked like a castle. The performers dressed like half man, half beast with fire shooting out of their nostrils. Some had beast costumes on, pretending to hang clothes made of fire on clotheslines made of fire. Enormous phallic symbols shot fireworks out into the sky that exploded in the most magnificent display. My friend Doug Cooney and I looked at each other with gaping mouths. Doug was an acting student at Rhode Island College and he played Socrates in one of our plays. I actually think we ran through the streets in laughter, exhilaration, and in awe at what we had just seen. It's the sheer supernatural power of artistry that is a life-giving, God-injected drug. When you are in the presence of it, you feel like you can fly!

Nighttime was my favorite. Amid all the actors in a large apartment, talking, sharing, laughing, drinking scotch, playing spades, talking about the process of acting, I slowly felt like a part of something. Usually, I clicked with one or two people in a group but this time, we were all together.

I flew to San Diego after the Fringe Festival for a week with David who was acting in the theater. Then, I took a bus from San Diego to Los Angeles, stayed at my friend Gary's apartment, and planned to fly to New York to start my first day at Juilliard the next morning. I took a bus from San Diego to Los Angeles. Halfway through the trip the bus abruptly stopped and police came in and removed 80 percent of the people on the bus for not having proper identification. We got into LA and I saw my friend Gary waving frantically.

"Hey, Gary!"

"Get your bags and run!"

If I hadn't experienced it, I would call myself a liar but a wave of displaced, homeless people started enclosing us and grabbing. They were trying to grab my arm, bags. Gary got into the car. I threw my bags in and jumped in almost at the same time the car was moving.

Someone should have told me, *Viola, you don't start your new life like that. Don't squeeze in the start of your new life.* But I decided I'd fly into New York, dump my stuff in Susan Lawson's apartment—which I had sublet sight unseen—and go to my orientation.

I took a cab from the airport and when I arrived at

the building, I thought, *Oh. Okay, the outside looks like crap but it's Susan Lawson's apartment.* I lugged all my suitcases to the fourth-floor walk-up. When I opened the door, I stood in that doorway for twenty minutes. I kid you not. It was a traumatic experience, like having dissociative disorder. I dumped my stuff in the apartment. Completely depressed, almost catatonic, I took the subway to Juilliard to start my orientation.

I was about to go into the belly of the beast. Juilliard was about to rip apart my world. I would come face-to-face not with God, but with me.

Chapter 14
Coming Into Me

"I did not come here for food. My stomach is full. I did not come here for food. I came for much more than that."

—MANDINKA RITUAL SONG

The orientation at Juilliard was a blur. Partly because I was squeezing in the start of a major part of my life and partly because of the apartment. Really, I didn't understand the living in New York. I just thought all the apartments look like George Jefferson's apartment.

Before I accepted my position at Juilliard, I really had to get my money lined up. I had Rhode Island Foundation money and savings from working as an actress and my day job at Providence Performing Arts Center. I was on a budget.

Subletting a cheap rent-stabilized apartment in New York from an avant-garde director who eventually headed the theater program at Columbia University seemed like the perfect solution. She came up to me after one of the plays that I did at Trinity Rep. I had told her I had been accepted to Juilliard. She was impressed and said, "I have an apartment for you."

"Oh my God. You see how God works. Oh my God."

"Yeah. I have an apartment for you. It's my apartment." Susan is a classy woman. She was becoming the artistic director at Trinity Rep taking over after Adrian Hall. She would be in Providence. I would be in New York. How perfect!

"Oh my God. Do I have to fill out an application?"

"No, if you want it, it's yours."

"How much is it?"

"$290 a month."

"Oh my gosh. Absolutely, I'll take it. Absolutely. No problem."

She may have asked me "Do you want to see it first?" but I didn't have time for that and only asked: "What's it like?"

"I love it. I've had it for years. It's a studio apartment." She really talked it up.

I thought, *It's her apartment, and she loves it. A top director. Her apartment. In the Village.* "Yeah, I'll take it."

When I arrived at the apartment building, on First Avenue between Second and Third Streets, what kept playing through my mind was what she said, *Oh, we love the apartment.* Walking up the stairs I felt I was in one of those Booking.com commercials where after being on the road where you've lost your shoes, your kids are throwing up, you're tired, you open the hotel room door to behold a massive, palatial suite overlooking the ocean. That's what I expected from Susan's apartment, the setting for my years at Juilliard. I was expecting to be amazed! Hell, when I opened that damn door, that shit did not happen. It was horrific.

The apartment was maybe 450 square feet. There was a small stove on the right side of the apartment and makeshift wooden shelves. Underneath the shelves was a large rusted white sink. It was one of those sinks you usually find in a basement. Next to the sink was the tub. Yup. Right in the center of the apartment was a tub that had rust stains on it. I thought, *Where's the toilet?* I found it in what I thought was a tiny closet. It was one of those toilets that you had to pull a chain to flush. It was infested with mice. Infested. They were coming out of holes in the floorboards. At night you could hear them coming up eating all the food on the shelves. It was no surprise that because of my childhood that totally set me off. I was killing up to a dozen mice a day. I could hear the traps snapping. I would then toss the entire trap, mice and all, in the trash. No way would I touch it!

I called her one weekend: "Susan! You have mice in this apartment."

She said, "I never remember us having mice, Viola."

"Susan, there are mice. I'm killing up to a dozen a day. You've got to help me out. Call the landlord."

I can't go back, is what I was thinking.

Nothing.

I told Susan, "I'm only keeping it to the end of the year." She may have given me some money off the rent. As I mentioned, it was rent stabilized. She had had it for decades. Years later, maybe the mid-'90s, I was working with someone in San Francisco to whom I told this apartment story, and in the middle of the conversation he said to me, "I remember Susan Lawson. People said that she had the worst apartment that anyone had ever seen in their life. It was common knowledge among actors in New York."

In defense of Susan, this was life in NYC. The concrete jungle filled with fast-moving, hardworking, dream-filled people trying to make it. All cramped into a high-rise apartment building whose landlord's only goal is to see how many people they can cram in there. I loved the hardness of it. I love how alive NYC is. I just don't like the living. I needed a place that kept the hardness of the city out.

At the time, the area wasn't all that much better than the apartment. The F train almost never worked. When I got off the train, I saw the same homeless people. The same woman always had a new bruise on her. You could tell she was being beaten within an inch of her life every day. Then I would walk to my building and often find blood at the front door cordoned off with police tape. This was because of CBGB, a former biker bar, now dive club where some of the greatest rockers started—Patti Smith, The B-52s, Blondie, Joan Jett and the Blackhearts, the Talking Heads. At night, that place was rowdy and the rowdiness culminated in a lot of vomit and blood at my front door.

The apartment was never cold. It kept heat. I always had hot water. The toilet always flushed. That's the extent of whatever good came from living there. I was in school all day and only went back to that apartment at night, but during the weekend, I was at home. All I did was eat all day. Eat, eat, eat. I wasn't a drinker, but more than a few times I would drink a forty-ounce beer with my meal. I gained about twenty pounds on Genoa salami, cheese, tomatoes, and mustard on baguette bread; a pot of pasta every day; and a pint of rum raisin Häagen-Dazs ice cream.

I started Juilliard with eighteen other classmates in my group. By the end of the first year, we only had fourteen students. One was thrown out. One was cut. The other two dropped out; those were Black students. There are four different groups at the Jailyard, as we called it. Each group is given a number. So, our first year was group 22. The second year was group 21, third was 20, and fourth year was group 19.

The minute I walked through those doors at Sixty-Fifth and Broadway, it was apparent why so many were either thrown out or ran out screaming on their own. It was hard. What got you admitted to the school was put on the back burner immediately. They weren't as interested in what you did well but what you didn't do well. If you were a willowy ingenue, they wanted to see you play a grounded matriarch. If you came off as strong and emotional, they wanted to see your lighter side, even if they had to beat it out of you.

John Styk, Robert Williams, Marian Seldes, Moni Yakim, Judy Leibowitz—these were our first-year teachers. We started early every morning around 8 a.m. and almost never finished until late at night. We were trained in speech, voice, Alexander technique, movement, and scene study.

The Alexander technique is a technique to teach the actor how to use their body without stress and tension. First-year students didn't act with second-year, third-year, or fourth-year students, because each year had its own objectives and was its own group. First year is about discovery. We did a Shakespearean play, *Pericles*.

They just want to see what you got. It was directed by a great actor, who's now gone, named Marian Seldes. You could do whatever you wanted. For the next project, you're given a role that is completely different from you, a role nobody would cast you in. I played a character named Lily in *Ah! Wilderness* by Eugene O'Neill. She was completely self-effacing, walked in really small steps, had a unique voice, barely audible, always shy. I am shy but that's not how I come off. My voice is very rooted and grounded and strong. This is a role no one would cast me in. This was the method at Juilliard. A structure based and steeped in transformation. They picked the material. They chose the plays and roles that they felt had value.

Between all day at school, a crappy apartment, undiagnosed trauma and anxiety issues, and being on my own in NYC, I was overwhelmed. I fell asleep in class all the time. My friend Michelle would wake me the hell up. Great actors would come to the school to perform and I would feign excitement, take a front row seat to these events, and within a time, my head was back, my mouth open and my eyes would be rolling back. Michelle would wave frantically, mouthing, *Wake the fuck up!!!* and she looked mad.

It was arduous listening and watching white guest actors perform, white playwrights coming in to speak, white projects, white characters, a European approach to the work, speech, voice, movement. Everyone was geared toward molding and shaping you into a perfect white actor. The unspoken language was that they set the standard. That they're better. I'm a dark-skinned Black actress with a deep voice. No matter how much I adhere to the training, when I walk out into the world I will be seen as a dark-skinned Black woman with a deep voice. Hell, when I got out there in the world, I would be called for jobs based on . . . me. I had to make peace with that. And I admit, there are some classical playwrights and contemporary ones that I never want to perform anyway!

The one other Black person in my class group was Cedric Harris. Only thirty Black students in a total of 856 students at Juilliard were enrolled in all the disciplines: drama, music, and dance. We called ourselves the Black Caucus. I was a part of that Black Caucus. Every January we had our Martin Luther King celebration, a variety show. To this day, I would say it's some of the greatest work I've ever seen by artists. In dance, music, drama. Creative pieces were put together to honor Black history, Black autonomy . . . us . . . me. Everything was included from Zulu dancers to great opera and gospel. We were forbidden to perform anything other than opera, ballet, European classics. Period. We were warned NOT to perform in the MLK celebration.

If actors came into the school and were already working, they were strongly told to stop. Jazz, gospel, tap, modern, any ethnic material was on the forbidden list. We called on all of the above when we created the MLK celebration. It was our rebellion. We were told it would ruin our instrument. Well, our soul was our instrument too.

Very few members of the faculty would even come. We felt racially and individually neutered by a philosophy built on forgetting about ourselves and birthing someone artistically acceptable. Someone whites could understand. Nevertheless, our passion and will to perform matched the lack of acknowledgment of our contribution to the school. In other words, their ignorance made us fight harder for ourselves and our craft.

Juilliard forced me to understand the power of my Blackness. I spent so much of my childhood defending it, being ridiculed for it. Then in college proving

I was good enough. I had compartmentalized me. At Julliard, I was mad.

I was always assigned the opening speech for the MLK celebration and Laurie Carter, who was Black and the dean, always said, "Let it rip! Speak your mind." It was a validation of a voice weighed down by trauma, shame, insecurity. Here was Laurie who found that small space inside of me that still had life and hope and she pulled it out.

The first ceremony at Avery Fisher Hall, I walked out onstage and told a story. It was a story of a slave in the Caribbean. He was always running away. He was a big, strong man who didn't want to be controlled. Every time he ran away, he would be found and beaten. Once he was beaten, he would run away again. Finally, to stop him once and for all they decided to kill another slave. The body of the dead slave was put on the runaway slave's back. They tied it tight. They made him work in the hot sun all day and night with that dead body on his back. They made him sleep and eat with it on his back. The body started decomposing. This big strong man began to lose his appetite. His body became infected by the carcass and he began to waste away and finally died.

I asked, "How many Black people in this audience feel like you have a body tied to your back? How many are trying to live and strive in a culture that has weighed us down and is more interested in our demise than our life?"

There was silence. I was speaking my truth. It was a truth fraught with the pain of everything that had ever been dumped on me consciously or unconsciously. Suddenly like an elephant who is being slayed for its tusk, I was fighting back, fighting for my space.

Every year, I would try to squeeze myself into every project and every character. I thought I had to. Corsets and huge European wigs that never fit over my braids. Listening to classmates "ooh" and "aah" over the beautiful costumes and imagining how awesome life would be back in the 1780s. I kept wanting to scream it. "Shit!!! I'm different than you!! If we went back to 1780, we couldn't exist in the same world! I'm not white!" The absolute shameful objective of this training was clear—make every aspect of your Blackness disappear. How the hell do I do that? And more importantly, WHY??!!! None of my counterparts had to perfect Jamaican, southern, urban dialect to be considered excellent. "I am BLACK!!! I'm dark with big lips and a wide nose and thighs. I'm Viola!!"

Manifestation has always been a part of my life. Either getting on my knees physically or praying silently. And God intervened. In my second year,

Juilliard was offering a $2,500 scholarship for any student who wanted to do a summer program that opened them up as artists, helped with their growth, unleashed something within. We had to write a five-page essay explaining it. I wrote that I was lost. That there was no way to unleash passion when you were asked to perform material that not only didn't touch your heart but wasn't written for you. I told them of the burden and myopic scope of Eurocentric training. I got the scholarship.

My friend Kris World, who was in the dance program, went to Africa every summer with Chuck Davis, an African dance choreographer out of the North Carolina School of the Arts. Every year he took a group of people, not all artists, to a different country in Africa to study the dance, music, and folklore of different tribes. This summer, he was going to The Gambia, West Africa, to study the Wolof, Jola, Mandinka, and SouSou tribes.

The lead-up, travel, and experience in Africa caused a cataclysmic change in my life. It busted a hole in my existence.

I got every shot known to mankind before the trip. I wanted to eat everything I saw when I got there without worrying about any sickness. I counted down the days, took the bus to JFK from Providence, and flew out of JFK with the entire group—all women and most not actors. One was a nurse. One was a teacher. One would stand off to the side. She looked mad. She took her seat and curled up. Not curled up as in sleeping but curled up, in pain. She would cry and stare out of the window. A Jamaican woman was a nurse and very nice but extremely shy. Then there was me and Kris World. I was bouncing out of my seat I was so excited!

We arrived in The Gambia after a long layover in Amsterdam. It was nighttime. The airport was tiny and without a baggage claim. Bags were placed in a big pile. Strong uniformed African men with semiautomatic weapons were everywhere. We found our bags and walked out. It was love. It was as potent as a first kiss or a great prayer session. The air smelled different. Oranges and blues and purples painted the sky as the sun went down. The faint tinge of incense mixed with the ocean wind. Africa was waiting for me.

We stayed at the Bungalow Beach Hotel right on the ocean. It might as well have been the Four Seasons, but it was more like Motel 6. Kris World and I shared a suite.

Man, it was hot. To this day whenever it's dripping hot, I refer to it as "Africa hot." It was so humid that when I washed my underwear, it took three days to dry. We would wake up at 5 a.m. and meet on the beach. Chuck would teach us about the tribe we would meet that day and teach us some of the dance moves. We would pray and run into the ocean fully clothed. Then we would go to the hotel and get dressed. Chuck had various people he hired as drivers, "ambassadors." They would pick us up in front of the hotel and take us to the compounds. In the car, we would laugh and sing. The driver would teach us a song from their tribe. The first tribe was Mandinka. The Mandinkas were the people of the celebrated writer of *Roots* and *The Autobiography of Malcolm X*, Alex Haley. We spent most of our time with them. We went into the compound, which was a cluster of four or five adobe houses where family members lived. We learned about djembe drums, the talking drum . . . They're called talking drums because the sound imitates speech.

We would enter the clearing in the compound and the extended family would bring out every chair they had. They greeted us like long-lost family members. The joy, the excitement! Children would run into your arms. Then came the drummers who were all men. The intricacy of each role that the drummers played was unreal. The women would enter the circle ready to do a dance called the lingen, which is a bird in flight. Kris whispered in my ear, "They getting ready to bust loose!"

A woman would enter and begin to dance. She wore a lapa (skirt) wrapped around her body and her head-wrap. As she smiled with unbridled joy, her feet would stomp with the drummers following her rhythm. She would stomp and slowly but surely her arms would fly up and her feet would go from stomping to leaping off the ground. Pretty soon, it looked like she was in flight. Other women would begin to ululate and another woman would leap into the circle and come face-to-face with the first woman. They would stare at each other intensely and begin to hold on to each other's head and begin to fly together. The entire earth seemed to move. Loose dirt swirled around us. We were witnessing something divine.

The dancing would go on for hours. More women would jump in. Some young and some old. When they were finished, they would get down to the ground and rub each other's feet and ululate. While all this was going on, they sang a song over and over again. It translates to, "I did not come here for food. My stomach is full. I did not come here for food. I came for much more than that."

I sang it so much it became a prayer. I was here for . . . something. I was crying out for something.

We each had to get up in front of the tribe and sing

and dance the lingen. We also had to learn a series of greetings.

"Sumole"—Hello, how are you?

"Ibije"—I am fine.

"Kon te na te"—How's your family?

"Te na te"—They are fine.

"Kara be"—I am here.

"Kara jon"—I see you.

By the way, we had to go through this greeting anytime we started a conversation with someone. Even if you only stopped to ask for a mango!

It made them so happy. To be seen, to feel their worth. Africa made me giddy with joy. Every smell, sound, color affected my senses in a passionate way. No shade of yellow or green or blue was the same. Fabric artists made the dye themselves. They would then make lapas, kufi (hats), grad boo boos (muumuus). Beautiful dark skin was unapologetically darkened by the sun. Every child had many women who would mother them. The ease in which people served each other. The kinky, curly hair, the complexity of the rituals, the numerous different languages.

We went to a baby-naming ceremony. After seven days the baby is given a name. The infant mortality rate was so high that parents waited seven days before they named their child. The baby was usually at a low weight but would surely live after making it past the week. We would wait in the compound for the parents with the baby to come out of the small adobe house. Women breastfed their babies while waiting to celebrate.

It was a cloudy day and the women were sitting laughing among themselves. They had calabashes, large wooden bowls, in front of them and buckets of water. When the parents emerged from the house, the women put their babies to the side on some cloth. They put their breasts in their wraps, turned the bowls over into the bucket of water, picked up two sticks, and began to drum in unison. With honor. With a sisterhood that went deep. We gasped! Kris World and I were coming from a school where we were being classically trained to become auteurs and we were witnessing it in front of our eyes. This was genius. This was art! Expression that is born out of the necessity of ritual to navigate life. When they were done, they simply put down the sticks, turned the calabashes back in the bucket of water, and picked up their babies to begin breastfeeding again.

Juilliard's academic approach did not connect the work to our lives. It missed the true potency of artistry, which is that it shifts humanity. Art has the power to heal the soul.

I needed healing. Before I left for Africa, I had found out finally that my relationship wasn't what I thought it was. David had other relationships the entire time. I was devastated. Anita comforted me, utterly confused by my wailing.

"Well, what made you think you were in an exclusive relationship?"

"Because, Anita, we just were! I was living there! In his apartment."

Silence.

"Living with him or just staying there when you came home on the weekends from school?"

"Anita!! I've been with him for years now," I continued to cry.

"Viola? If there was no conversation about being exclusive in the relationship, then you weren't. I'm sorry. You just thought you were because . . . what . . . you love him?"

Anita was very matter-of-fact. Loving and logical. The honesty sobered me up and hurt like a motherfucker.

"Of course I love him, Anita."

"How do you know? Viola, how many boyfriends have you even had? You don't know what love is."

It was an exchange I wished I had had before I started dating. I never knew love had to actually serve the two people involved, establish boundaries and communication. I thought all that just happened.

In Africa at age twenty-five, I felt my life both starting and ending. I was in an in-between time. Africa was an elixir. We ate benachin every day outside the hotel and in the compounds. It was rice, white fish, white sweet potato cooked in the ground and a spicy red sauce on top of the fish. It cost five dalasi, which equaled fifty cents. You brought your own bowl no matter how big and they would fill it up for fifty cents. My greediness followed me from childhood. I could never get enough food so I found the biggest bowl. Women would set up a makeshift shop outside of the hotel. Mostly, you ate with your hands. There were almost never utensils. You would squeeze the palm oil from the food with your right hand and pop it in your mouth. The left hand was used to . . . well . . . wipe yourself after going to the bathroom. I couldn't get with that.

We went to an African wrestling match that was more about theater than wrestling. The wrestlers would march around a field with drummers behind them and you would throw them coins. After doing this for the longest time, they would wrestle. The Wolofs had a dance called the "turtle dance" that was the equivalent of twerking. Women would bend over with their butts toward the man and twist, shake, and move at a rapid speed accompanied by not only drums but balafons, which were xylophones, and koras, which were guitars.

Drums from goat skin, and batiks were exquisite works of art. Sculptures were carved from mahogany wood and usually were in worship of tribal deities.

Africa was God's playground.

I found out that the woman who came on the trip who looked like she was in pain was. She had lost her sister and mother within weeks of each other. She could not see her way through the grief. She was consumed by it. She came to Africa in search of comfort, answers. We all did. The shy nurse was looking to get out of her head and comfort zone. She was so shy she would just sit in the background whenever we went to a compound. I never saw her there, she was that quiet. Sometimes she would cry if she were asked to dance even during our morning prayer circle.

But there was no mistaking the supernatural enchantment that was happening in Banjul, Bakau, and Serekunda, The Gambia, West Africa. There was no mistaking the transformation that was happening. Suddenly the anxiety that always existed in the pit of my gut went away completely. I almost felt drugged. My skin came alive.

A group of girls braided my hair one day. They laughed, giggled while doing it. They couldn't have been older than fifteen, and there were nine of them. All they wanted to hear about was my sister Danielle and our relationship. They didn't want to hear about Juilliard, New York, being an actress. They didn't want to hear about what I wanted to become. They wanted to hear about me. Just me. They would squeal, laugh, and clap when I told them the most inconsequential detail about me, like the day Danielle was born.

One day, we went to the Mandinka compound and a group of women came in with clownish makeup on, oversized clothes, shoes, and djembe drums. Chuck said they were comedians. I was fascinated. They were laughing and made funny faces and then would play the drums, loud but not well. When everyone saw them, they would get loud, scream, become animated and laugh in an exaggerated way. People gathered around these women until there was a mob of women hugging, rousing, laughing loudly, singing loudly, "I did not come here for food. My stomach is full. I did not come here for food. I came for much more!" Then they began to pass a calabash around with mush inside. It tasted like peanut butter oatmeal. Everyone dug in, ate some, and passed it down. These "comedians" were actually infertile women.

In The Gambia, to have a child is the greatest blessing. When you couldn't, the belief was that God did not hear your deepest wish and had passed you by. The intent is to make as much noise as possible so God can hear you in heaven and pour down a blessing. The noise stopped and I looked around at the faces of the women smiling, laughing, screaming in manic desperation. They were trying to wake God up.

I wept. Despite the nature of the roles I get, I'm not a crier. But I wept. I cried again when I saw a woman who looked like my mom dancing in the rain at her daughter's wedding. She was doing the lingen dance and seemed to fly off the ground. I cried when many of the people we met in the compounds came to our hotel so that we could perform for them. We even had food. Everything we performed they squealed with joy, laughter, tears, and they didn't even understand English. I performed Topsy from George C. Wolfe's *The Colored Museum*. It's a character that imagines herself at a party with Martin Luther King drinking champagne out of Eartha Kitt's slipper, Malcolm X having existentialist conversation. Then this party gets so rowdy that the floor started to shake, the walls started to move, and the entire room lifted up off the ground and went spinning and spinning until it disappeared, inside of her head.

"Yes, chile! That's right. There's a party going on right here because I'm dancing to the music of the madness in me. That's why every time I walk down the street, my hips sashay from side to side because I'm dancing to the music of the madness in ME! And here all this time I thought we had given up our drums. But now still got 'em. They're here. In my walk, my dress, my style, my smile, and my eyes. They're inside here connecting me to everything and everyone that ever was. So . . . honey don't try to label or define me, cuz I'm not who I was ten years ago or ten minutes ago. I'm all of that and then some. And whereas I can't live inside yesterday's pain, I can't live without it."

They roared!!!! I had lost every bit of potency and belief in my work since entering Juilliard. In The Gambia, in the midst of my people, I found it. I found the party inside me. The celebration that needs to happen to combat the pain and trauma of memory. I found that there is no creating without using you.

For two years I thought the rule was to erase and negate oneself. That's what I was doing. Lose the voice, speech, walk, face . . . lose the Blackness. Lose and bury the very essence of what makes you *you* and create something void of joy but steeped in technique.

After the thunderous roar, Chuck quieted everyone down and had us form a circle to pray. We said a prayer of thanks. We thanked them for their hospitality, wisdom. We thanked them for their love and said we would never forget them. They wept and cried and began to ululate. Then they began to dance and take out their drums, in the hotel. It, ironically, was that party I spoke about in my monologue. We were all dripping with sweat. Suddenly I saw Kris World's face change. She shouted, "Viola. Look." The crowd parted and behind the room was the shy nurse! I didn't even know she was there. She was coming into the circle dancing!!! She was doing the dance we learned with the Jolas and she was doing it perfectly!! She was almost in a trance and she kept dancing until she was face-to-face with the choreographer Chuck Davis. He was staring at her, and she danced and danced until sweat, tears were pouring down.

I left Africa fifteen pounds lighter, four shades darker, and so shifted that I couldn't go back to what I was.

I was always on the outside of Juilliard because I wasn't on the inside of me. I was fighting an ideology about what an actor was, and it was all born in the depth of white superiority. The notion of "the classics" being the basis for everything. Yet I was in the land of the classics. In Africa, there is the equivalent of every "classical" instrument known to man and it predates any European instrument. There was a "technical" proficiency attached to drumming, dance, music, storytelling. Why is it "limiting" to play Black characters but white actors are "versatile" playing white characterizers? Why do I have to be small, willowy, and lighter than a paper bag to be sexual? I'm playing a character. It's not porn. I was sold lies for two years and the worst part is that I believed it because I couldn't combat it with anything else.

Africa exorcised those demons.

When I got back, no one recognized me. I performed my one-woman show in my third year with all I had learned in The Gambia. I could do anything I wanted and I wanted to use me. It was a true Coming-Out. I wasn't weighed down with speech, voice, and all that I had been taught that was drowning me. I heeded the saying, "Stop making love to something that's killing you."

A year later Mark Schlegel was an agent at a top agency back in the day, J. Michael Bloom. It was the agency everybody wanted to get into. They represented major names. They had Tom Hanks, Alec Baldwin, Wesley Snipes, Ethan Hawke, Sigourney Weaver, Kathleen Turner, and Macaulay Culkin. They had everyone. It was also the hot agency, probably the equivalent of William Morris, CAA, and UTA today. Mark came to see *Journey of the Fifth Horse* where I played a character who was an older Russian woman. It was part fantasy, part realism. I was in heavy makeup. He saw me in that role and left me a message in the Juilliard office saying that he wanted to meet with me.

I met with him. He said he loved my work, saw something in me. "Viola, it just popped out. Your talent, your power popped out. I wanted to meet you." Our meeting was one of synergy, kismet, a perfect moment. Sometimes actors meet an agent and the vibe is *What can you do for me? You're a big agent. Just get me auditions for a job. Get me a lot of money.* But this was someone who saw me, saw my talent, saw my possibilities. He introduced me to the other agents and said, "We want to sign you."

"Okay. Let's do it." That's what I was at Juilliard for. They signed me before I even graduated from Juilliard. By the time we got to the auditions at the end of fourth year, I didn't have any stress about signing with an agent. Friends at school said, "You should have waited until after you did your scenes because you probably would have had more choices."

All I needed was one agent. Agent and actor are like a marriage. The agent has to "get" you. I was dark-skinned, not a size two, not considered "beautiful." After all the trials and tribulations I'd experienced at Juilliard for these reasons, I felt like it behooved me to get an agent who did "see" me. That agent would be the driving force in my career, my advocate. I got maybe twenty-two callbacks after my scenes—which was good, although some people got sixty callbacks—but I never regretted that I signed before I did my scenes.

The reality and social media fantasy of being an actor are diametrically opposed. Most actors don't want to be an artist—they want to be famous. Many believe if they're pretty, young, have a great agent, then "Voila!" It's a business that is way more fickle than that. No words can describe that one-two combo of luck meeting talent. Me? I just wanted to work. I didn't want to go back to Rhode Island. I compared going back to death.

I was finally two weeks from graduating from Juilliard. The last two weeks were meant to be the jump-off to my new life. After four years of honing my craft, this was it. All the pain, joy, suffering, and triumphs, and suddenly . . . exactly two weeks before graduation day . . . I woke up sick!

Chapter 15
The Wake-Up

"Girl, get up! Girl, get your fight back!
Girl, get your power back! Girl, start acting
like you are a King's daughter and there has always
been a crown attached to your head. Even when
I was sick, I was still His! Even when I was dead,
I was still His. Do you know who I am?"

—SARAH JAKES ROBERTS

Everybody has secrets. Everybody. I guess the difference is that we either die with them and let them eat us up, or we put them out there, wrestle with them (or they wrestle with us) until we . . . reconcile. Secrets are what swallow us.

There's always one secret that drives the nail in the

coffin for me. . . . It's as fresh in my memory as if it happened yesterday and yet . . . distant.

Two weeks before graduation, I woke up sick to my stomach and just knew. I got pregnant by my boyfriend of seven years. I remember taking my headshots that week and going to see *Beauty and the Beast* at the movie theater and all I kept thinking was *I'm pregnant*. I didn't know what the fuck to do with that. It was an emotion far beyond scared. It was as if all the irresponsible decisions I had made had culminated into this. Ever since I started having sex, which was late in life, I didn't know what I was doing. Yeah, you can learn about birth control but . . . how to love? How to be consistent and responsible, in control, create boundaries? Hell, even making sure you had the money to access condoms or birth control pills? The only commitment I had down, I felt, was my career, and that took EVERYTHING I had. All the other facets in my life overwhelmed me. Now . . . I was pregnant.

I remember I went to a clinic near Juilliard. I went early in the morning and had to cancel the first appointment because I had eaten. I came back the next day. I remember going into a lot of rooms. One room to check in and pay. One room to take another pregnancy test. Another room to put on a surgical gown. Each room was something out of a Stanley Kubrick film where you were getting closer to your demise. There were some very nice doctors who put me on a surgical table and I was put under.

I woke up terrified. I woke up as if being attacked. The pain was excruciating! More than any pain I'd ever experienced. They had told me there may be some pain, but man . . . . There is "what is said," "what you heard," and how it actually is, and this pain was NOT what I thought it would be. The recovery room was a bunch of folding chairs arranged in a circle. They placed huge pads on each chair to hold the bleeding from surgery. There was a woman in each one, and there were at least a dozen of them. They gave us apple juice and crackers. All around me were women vomiting in bowls and screaming or moaning in pain. One woman kept crying, "I couldn't keep this one! I couldn't! I already have five and no money!" Another girl who looked fifteen kept screaming, "MOMMY!!!! MOMMY!! I want my MOMMY!!!" Me? I just cried . . . and vomited . . . and cried through the pain until it was gone. I went home and bled profusely for two weeks and fell into a life-altering depression.

Hell, I remember calling my boyfriend, yelling at him, "Where are you! Why aren't you here?" He thought what I did was wrong, and yet there was every probability that he wouldn't be there for me or the baby. There were no resources financially or emotionally—at all. Once again in my life, I had to rely on the Santa Claus theory to get through major, life-changing obstacles. I was always asked to rely on miracles. My boyfriend finally came to New York to hold me for a day and then left. It was a perfect reminder that as much as I thought I had evolved into a mature woman, I hadn't. There was no escaping brutal life accidents that can stop you and render you completely frozen.

The big clots of blood were a constant reminder that I terminated a life, and I absolutely, without question, knew it was a life . . . which I had traded for my own life. Try dealing with the weight of that shit!!!

My mom started having children when she was fifteen, and I wanted my life to be different. This baby didn't fit into my dreams. Who was I without my dreams? The bigger the dream, the more the shame of that little third-grade Viola could disappear. The bigger the dream, the more people would not call me those names I was running from. The bigger the dream . . . I could be worthy.

I felt almost desperate to explain this to God in exchange for forgiveness . . . to be cleansed.

I have a Jewish friend who is Modern Orthodox. He said one of his rabbis said, "It's futile to ask why. Instead ask yourself, 'What did I learn from this?'"

What have I learned from all of it? There is absolutely no way whatsoever to get through this life without scars. No way!! It's a friggin' emotional boxing ring, and either you go one round, four rounds, or forty rounds, depending on your opponent. And by God, if your opponent is you . . . you will go forty. If it's God, you'll barely go one because Big Daddy has rope-a-dope down! He's a shape-shifter. You think you're fighting him, screaming, punching, begging him for help. And he leaves you with . . . YOU.

Anton Chekhov, the great Russian playwright, once said, "The same time you're laughing hysterically, your life is falling apart." It is the definition of living.

My graduation meal when I finished Juilliard was joyous and hysterical. Me and one of my great friends, Cedric, who graduated with me from Juilliard, sat on the floor of his room and ate pickled pigs' feet and Champale. We sucked on the cartilage, fat rich pig bones soaked in vinegar. Loudly proclaiming through laughter that we would never tell anyone about this. We were done! We had made it through an emotional, ego- and soul-crushing artistic war zone.

I graduated from Juilliard. Let me tell you something. I was a poor kid and now I was a poor adult. I had a hotshot agent and . . . nothing happened. I would audition, get a callback, and then someone else would get it. Or I wouldn't get the audition at all because I was too young, too old, too dark, not sexy. In the meantime, life keeps moving. Rent is due. Phone bill is due, subway fare, food, student loans. All the stone-cold reality stuff I hadn't factored in. Well, I had, but I just didn't understand the weight of it. At this point, I was sharing a brownstone with six other students from Juilliard and they were having a hard time, too. Eventually, one got dozens of commercials and a soap opera. One got a big job out of school but when it was over was back to auditioning. One left NYC entirely and the other was still in school.

I had a couple of big "aha" moments. The first was that we were living the reality of being artists. The mentality pervasive in social media is that you have to be "The boss bitch." You have to call your agent and tell THEM the roles you want or, hell, write it yourself. I beg young actors not to listen to that.

The actors who are privileged are the ones who have the mic. They are being interviewed because they've reached the height of their careers and those testimonies are released on social media like vomit. We consume them and, having no way into the reality of the acting business, we take it in as truth. If you hit big when you're young and turn down a six-figure salary, You. Are. Privileged. That's not throwing shade. Hell, anyone would love it if that were their path. But struggle is defined by not having choices, and the actor who takes the Geico commercial to get their insurance has just as much integrity as someone who doesn't take it waiting for their Academy Award–winning role.

An actor called me ecstatic because her commercial got picked up and she qualified for Plan 1 insurance for her family. She has two children, one of which had health issues. Life is happening as your career is happening. Stone-cold life. I realized my joy is not just attached to artistic fulfillment, but life fulfillment. I had $56,000 in student loans. My fibroids were growing. I would bleed for weeks at a time. I was badly anemic. I had alopecia areata. I woke up and on the right side of my head, my hair was gone. It was clean as a baby's butt. The knee-jerk response is go to the doctor. I would've if I had had health insurance. I could go to cheap clinics, but fibroids, anemia, alopecia required comprehensive care. Ongoing help from qualified ob-gyns and dermatologists. It would be years before I made enough to qualify for Plan 1 health insurance or Equity insurance.

My other "aha" moment was the power, potency, and life force of the one-two punch of colorism and sexism. Almost every role I auditioned for were drug-addicted mothers. I auditioned for a few roles that were low-budget for a woman of color, but all of them were described as light-skinned. All! The others were soap operas where I would be sitting in the audition waiting room with models.

Black rom-coms were happening. There were awesome shows on TV that displayed the cute Black girl who had autonomy and material wealth. But none of those women looked like me. An agent told me the word all the casting directors used when on the phone: "interchangeable." That means even if you are a little darker, you have to have smaller, classical (read whiter) features. That wasn't me.

What made it worse is that it's not just presented by white executives, but also Black artists and producers. You begin to adopt the ideology of the "oppressor." It becomes the key to success. Culturally speaking, many believe it and they have adopted the belief that if you are dark, you're uglier, harder, more masculine, more maternal than your lighter-skinned counterparts. It's the paper bag test mentality that many still refuse to believe.

In finding my way, the great role was not the biggest objective. Waiting tables to make ends meet until that awesome role came along was not the objective. I had to live: that was the objective. This was before streaming services. Studios weren't churning out great roles for Black actors, at least not Black actresses my shade. It was either a great role or a good payday or a good profile or just a friggin' job. You have no leverage if you do not work.

Here's the truth. If you have a choice between auditioning for a great role over a bad role, you are privileged. That means not only do you have a top agent who can get you in, you are at a level that you would be considered for it. Our profession at any given time has a 95 percent unemployment rate. Only 1 percent of actors make $50,000 a year or more and only 0.04 percent of actors are famous, and we won't get into defining famous. The 0.04 percent are the stories you read about in the media. "Being picky," "dropping agents," making far less than male counterparts. Never having any regrets in terms of roles they've taken. Yada, yada, yada.

He who has choices has resources. And the life needs of some twentysomething actor are not the life needs of everyone. Health insurance, mortgage, children are not the top priority of most twentysomethings. Yet the people who are aspiring to be actors and have no knowledge as to a way in listen to the testimonies of the privileged. The ones who were extremely talented, but also extraordinarily lucky. Luck is an elusive monster who chooses when to come out of its cave to strike and who will be its recipient. It's a business of deprivation.

For every one actor who makes it to fame there are fifty thousand more who did exactly the same things, yet didn't make it. Most of the actors I went with to Juilliard, Rhode Island College, Circle in the Square Theatre, the Arts Recognition Talent Search competition are not in the business anymore. I think I can name six, and many, you wouldn't even know. It doesn't speak to their talent, it speaks to the nature of the business. Trust me when I say most were beautiful and talented, and some had incredible agents. It's an eenie, meenie, miny, mo game of luck, relationships, chance, how long you've been out there, and sometimes talent.

You get auditions based on the level you are at. It's hard to see when your journey to the top had more ease, but in reality, there is no ease. You do what the lucky person did, you have a 99 percent chance of it not ever happening for you. Only about 4 percent of actors in the Screen Actors Guild and American Federation of Television and Radio Artists (SAG-AFTRA) union make enough for Plan 1 health insurance and that's $20,000 a year. That is our reality.

There is a way of thinking in our zeitgeist of not taking anything that is beneath you. That "I deserve" way of thinking is hard to reconcile in this business. A better question is this: Do you want to be an actor or do you want to be a famous actor? If you want to be famous, as the great Alan Arkin said, you will have a hard time. If you want to be an actor, you will find a way. Beware of the actor who says they've always turned down work but never made the choice to go do theater for $250 a week to feel fulfilled. Fame is intoxicating.

I was twenty-eight and waking up to reality. I was waking up to being an adult and taking care of myself but also navigating feeling fulfilled in my craft. They were diametrically opposed. I was also full of shit. On one hand, I was frozen. I was too scared of navigating the city and finding a "survival" job. I had so many survival jobs in the past and the thought of juggling that and auditions was becoming too much. On the other hand, because I auditioned for theater, film, and TV, I needed more space to prepare. I spent years preparing on buses and subways and stoops. I needed room to just focus on the work. That first year everything was hard and claustrophobic. I had moments, not of starvation, but of struggle. It was the real world of actually being an actor. My rent was $250 and even that was sometimes hard to raise, but I wanted to be great at what I did, despite not knowing how I was going to pay the bills. Speaking of bills, I talked on the phone way too much, I would ring up hundreds of dollars and would have enormous phone bills. This is before cell phones and when you had to pay for long distance.

I ate wings every day. The quart of white rice at Chinese restaurants was $1.20. The pint cost 60 cents. The chicken wings were $3 and I got them when I could afford it. Otherwise, my protein was the dried salty smoked herring I'd buy at the Spanish markets. I slept on a futon on the floor in a room I shared with my friend Pilar. My entire life had been struggle and survival. I'd been on my own since age seventeen. The fact that it was hard, shitty, was nothing new, but the biggest struggle was keeping hope and a belief in myself. Then, finding an artistic community for support while fighting my ass off to stay alive. Acting was my choice, maybe a masochistic choice.

My first job out of school was understudying Danitra Vance in a play at Joseph Papp's Public Theater called *Marisol* by José Rivera. Danitra was the first Black woman on *Saturday Night Live* and created a famous sketch called "That Black Girl." It was a parody of Marlo Thomas's show in the '70s, *That Girl.* Danitra was extraordinary. She wrote, sang, acted. She had metastasized breast cancer when I was brought in to understudy.

Danitra was doing chemo during the day and at night doing the show. The tumors had spread to her spine. I didn't know until I was chatting with her one day in the dressing room and she took her shirt off. It was the first time I had seen a mastectomy scar.

I made $250 a week and loved it. I never went on the entire four or five weeks I worked. But I connected to Danitra. I remember helping her move and listening to her stories. I love listening to stories. When I heard she was dying, I called her and her voice was so weak.

She said, "How're you?"

I said, "I'm fine." I was going to complain about how hard it was to get work and to work consistently but it seemed too small now.

"How are you?" I asked.

"I'm angry."

Silence.

"Tell me what you're angry at, Danitra." I just wanted her to talk. Her voice was so weak and raspy. The cancer had spread and there was nothing the doctors could do. She was dying.

"I'm angry at this. I'm angry about dying."

"Danitra, I'm so sorry."

"I know. I love you. I'm tired. I gotta go."

A mutual friend of ours, Tommy Hollis, told me a story about Danitra. He said he saw a performance art piece of hers called "The Feminist Stripper." She came onstage and began to take off items of clothing. She had music playing and was cracking jokes while stripping. Everyone was on the floor laughing and egging her on! She got down to her thong and her back turned to the audience, tantalizing them before ripping off her bra. She then turns around and reveals her mastectomy scar; a big X made of tape covered the scar. There was a collective silence, a brutal quiet in the room. They were forced to contend with the woman who was in that body and not just the body itself. Tommy said his heart stopped and he would never forget that experience.

She died about two months later. When she passed her final words were, "Y'all have a parade."

Death, adulthood, responsibilities. All the stuff I never studied in school and no one talks about. And through it all, the work and auditions slowly started trickling in. There are not enough pages or memory cells to explain auditions. The casting director hired for a movie calls the agent based on the needs of the movie, TV show, or play involved. If you fit the breakdown, aka description, and if you have the visibility based on the pedigree of the project and if your agency is powerful enough, you will be called to the audition.

The roles, almost all where I fit the description, were drug-addicted mothers. My agent would send me in for the others. The roles for Black actresses that were described as "pretty" or "attractive." I would put on my makeup, do my hair, and never, ever get those roles, even if the producers were Black. I took the jobs that were given to me. I went back to Trinity Rep and did two plays. I went on to work at the Guthrie Theater and worked with famed director JoAnne Akalaitis in a play called *The Rover* by Aphra Behn. I came back to Trinity Rep to do Dickens's *A Christmas Carol* and *Red Noses* by Peter Barnes. It was during *Red Noses* when I got the call from my agent in NYC about August Wilson's *Seven Guitars*.

The great Lloyd Richards would be directing it. I was so excited. It would go to Broadway but beforehand, it would be developed at the Goodman Theatre in Chicago, the Huntington Theatre Company in Boston, A.C.T. (American Conservatory Theater) in San Francisco, and the Ahmanson Theatre in LA. We would open a year later at the Walter Kerr Theatre in NYC.

I studied that script like crazy. The role was Vera. She had been dumped by her boyfriend, Floyd Barton, who went to jail and while in jail, the song he recorded hit it big. Now he was out and wanted me by his side. It was a beautiful scene of hurt, pain, longing, love. It was me. It didn't require much for me to tap into that part of myself. I was so nervous for that audition but so excited. It was a big deal. I took the train to NYC and went in memorized or "off book," as actors say. I was not off book back in the day for most theater auditions because they were always a lot of pages.

A TV/film audition was maybe a page or two. A theater audition could be nine, ten, or more. When you got them at the last minute, studying the character, play, background sometimes left very little room for memorization. But this was one of those rare occasions when I was off book. The words from the beginning were a part of me.

Lloyd Richards was a small, quiet man. He had directed the original production of *A Raisin in the Sun* with Sidney Poitier, Ruby Dee, Diana Sands, and Glynn Turman. I really wanted this job. I was never an actor who was supercompetitive or had the courage to admit when I wanted something. I went with the flow. I was happy to say, "Hi! Yeah, my name is Viola Davis and I'm an actor." But this day, I wanted it. And the casting director, Meg Simon, wanted it for me. She'd seen me come in and out over the years for so many roles and never book anything. The audition started and I felt good but not great. It was a scene that ended with a monologue about how angry Vera was about being left and how she longed for Floyd. It starts with anger and slowly morphs into her remembering how much she missed him, his touch.

There was silence.

Lloyd smiled at me and said in his soft voice, "I want you to do it again. This time I want you to think this, she doesn't want to go there." He was asking me to hold back until I couldn't anymore. Those moments in life that you start off trying to communicate a thought to a significant other and suddenly a huge wellspring of hurt, vulnerability opens up and surprises you. So I did it again. It was a magic moment. The moment that is about preparation but also about luck, kismet, God. It's where everything aligns. I finished and Lloyd said, "Thank you."

I took the train back to Providence after talking to my agent and saying, "I think I had a great audition." I have a tendency to downplay auditions. You may think you've had a great audition and get feedback and find out it was great but you didn't get the part. Or you find out it was good, not great. Or you find, in the eyes of the producer, director, you simply sucked. It's like Whoopi Goldberg said, "I've been bad, a lot. I've been good sometimes and I've been great just a few times."

The next day, I found out I had gotten the part. I cried. I've only cried a couple of times when I got roles. But, man oh man. It was the first really big job in my career and I was over the moon.

By the time I got *Seven Guitars*, I had given up my apartment in NYC. I was never there. I was always on the road. That's another aspect of the business no one talks about. Being away from home or never having one. It's nomadic. Whatever housing they put you in becomes your home until it doesn't.

The first stop in Chicago was brutal. The temperatures reached 38 degrees below zero. I spent my days off sitting on my couch with the heat blasting, another portable heater, and a huge blanket over me. I still shivered. Working in Chicago, Michigan Avenue, grocery shopping, working out during the day, and performing at night was the joy of my life. I was happy. I felt like I was growing and changing in a way that was surprising. I felt independent and safe.

Seven Guitars was a long haul. We went to the freezing cold of Chicago to the Huntington Theatre Company in Boston that at that particular time had a rat problem. Can you believe it? We would be chilling in the common room and a rat would run across the room! Geez. The great South African actor Zakes Mokae had joined the cast and little did we know, he was in the beginning stages of Alzheimer's. He was a beautiful man but could not remember his lines. It was so bad in Boston that the production had four people with scripts stationed at various points near the stage ready to scream lines. And I mean scream.

Then, he would carry his script onstage . . . during the performance . . . with an audience. It became cruel and difficult. It epitomized the whole adage that the

"Show must go on." It also encapsulates the whole notion that in theater anything can happen when it's live. It's a preparation that you cannot even fathom. And it just got worse. By the time we got to San Francisco, they had let Mokae go, which was heartbreaking. They hired an actor named Roger Robinson who was wonderful.

When you are doing a pre-Broadway run, the script is still changing. There are still rewrites, rehearsals. When we were in San Francisco at A.C.T., the play was four hours long and we were performing nine shows a week instead of eight. During the day, we rehearsed for eight hours. We were exhausted. During this time, I learned the hard-core lesson of what makes a great producer. The actor's energy and health has got to be paramount. No one was sleeping or no one was sleeping enough. We literally were falling asleep onstage. I fell asleep on the set waiting to go onstage during a tech rehearsal. I woke up petrified not knowing where I was. But sweet, special, unforgettable moments were created as well. Tommy Hollis, who has since passed, played the character of Red Carter in the play. He was real country. I loved him.

We talked for hours at night. We talked about everything and anything. We complained about the show. We talked about the different comments from people who had come to see it. We talked about fears, hopes, dreams. He would make me neckbone sandwiches with hot sauce on it. Yup. And I ate it. He would leave me turkey, cornbread dressing, and cranberry sauce sandwiches at my door. Years later, after 9/11, I tried calling him like I always do and I couldn't reach him. After a few days, I tried calling anyone I knew in NYC to go to his apartment. Roger Robinson finally did. He said he could smell the decomposition of his body when he went to his door. He had to get the apartment manager to open it. He had been dead for a week. Tommy was a beautiful, conflicted soul. I was devastated.

By the time we got to Los Angeles, we were swinging and dancing. Oh my God. Everyone came to see the show—Halle Berry, Angela Bassett, everyone. The driving was a pain in the ass. But when we left LA and rolled into NYC on a rainy day in late March 1996, we had a well-oiled machine. A lot about this business is anticlimactic.

It's not as glamorous as you think, and it's way more isolating. But man, Broadway? It lives up to everything you ever believed about what this business could be. It fulfills both the glamour and the work. It fulfills the community and comradery. It's the stuff of dreams. More than Oscars. More than Emmys. Each of those has its own disillusionment. Broadway is everything; it lives up to every bit of that dream.

There are other moments in life that absolutely live up to the hype, like adopting my baby—the love you have for your children (even when they drive you crazy) is everything, absolute perfection as far as I'm concerned. Okay, that's number one. Number two, getting married. I loved it! I didn't have any stress. That's why I had three ceremonies with my husband. Every one of them was among the most perfect days in my entire life. Winning an Oscar, a Screen Actors Guild Award—some perfect moments. But opening on Broadway on March 28, 1996, absolutely lived up to the hype. Perfect. It was everything that I dreamed it could be.

When I was a little girl dreaming of becoming an actress, I would say, "I want people to throw flowers at me onstage." The opening night on Broadway of *Seven Guitars* was beyond fucking fantastic. It was like someone giving you a big jolt of adrenaline and the happiest drug in the world. Flowers are in your room. You get presents. And then you do the play! I'm never very good on opening night on Broadway. I'm always too nervous. But it doesn't matter. When the play opens, critics have already been there. After opening night is when all the reviews come out.

I remember being so nervous from the anticipation of it all. Waiting for the reviews and how or if the plays land is anxiety inducing. Especially when you've worked on a play for a year, developing it, cutting, replacing actors . . . etc. *Seven Guitars* was just that, seven characters in harmony. Vera gets to her final monologue. She talks about a vision she had after burying Floyd Schoolboy Barton, the love of her life.

". . . I tried to call Floyd's name but wouldn't nothing come out my mouth. Seem like he started to move faster. I say the only thing I can do here is say goodbye. I waved at him and he went on up in the sky."

A brutal piece of writing and one I knew would land with my parents who were believers in myths, spirits, and rituals. It was a play where they not only could see my work but writing that was about THEM. When we ended our opening Broadway show of *Seven Guitars* after the curtain call, the lights came up, cameras from the television station glared in my face, everybody in their tuxedos and gowns was standing up clapping and shouting in thunderous applause and I saw MaMama and Daddy. Daddy was crying, clapping, staring at everybody, and I could tell his heart was pounding out of his chest. He looked beautiful; he had on a black tuxedo; he could always "clean up nice." My mom was clapping uncontrollably. I had put them in a hotel across from the theater and they were so happy. It was a Best Western but it might as well have been the Four

Seasons. Having my family there, my friends, was everything I could possibly imagine.

The after-party was in the big ballroom at the Marriott Marquis. Halle Berry, Laurence Fishburne, other wonderful actors I had always admired were there.

Everybody comes to Broadway. There was an intercom in everybody's dressing room. After every performance, the stage manager downstairs would get on the intercom and say, "Vanessa Redgrave is here to see the cast members from *Seven Guitars*. Denzel and Pauletta Washington are here to see the cast. Barbra Streisand here to see Viola Davis, Rosalyn Coleman, Ruben Santiago-Hudson, Michelle Shay, Tommy Hollis, Keith David." Everybody comes to meet you. Literally. I can't tell you how many people I ran into—producers, directors, agents—who saw me back then doing *Seven Guitars*.

But before opening night, it's the work. It's the payoff of the work. Lloyd Richards was very big on ensemble work, actors becoming a company. He wasn't big on above-the-title names and single-card billing; the business of acting, he wasn't into. He believed that it took a lot of time for a whole cast to become a company of actors who were in sync with one another. It wasn't until the last rehearsal in New York where he gathered us onstage, talked about his experience and how awesome it was to work with us, that he finally looked at us with laser focus and said, after a long pause: "And now, you are a company!" Lloyd represented the last vestiges of the old-school mentality. One that has indeed become a relic.

Everything was earned. *Seven Guitars* was a huge part of my growth as an actor. It was the difference between making the decision to become an actor, then training to become the best actor I could be, and finally putting everything that I learned to task. It also taught me a lot about life. There are no words to describe "The stage door." It's the door of the theater that you exit after the performance. Usually, people in the audience wait there to see you. It's not something that is present when you do TV/film.

Sometimes you never meet your fans or foes unless you're at the grocery store or Target. In theater, you are face-to-face with them every night. I learned about the graciousness of other actors and commitment to support and community. I have also experienced the other side. The cruelty and jealousy that is rampant in a business that has a lot of depravity. Jealousy is the cruelest of emotions. The part that makes it cruel is its lack of ownership.

Despite the good and the bad, I got a Tony nomination. I watched the Tonys every year. I would always run into school and ask anyone, "Did you see the Tonys last night?" I was always alone on that front. It usually was just me and my high school friend Angelo. Well, here I was getting a Tony nomination. I found out by checking my answering service. This was back in the day when you had to purchase an answering service. It was usually $6 or $10 a month. You could call from any phone at any time and check your messages. I went home to Rhode Island to relax the morning of the Tony nominations. Then I checked my messages and it was my agent Mark Schlegel telling me to call him. I got him on the phone and he said, "Viola. You got a Tony nomination!" I flipped out. I was at a pay phone. I flipped! I took the bus to my parents' house and ran in screaming, "I GOT A TONY NOMINATION!"

My mom, dad, and baby nieces and nephews started screaming, "Yay, Auntie." They didn't know what it meant but they were happy for me. They jumped all over me. In a world and in a business where friendships morph, change, where trust, love, and loyalty are elusive, this stands out as a great memory.

My agent Mark said to me, "Viola, you have great parents." His statement shocked me. I said, "I do?" He said, "Yes. They are great." I asked him why he said that. He said, "I've been in this business a while and have seen a lot of stage parents. It becomes more about them and not about their kids. Your parents are not that way at all. They just want to see you fly. They're just happy for you." It was a seed planted that made me look at my parents in a completely different light. It woke me up.

My first awards show was the Tonys. I remember Nathan Lane hosting. Savion Glover from *Bring in da Noise! Bring in da Funk*, directed by George C. Wolfe, performed. The cast from *Rent* performed. My sister Dianne came with me and she just kept saying, "Wow! Omg! I can't believe this. I can't. I can't believe I'm here." Seeing the great Zoe Caldwell win for *Master Class* and Audra McDonald for the same play. In my world, I had made it, whatever it was. I had made it because I was simply in their company. And just like film, with all the awards precursors, theater has its awards precursors.

The Outer Critics Circle Awards, the Drama Desk, the Drama League, and the Theatre World Awards for Outstanding Broadway debut—I won that one and I was over the moon. I didn't have to hear about awards prognosticators. This was before Google and awards sites and unknown people being given a media platform weighing in on who gave the best performance. It was untouched by outside influencers with little knowledge of what we do as artists. Except of course the critics of the day: John Simon, Frank Rich, Vincent Canby. But even they had a certain amount of weight and aesthetic that was earned. It was good times.

But this renewed joy was like a seesaw. My sister Danielle had her first child at seventeen. We all tried to keep her on the right track but she went through the teen years and started to rebel. None of us were around at that point. Her first baby's name was Derek. A beautiful baby. My parents were still living in poverty. I helped in every way I could while living in NYC, paying student loans, managing expenses; that little girl with the snot dripping down her nose and running for her life felt a huge responsibility. I was driven by the need to save everyone. I felt if I saved anyone, I had found my purpose, and that was the way it was supposed to work. You make it out and go back to pull everyone else out.

My parents were living on Parker Street in the first-floor apartment now. A low salary as an actor on Broadway is $1,500 a week. When I got on Broadway with *Seven Guitars* I was making $2,500 plus a $500 bonus because I got the Tony Award nomination. It felt like real money especially when combined with other gigs, or whatever, on the side. *Seven Guitars* ran for over a year in various cities, which is a long run for a show. On the road, I was making $1,500 a week and I was put up in, at the time, what I felt were really nice apartments. By the time it got to NYC, you're on your own. I had to look for another place to live because I had given up my apartment the year before.

Looking for a place to live in NYC is a harrowing undertaking. One that can bring you to your knees. I found a place with three other people. One was an actor I knew from Trinity Rep. It was a huge apartment on the Upper West side. I, once again, agreed to it sight unseen because I was on the road and didn't want the stress of looking for a place and juggling a Broadway opening. Thankfully, it did not mirror my experience with Susan's apartment. But, man, did I hold my breath when I opened that door.

A change started happening regarding the kind of money my family would ask me for. When you're making maybe $600 a week and you're working more than anyone else in the family, they'll ask for $20, $25. When you're on Broadway, they'll ask for $100 and $200. Family starts counting your money because they always feel like you're making more than you are. Later, it starts getting into the territory of "Buy me a house. Buy me a car." If you're not careful, you will go under, because the need is too great, too consistent.

I have gotten more calls than I can remember to pay

gas bills, grocery bills. At first, I would send money for food. The food would last for two or three days. Then they'd ask me for more. Then I started buying the food myself, getting it delivered, once that service was available. The need is endless. It's depleting. You're in the process of healing yourself, you're running on reserves. Success is absolutely wonderful, but it's not who you are. Who you are is measured by something way more abstract and emotional, ethereal, than outward success. *Seven Guitars* began a domino effect.

My dad changed considerably. He was still drinking a lot, but his rage binges had just about stopped cold. A kind, loving gentleman emerged. It was all about helping my mom, catering to her needs. They had gained custody of my brother's sons. John, my brother's firstborn, was born with withdrawal symptoms. His mom, my brother's girlfriend, gave birth while she was on the street and high on crack cocaine. It was literally subzero weather and she was prostituting and went into labor.

Little John's withdrawal symptoms were so bad, you felt you had to hold him tight or else he would just bounce out of your arms. He was in the hospital for a long time. I would come early in the morning around 8:30 a.m. or 9 a.m. By the time I got there, my dad had already been there for hours. He would walk from

Central Falls to Pawtucket, take the bus to downtown Providence, and walk the rest of the way to Hasbro Hospital. It was a brutal journey in the dead of winter but he and my mom, but mostly my dad, was there every day. My dad would just hold the baby and continually whisper to him how much he was loved. My brother's second child, Daniel, was born a few years later and my parents gained custody of him, too. My brother and his girlfriend had none of the resources to help.

Their burden became my burden. I didn't know how to say no to requests for food, money, payment for utilities. The needs were so great and began to escalate. I didn't know that my brother's problems were not my problems. I had created a life for myself and I would ask God constantly, *When do I get to enjoy it fully?* Plus, I simply didn't have the money.

The only predictor of a play closing is how many tickets it sells. If it doesn't sell, you're looking at a very short run, and when it's over, you will be collecting unemployment if you don't have a job lined up.

All the weekly payments are before taxes and before paying your agents. Your agents receive 10 percent of anything you earn in acting and Uncle Sam takes his cut. When you work in theater, film, or TV, they fly you out and put you up. In theater, they choose the housing and they fly you economy. In film and TV, they fly you first class and put you up in five-star accommodations and give you a per diem. Not everyone's five-star accommodations are the same and not everyone's per diem is the same. It's all based on clout, box office potency, and the serious negotiating skills of your agent. If an actor is blessed and fortunate enough to see a million dollars, deduct taxes, 10 percent for your agent, 10 percent to your manager if you have one, 2 to 5 percent to a lawyer, and at least $3,000 to $15,000 a month to a publicist.

Why do you need a lawyer? The lawyer knows how much money is on the table. Legally makes sure everything has the right jargon in your contract, and most importantly lawyers have the inside track on what other actors on your level get paid. The budget of the film, your role, and your standings in the business determine your pay. The fucked-up part is that you don't necessarily get paid for talent. You get paid for "getting butts in the seat." The caveat is that with most people of color, your films are not distributed and promoted enough to ensure butts in the seat and it keeps you hustling as far as pay is concerned.

Theater is a different beast. I never thought of myself as struggling during this time period. Even though at one point, I did a play in Newton, Massachusetts. I stayed in my sister's unfinished basement in Pawtucket, Rhode Island. Walked to the bus stop thirty minutes away to catch the greyhound to Boston. Yup! The bus again. Once I got to Boston, I would walk to the T and take the train thirty minutes to Newton where I performed in a church.

The play was *Jar the Floor* by Cheryl West directed by Woodie King Jr. Then Keith Glover's *Coming of the Hurricane* at the historic Black theater Crossroads in New Jersey. *God's Heart* by Craig Lucas at the Mitzi E. Newhouse Theater at Lincoln Center. Then *Everybody's Ruby* by Thulani Davis directed by Kenny Leon. I just followed the work.

Earlier in my career when I did *The Rover* at the Guthrie Theater, I lived in Minneapolis for six months and it was a turning point for me. I was twenty-eight and when I went back to NYC when the play was done, I had an epiphany. I was in the living room of our brownstone in Brooklyn and I was talking to my friend, housemate, Juilliard classmate Michelle O'Neil. In the middle of the conversation, I just threw out a random statement, "I wonder why I keep meeting assholes?"

She looked right through me and said, "Did you ever think it could be you?" At first, I thought the statement was born out of a grudge she had against me for never sharing my food at school. I was downright hostile toward anyone who asked me for food, and she was one of them. But she said it so matter-of-fact. The kind of truth that's like a hundred-pound hammer that knocks the wind out of you.

I remember I had my short, black minidress with my platform '70s-style heels. I had my braids and cowry-shell necklace. I thought I had my signature style, look. It was unapologetic, authentic, but it was clothing. She wasn't looking at that. She was looking at me. I was trying hard not to be seen. My style was my distraction. As fate would have it, soon after that my friend Gary who lived in LA suggested therapy because he was in it. I said I couldn't afford it. It hovered there through all our conversations.

The thought of sifting through all my shit and reconciling me . . . it almost felt like cleaning all that trash and miscellaneous junk under our beds at 128 and fearing rats jumping out and biting us. My last image of the rats was our basement after a major flash flood. The basement was flooded, killing the whole litter of our dog Cocoa's pups. She tried to swim and swim, whimpering to save them. Every time we tried to grab her, she growled, bit, and jumped back into the flooded basement searching for her babies. When the water subsided, they were found dead and partially eaten by the rats. I was afraid of being consumed, drowned, left, abandoned. Unloading my shit felt like major surgery that had a high propensity for death.

Another obstacle to getting therapy was the fact that I just couldn't find a way into TV and film. Screen Actors Guild health insurance would pay for ten free sessions a year of therapy. I'm sure my agents were frustrated that I hadn't booked anything onscreen. At first, I thought it was my hair. I had started doing my own hair to save money. I would buy ZZ curl hair from His and Her Hair shop in LA. It's crinkly curly hair but silkier and longer. I would buy it and get it shipped to me and sit down in front of the TV and proceed to braid it into my hair. I braided in a lot of hair. By the time I finished, it looked like a huge Afro of loose curls. I loved it! It was me but I don't know if the industry shared my sentiment. In hindsight, I could see their eyes widen when I walked in the room. I just ignored it because, really, I didn't know what to do about it. I couldn't be another me.

One day I got an audition for a Steven Soderbergh movie called *Out of Sight*. My agents put me on tape at their offices. I remember by this point I was so tired of going to audition after audition for TV/film that I just said the lines. I put nothing on them. The character was Moselle, who was very stoic and was just over it. So every line was, "I don't know where he is? Nope. He ain't home." I also had absolutely no hope I would get it because I had to play Don Cheadle's girlfriend.

I never got girlfriend roles, even if you saw the girlfriend without the boyfriend. It was almost as if there was a type called "Girls that nobody desires." I did it and forgot about it. I especially forgot because I hate being put on tape. Auditions are way more potent in the room. Nevertheless, I forgot about it. Three weeks later my agent called and said, "You know that role you auditioned for in the Steven Soderbergh movie?" Oh my God. I waited for the bad feedback; by the way, you will absolutely, without question, get bad feedback in your career. I waited for him to tell me that they thought my damn hair was too big.

I said, "Yeah," in my little girl voice. He said, "Well, you got the part." I was in shock. Shock. It was three days of work in Los Angeles and Detroit. My scenes were with Jennifer Lopez, Don Cheadle, and Isaiah Washington. I was in shock. I danced around my apartment. I was going to make more than $1,000 a day. Compare that to the theater. So imagine my excitement. I asked Steven later what got me the role and he said, "It was the combination of your stillness and that big hair." Bam! The damn hair did something.

Shortly after that, I booked a role in an HBO movie called *The Pentagon Wars* that shot the same time as

Out of Sight in LA! Once you get one role in TV/film it's a domino effect. All of a sudden, the same people who didn't cast you look at you and say, "Where have you been?"

I arrived in LA to shoot both projects. For *The Pentagon Wars*, I shaved my head. Which in hindsight, I think, *What?* But I was playing a woman in the military and wanted to be authentic. I always wanted to be authentic.

I stayed at the Sportsmen's Lodge in LA and was lonely as hell. They gave me a car, but I was terrified of driving. Literally. I would have the biggest panic attacks in LA behind the wheel of the car. Luckily, the soundstage where we shot was right down the street, so I didn't have to drive far. I worked with Cary Elwes, Kelsey Grammer, and Olympia Dukakis. Yup. I thought I had broken the barrier of being a working actor making money.

I worked out every day. Ate great food and had found a therapist who lived right up the street. I loved her, well, as much as you could love a person who pulled your insides out. She would tell me that I wouldn't know how to cross the street if it weren't covered in piss and shit. I had normalized the piss and shit. She would also say, "Viola, what if you didn't change all the parts of yourself that you are not happy with? What if you just stayed, you? Could you be happy with that? Could you still love yourself?" It almost became a moment like the one I had with a different therapist years later who told me to allow my younger self to hug me. Hell, SAG was paying her $100 per hour to tell me that? It took me the longest time to answer that question verbally and even longer to answer it internally.

I still felt awkward. I was still trying to fit in—I don't know where—just feel right. I just wanted to feel like who I was meant to be. I was still running from those boys. I was still staring into the hate-filled, disgusted eyes of my tormentors and feeling like they represented the overall consensus that I was worthless.

I finished *The Pentagon Wars* and had my hair done. This time, Universal hired a professional to do my hair extensions. I shot my scene in *Out of Sight* with Don Cheadle and Isaiah Washington and felt like a real, respected actor. The hair, makeup, trailer, and set just blew my mind. No audience present like theater. No rehearsal. No spending weeks with other actors trying different choices, seeing what works and doesn't work. No time to establish trust. Film and TV is about preparing and leaping. When the movie is finished you watch yourself. I love it but the trap has always been the self-consciousness that comes from watching oneself. No one watches themselves in life, which is what we as actors are mirroring. We just . . . live.

I was trying to connect where the beginning of the dream started to getting to this moment. They put me in a leopard print robe. I had to smoke a cigarette. I remember being introduced to Jennifer Lopez for the first time. We got along great. She said it was her first big job, too.

I had to finish up another part of my scene in Detroit a few weeks later with Jennifer. Detroit was freezing. They put me in a huge suite in a hotel and I was stunned. I remember looking around with my jaw to the ground. Then, ironically, I couldn't sleep in the bed. It was a nice king-size bed, but it sort of dipped in the middle. The suite was cold and really dark when the lights went out. I had flashbacks of my childhood. Images of urine-soaked mattresses and cold rooms because the heat was cut off. I slept on the couch and kept the lights on all night. I really didn't sleep. But filming was awesome. Jennifer wanted me to drive in her car with her. We chatted about all kinds of things and shivered. Then it was over.

Soon after that, I had made enough money for health insurance. My fibroids were so bad I looked six months pregnant. I was so anemic from constant bleeding that I would fall asleep standing up in the subway. I also developed a really bad habit of eating cornstarch. My mom would eat it growing up as did many people down south. I later found out it was from a condition caused by low iron levels called pica. The symptoms are cravings for weird textures such as ice, rubber, and even starch. It was an embarrassing habit because I was always trying to hide it. Finally, I decided my fibroids needed to be removed. I had them removed during Thanksgiving and I had nine of them. They were enormous.

My mom was there with me in NYC. I remember the head resident came into the room with five residents behind him. "Okay. This is a patient who had a myomectomy. Uhh . . ." He looked at my mom sitting in a chair beside me. "Uhh . . . Ma'am, can you please leave the room?" My mom, without missing a beat, said loudly, "No." He was in shock. "You heard what I said; no. I know my rights. You can talk all you want to but Imma stay right here." He was silent. Turned around and walked out. When he left my mom whispered, "Vahla. Me and ya daddy saw this on a program late one night. They said never leave anyone in the room alone with the doctor. You don't know what they gon' do when you leave." I'm sure she was having flashbacks to the time the doctor wanted to break my legs when I was two. She stayed by my side. She ate all my food because I had little appetite. My friend Michelle came one day to visit me. My mom was just sitting there. "Vahla? You ain't gon' eat that food? Give it to me." Michelle, who was trying to get pregnant, said, "Mrs. Davis? Do you remember giving birth?"

"Yup," in between eating the hell out of a turkey gravy meal. "Dianne cost $25. John cost $25. Vahla cost $25. Deloris was expensive. She cost $30." By this point we were laughing. "What do you mean, Mom?" I said.

"Vahla! That's what we had to pay Miss Clara Johnson, the midwife."

"But Mom, Michelle wanted to know what it was like giving birth."

"I don't remember no pain." She was quiet. "But MaMama and Daddy did lie to me about the pain with ya brother John when I was fifteen. They say it wasn't gon' hurt. They lied to me. I don't remember no pain after that. All this stuff that people do now and tellin' you what you can and can't do. What you can or can't eat. Shiiitt. I didn't do nothing like that and I had six children."

It was the first time I felt the weight of the operation I just had. The benign tumors that had been removed would form scar tissue and adhesions. I would have a small window of time after recovery to have a baby or would be rendered infertile. I had no significant other in my life and was already in my early thirties. Once again, the reminder that life was happening as my career was happening. I just suppressed it. I had time. Right?

Soon after my recovery I would get a fateful job at Williamstown Theatre Festival in Massachusetts. I played the role of Ruth in *A Raisin in the Sun*. I had gone to Los Angeles before this time to shoot *The Shrink Is In* with Courtney Cox and David Arquette. Richard Benjamin, who directed *The Pentagon Wars*, cast me. Like I said, getting one job in TV/film creates a domino effect of relationships and connection.

While I was in LA, Steven Bochco called me to audition for *City of Angels*. It was touted as an all-Black drama. Blair Underwood was cast in the lead role. Steven Bochco created *Hill Street Blues* and *LA Law*. I had a great audition, but I got feedback that I wasn't right for the part. They kept saying things like, "Uhh . . . she was great, but too quirky, too different." In reality, I wasn't pretty enough. At this point, it was the story of my career. So I just forgot about it and went back home to Harlem where I now lived.

I then booked *A Raisin in the Sun* by Lorraine Hansberry. I played Ruth. Kimberly Elise played Beneatha, Gloria Foster was Mama, and Ruben Santiago-

Hudson, who wrote the screenplay to August Wilson's *Ma Rainey's Black Bottom,* was Walter Lee. Jack Hofsiss directed.

Williamstown is a summer stock theater where all actors go to legitimize themselves or just get back to the work. It takes place on the Williams College campus. All the actors live in dorms or homes. It's about getting down to the bare bones minimum and just focusing on the craft. I lived in the dorms. I loved hanging and talking with the actors at night. I was in therapy and would have phone sessions once a week. My therapists would always say, "You're not poor anymore. You're not that little girl with no shoes or hot running water."

During *Raisin* one of my castmates, Joseph Edward, who played Bobo, asked me a more potent question, "Why don't you have anyone in your life? You seem really smart. You're a nice woman. Why don't you have someone in your life?"

Joseph and I had a great friendship of transparency and respect.

"I don't know." I almost cried when he asked me that.

It was a question that seared through my soul. One that I refused to even ask myself. By this point, I was a few years from my fibroid surgery. I was alone but not lonely, or so I thought. I was good if I didn't think too deep.

"Have you prayed for someone to come into your life?" He just stared at me.

That's what he asked me next. It was a big moment for me. I said, "No, but I'm doing the work. I'm in therapy. I've gotta clean things up before I can invite anyone into my life to love me."

There was silence.

He said, "This is what I want you to do."

I was so sensitive about not having anyone in my life that I paid attention to him.

He said, "Do you know what you want?"

"Yes, I know what I want," I said.

"Are you sure you know what you want? You gotta be sure you know what you want."

"Joseph, I'm sure about what I want," I said. "I'm a grown woman."

"Okay, this is what I want you to do. When you go to bed at night, I want you to get on your knees and ask God for exactly what you want."

I did not have anyone in my life but I had no response to this surprise advice.

He said, "You just give God your list. The frivolous stuff and the meaningful stuff."

I was skeptical that this advice would change my situation.

He said, "You got it?"

"Okay, Joseph."

He said, "Are you gonna do it?"

"I will. I'll do that."

He said, "Are you sure?"

"Yeah, I'll do it."

He said, "You gotta be really specific."

"Mm-hmm. I will do it."

I don't pray at night. At least, up to that point I didn't. I got in bed that night and I remembered Joseph's words. I thought, *I'm not getting down on my knees.* After twenty or thirty minutes lying in bed, I thought *Okay!* I got out of bed. I got down on my knees. I clearly remember how I opened my prayer: "God, you have not heard from me in a long time. I know you're surprised. My name is Viola Davis." I continued like this, repeating my name since God and I hadn't been acquainted for such a long time: "I'm Viola Davis. I'm at Williamstown Theatre Festival right now. A friend of mine told me to pray and ask you for what I want. I believe in you. I'm gonna believe that you're gonna deliver and I'm gonna ask you for what I want."

I brainstormed a list. I told God the list. I said I wanted a big, Black man who was an ex-athlete, preferably a football player, because I love football players. "I really want him to be Black, but he doesn't *have* to be Black, God. I mean at the end of the day, I really,

really want him to be Black, God. And I love southern men, I love country men, God, so I want someone real country.

"And I don't want any pressure to have children, so I want him to have had a wife before me and children already, so that's settled. I want someone who trusts in you and loves you, God, because then he will be accountable to someone—you, God." None of the men I've ever dated were accountable to anybody. They just did and said what they wanted. And they were completely emotionally unavailable and that's what I said, too. "I want him to be emotionally available and understand what I do as an actor." I was getting up off my knees and before I climbed back in bed, I said, "I promise I'll start going to church" and thought *If you give me what I want, the church may blow up when I walk in there.* After that last bit of bartering, I said, "Amen."

This was toward the end of the *Raisin* run. I learned I had landed the role in *City of Angels* but I almost didn't go back to LA to take it. They were giving me a series regular role but only paying me $5,600 per episode and only guaranteeing me ten episodes. $5,600 an episode sounds like a lot of money, but after New York City and New York State taxes—because I was still a New York resident—Los Angeles taxes, and federal taxes, I was left with $2,200. Most actors make at least three times more than that for their first series regular job. But the network was not sold on an all-Black drama, so Bochco had to use his own money. Hence the low salary.

My agent received 10 percent on top of the taxes I had to pay. I had to move and live in LA for seven months. I had to rent a car and an apartment. I had to pay housing in New York and LA because the pipes had burst in my apartment in New York and the ceiling had caved in, so I couldn't get anyone to sublet that Harlem rental. But I decided to take *City of Angels* even though it was not a lucrative job and it required the move to LA, which is as expensive as New York.

With three films under my belt, *The Shrink Is In, Pentagon Wars,* and *Out of Sight,* and TV work that had never seen the light of day, I moved to LA to start *City of Angels.* Despite the crappy salary I earned, it was still more money than I had ever made before, and I took it because I had never done a series regular role on TV. It was a chance to work with Steven Bochco—and Paris Barclay who was the new hotshot Black director.

I stayed in the Oakwood Apartments in Marina Del Rey for a month because it was close to the Culver Studios where we shot. I had to move out of there because I couldn't afford it and my credit was crap. I had defaulted on my student loans when I first got out of school and tried to catch up but my credit score was not moving. I had my first credit card but it was one of those cards that worked like a debit card and my credit limit was the money I had put into the account. I couldn't lease a car or sign for an apartment. I finally got my sister to cosign for a cheaper apartment on Vermont Avenue. It was an Oakwood Apartment but only $1,500 a month. My friend Patrice helped me find it.

I called her crying one day because I finally got tired of having it hard. I got tired of walking and taking buses and the loneliness and nomadic lifestyle. I just wanted to find home. Not find a home but find home. A safe place sanctuary that was peaceful, nurturing, reliable . . . and filled with love. I had gone from running from bullies, poverty, acting student, pounding the pavement, getting theater/film work to LA. I was ready to arrive at some destination.

Chapter 16
Harnessing Bliss

*"Fame is a vapor. Popularity is an accident.
Riches takes wings. And only one thing remains . . .
CHARACTER."*

—HORACE GREELEY

I moved to LA a few weeks after I prayed. And three weeks after I moved, I met Julius on the set of *City of Angels*. Julius Tennon was playing the anesthesiologist Dr. Holly. I was Nurse Lynette Peeler. We were working together in a scene, passing the blood. He was really nice, but he was messing up, playing with the little needle thing during the scene. He punctured his finger, but it wasn't a big deal. When the scene was over, I was at craft services eating a bagel. I had already said "Bye" to him, "It was nice meeting you," but he came back to set, to craft services, and said to me, "I overheard you say you don't know anyone in LA."

"No, I don't know anyone in LA," I said. "I do not like this city. I'm so nervous here and . . ."

"I understand. Have you ever been to Santa Monica Pier? I'll take you to Santa Monica Pier!"

"No, I've never been to Santa Monica Pier."

"I'll take you. Here's my card. You call me. I don't want you to be alone here."

I was thinking, *Oh my God, he's giving me his card.* I hoped it was not a card that's a headshot and he has no shirt on. That was so prevalent in LA. Every time a man would pass me a card, saying, "I'm an actor. Maybe we can do something together after work," these dudes' cards had them pictured showing their six-pack abs and chests. I would always toss those cards in the garbage. Julius gave me his card and he was pictured in a shirt. That was good.

We talked. Looking at him, he was big. Beautiful. I thought Julius was beautiful. He told me he was from Texas, used to play football, and "I have two kids, and a grandbaby." He gave me his card and I thought, *Oh, he's so nice. I need to have my stuff together. I have bad credit. I can't stand driving. I'm nervous. How am I going to drive to him and then go places? I can't do that.*

I was struggling to survive, struggling to figure out how to live in LA, struggling to rent a car to figure out how get groceries or get to the set on time. I didn't know how to navigate the city. I had a lot on my plate. I was a mess, in my opinion. I didn't have my life together. I couldn't think about anything other than sitting in my room in that apartment in Marina Del Ray and stressing. I couldn't think about no Santa Monica Pier.

I finally called him six weeks later after I went to my therapist. That was one place I knew how to drive to without ever getting on the freeway. My therapist asked, "What's new in your life?"

"I met someone really nice on set."

She was so excited. "Oh, who?"

"He's really, really nice. Really cute, too. But," I said, "I don't know, there's gotta be something wrong with him." I was so jaded. My relationship of seven years was over and I'd forgotten about that prayer, which seemed like wishing on a star.

"Call him."

"No, I'm not going to call him because he's probably no good."

"Viola, call the man. Call him. You don't know whether he's nice or not. You don't know who he is, but he's someone who extended himself. He saw that you were lonely. He sounds nice to me."

I didn't admit to her that I hadn't called him because of *me*, because I didn't have my shit together. I went back to my apartment and it took me the longest time to find his card. I called him. *Oh my God.* I expected him not to remember me because it'd been so long. "Hi, Julius."

"Heeey, Viola! How you doing?"

"You remember me?"

"Yeah, I remember you. How you doing? It's so nice to hear your voice."

After that phone call, my life just got better. For our first date we went to Santa Monica Pier to a restaurant called Crocodile. Everything that I had prayed for, the whole list, all of it, was checked off. Julius was an ex-football player from Austin, Texas. His manner was what I call "country." He had two kids, and he invited me to church.

When he said, "How are you doing?" I told him how I was struggling, and I felt he listened to me. He immediately invited me into his life, saying, "I want you to come and see where I work in Santa Monica." No man I ever dated invited me into his life. The men I had dated wanted to come over to my apartment to do the Boom Ghazi. He said, "It's a nice place to work. You should see the antique reproductions. It's in a beautiful area. And then, maybe we could sit down, get something to eat at my favorite restaurant." He seemed so excited about the high-end furniture store in Santa Monica called Prince of Wales that sold beautiful antique reproduction furniture. Celebrities would visit that store. He loved where he worked. He was so proud of it.

City of Angels was gearing up for publicity and I needed to attend a photo op event. I'm still shy but at least I can handle PR now. Back then I couldn't handle it at all. I knew it would help to have someone beside me and I had a plus-one. I knew no one else to take, so I called Julius. He sounded thrilled that I called him. Nervously, I said, "Well, okay. Well, I'm really calling because I need someone to come with me to a photo op for City of Angels, this publicity thing. I mean, I'm wondering if you would like to come with—"

"Yeah, I want to come with you to a photo op!"

"Oh my God."

"When you want me to come pick you up?"

"Oh no, no, I don't want you to come pick me up."

"I'll pick you up," he responded.

"I don't need you to pick me up. I can get there myself. I'll take a cab."

"You don't have to take a cab. I'll come pick you up."

"No, I don't want you to come pick me up. I'm telling you, I do not."

After a long pause, he said, "Okay. Well, all right."

But I could tell the conversation was unsettling to him. We made the date, I hung up, and right then Phylicia Rashad called me. I had done *Everybody's Ruby* with her at the Public Theater in New York and she was in town staying in a great hotel. She wanted to see me the same night as the *City of Angels* photo op. "Oh, Phylicia. I want to see you, too," I said, genuinely eager to reconnect. We agreed to meet at her hotel for appetizers. Then I remembered the photo op and that Julius would be with me. *Oh shit*, I thought, *It will sound pretentious to call him back and say, Phylicia Rashad—I just worked with her in New York—and she would like to get together* . . . but I called and asked him if he wanted to also come with me to meet Phylicia Rashad.

"Phylicia Rashad! Yeah. I want to go." Not only did he not make me feel I was being pretentious, Julius said something that reminded me why I so love folk who are country. "You know, I'm gonna wear my white jacket. I'm wearing my white jacket with black pants. It's a real nice white jacket."

The date was perfection. We went to the photo op and stopped by to visit with Phylicia. After the visit he said, "I'm driving you home, To. Your. Front. Door." At my front door, he shook my hand and said, "You are a beautiful woman. I had such a nice time with you. You are so sweet."

"I had a nice time with you, too," I said.

"You get some rest."

I went into my apartment. He left.

Twenty minutes later, my phone rang. I pick it up and it's Julius. "I just wanted to say again that I had such a nice time with you. You are a sweet woman."

"You're home already?" I asked.

"No, I'm at the Ralph's down the street. I had a very nice time."

Another twenty minutes and the phone rings again. I pick it up and it's Julius. "I just wanted to let you know I got home. I'm home now. You are such a sweet woman. I had such a good time."

"I had a good time with you, too, Julius."

"Well, get some rest."

That was the night that there was an earthquake at four o'clock in the morning. Right after the earthquake, my phone rings again. It's Julius: "I just wanted to call to see if you are okay." I thought, *One thing I will not have to worry about is this man calling me. I do not have to wonder where this man is.*

It is true, my life just got better once I met Julius. He just helped in every single way. If I asked, *How do I lease a car? How do I navigate this? Where is this place and that place?* he had an answer. It could be anything. He was a helpmate. We clicked. It was love in the best sense of the word. We were with each other every single day. He invited me to church again, and when I went it did not blow up.

Every day was a party. When Julius and I celebrated our first Thanksgiving together, we cooked, ate so much food—a whole pot of dressing—and drank, I don't know how many bottles of wine. We got in the Jacuzzi at the apartment every night except when we were working or when it rained.

We laughed and played tickle monster every night. Don't ask. I prefer to think that we were just ecstatically happy and that happiness brought out the child in both of us. We did Tae Bo together and played on the couch and watched hours of TV. We didn't spend one day apart. Then *City of Angels* got picked up for the second season, and he said, "Vee. You should come live with me. That way we could split the rent. I got a two-bedroom, two-bathroom apartment that only costs $850 a month. We can just split it right in half. It'll be a lot less expensive."

I was paying $1,500 for rent, so aside from love, I thought, *This is a good deal.* I moved in and my rent went down to $425. Everything got better. My life opened up. I was being catapulted into adulthood. Coming from a childhood of trauma I needed a radical transformation. I hadn't been taught how to navigate the world. I hadn't been taught what could help me grow or live better. I'd been taught how to run from the world. I'd been taught how to hide and fight. I hadn't been taught how to love and be still.

As soon as he came into my life, my life got better because I created a family with him, with someone who loved me. I was no longer solely defined by the family that raised me and my childhood memories. Julius and I created this new chapter in my life, starting from a blank slate. I could create my own family and I could create it intentionally with what I had learned.

What I earned from *City of Angels* went much further because I was living with Julius. And while I was living with Julius, I also got a movie. The movie was *Amy and Isabelle* starring Elisabeth Shue, Conchata Ferrell, Ann Dowd. It was an Oprah Winfrey Presents movie that she produced. I also got a play that would be very fateful because it would lead to my first Tony Award.

It's like Oprah said, "I know for sure what we dwell on is what we become." With this chapter in my life, I didn't want to dwell on little Viola running away anymore. I wanted to run toward joy, hand in hand with Julius. I wanted to feel alive. I wanted to become . . . me.

Julius is and was a protector and an awesome life partner. He is motivated by his love for me and his fierce protectiveness of our life. I see that in him even now, after twenty-one years. With both of us, like any human being, the nicks, obstacles, and scrapes still threaten. Little crumbs from the past come, memories that still carry some weight and power. They show up in anxiety-filled dreams. They show up at Thanksgiving when I cook too much food and he cleans within an inch of his life. But it's a matter of recognizing what stems from my childhood, being aware and not letting that control us. Toni Morrison in *The Bluest Eye* says that "a person's love is only as good as the person; a stupid person loves stupidly, a violent man loves violently." The love of a man who puts you first, who is evolved and who always wants to be better for you, is Julius's love capacity.

Coming home late one night after a late-night shoot on *City of Angels*, I was exhausted, driving to stay awake and get home quicker. I had bought my first car from a friend of Julius, a gold '86 Volvo for $2,500. It was a tank. I was driving so fast getting off the 101 to get to Van Nuys, the police stopped me. I had never in my life been stopped by the police. My ass was tight! Translation: I was scared to death. The police officer shone his flashlight and said, "What's going on?"

"Well, Officer. I'm exhausted. I just did an eighteen-hour day on a set." I then proceed to show him my script. "I'm on this show *City of Angels*, Steven Bochco. I know I was driving fast—"

"You weren't just driving fast," he interrupted, "you went through a red light!"

I was shocked. I did not know I had sped through a red light. I had no argument. I began begging and apologizing: "Oh, man! I'm so sorry. I'm here from New York. I'm overwhelmed here. You wanna see my license?"

He nodded his head. "Yeah, let me see it." At that point, he let me go. It took me less than five minutes to get home. As I was walking toward our apartment, Julius was coming out the door. He was half asleep. One eye was open. One arm was in his coat, which he was attempting to put on, and in his other hand was his baseball bat. I jumped. "Julius! Where're you going?"

"I was going to find you! It's late. Hell, you called from the set but that was a while ago. I thought something happened to you. I was going to put this bat on somebody's ass."

Julius had a whole system involving safety when we moved on to our condo. When I drove into the gated community, I had to keep the car door locked and the engine running until the gate closed behind me and then drive into our garage. If I was being attacked or followed, I should lay on the horn and he would be out with his baseball bat to lay it on someone's ass. That was the plan. I made the unfortunate mistake of coming home late one night and accidentally laying on the horn. I caught it fast but I literally counted to three and Julius had come out of the house like a grizzly bear. No shirt and in his pajama pants, with that baseball bat securely in hand ready to fight. He was audibly growling!

"Julius!! No!! It was an accident! I accidentally pressed the horn."

"I was gonna split somebody's ASS!!!!" he said.

Julius and I had not been together long when *King Hedley II* came along. I was not going to do the play. I said to Julius, "It's not a lead character. She's not on-stage a lot, even though she has that big monologue. It may be beneath me." Julius said nothing, but he stared at me. "What do you think, Julius?" He stared at me some more. *City of Angels* had come to an end after two seasons of thirteen episodes each. When we stopped shooting the first season, I went back to New York to do *Vagina Monologues*. Then *City of Angels* was canceled after its second season and I had only done ten episodes in the new season.

Julius kept staring at me. Finally, he said, "This is what I think. Yo' ass ain't got a job. You need to go on and do that job. That's what you need to do." I laughed my ass off and went on to do the job.

So I was Tonya in August Wilson's *King Hedley II*. We performed at the Kennedy Center before opening on Broadway. I remember in Washington, DC, at the Kennedy Center opening, Julius said, "You're gonna win the Tony." It was prophetic because I did. Joan Allen presented the award to me and I cried uncontrollably. The experience was perfect, first in the Virginia Theater at the Kennedy Center and then we took it to Broadway. Working with Brian Stokes Mitchell, Leslie Uggams, Charlie Brown, Monté Russell, and Stephen McKinley Henderson.

At any rate, I define this part of my life, moving in with Julius, as growing up. I started saving money, took my landlord to court to fix the apartment in Harlem and then sublet it so I didn't have two rent payments—LA and New York. And slowly but surely paid off my student loans. Within three years we had worked and saved enough to buy our first condo. It was $299,000. We had an excellent safety net in our account, so we said, "Let's go for it" and we moved in. We married in that condo a year later in 2003.

My biggest discovery was that you can literally recreate your life. You can redefine it. You don't have to live in the past. I found that not only did I have fight in me, I had love. By the time we clicked, I had had enough therapy and enough friendship and enough beautiful moments in my life to know what love is and what I wanted my life to feel and look like. When I got on my knees and I prayed to God for Julius, I wasn't just praying for a man. I was praying for a life that I was not taught to live, but for something that I had to learn. That's what Julius represented.

I was also waking up to the hard-core reality that life unexpectedly throws curveballs in your life. The one-two punch was the bombing of the Twin Towers and a week later, the death of my friend Tommy Hollis. I was speechless. Somehow the story I was telling myself was that I could actually do something that would make my life go exactly as I planned. I did. It's like Hedley says in *Seven Guitars*, "Man got plan but God? He got plan too." Well, I believed God loved me enough to cradle me and protect me from pain. THAT was the agreement. Man . . . but I had no idea that the pain can just keep coming.

Julius pointed out to me when we first met that I had never experienced the loss of a close loved one. He said, "Vee, you still have both parents. When that happens, it's brutal. Especially your mom." He had lost both of his. When his mom died, he sat with her body at the mortuary for six hours. I asked him, "What did you do that whole time?" He said that he cried and talked to her. He laughed and recounted certain memories and he slept some. That image was tattooed in my head. When I told him about my life and what was on my parents' plate as far as raising grandkids, he said, "That's just like my people. It's brutal. It wears down your health. My mom went from pretty good health to debilitating health in a short time taking care of her dad."

He advised me to get insurance on them, because when it happens, no one is going to know what to do or have the money to bury them. I was silent, knowing life happens, there's no pause button, no editor to change an outcome to something that fits the limitation of your heart. I got the insurance.

During this time, what healed completely from my childhood was my relationship with my father. I came to understand him with compassion, as a person, as I beheld Daddy's turnaround, becoming patriarch to his grandchildren. He'd begun to change, almost imperceptibly, when I was in college as my nieces and nephews were born. He began to be the one who kept it together, even a little bit together, in the house and the family. My father was radically transformed—docile, loving. Every time I talked to him, he'd say, "I love you so much, daughter. I love you so much." He turned the corner when he had to take custody of my nieces and nephews in the early '90s. Somewhere in there was a heart, a very fragile heart. I began to glimpse it in those moments when he wasn't drinking. Somewhere, inside, he was really trying to make amends. I think my dad just got tired of the anger, the rage, as an answer to his inner pain. Either you give yourself over to it in a sort of emotional suicide or you simply just get it. What do I think he got? That he was loved. That he was needed. That he mattered. I believe he changed as a way of asking for our forgiveness.

My parents took in my sister Danielle's three children at that time, one after another. She would later have three more. The last three, my parents couldn't take on. Some of my other nieces were in and out of their house. At least five of my siblings' children lived with my parents because my siblings Anita, John, and Danielle couldn't take care of them because of addiction and/or money issues. MaMama and Daddy raised them as their own. Those five were permanently there. Another three would come in and out at various times. The daily task of now parenting young children, keeping them alive and happy, was bigger than any demons. The fighting just got less and less until it was nonexistent. It was replaced by a bigger task that took every fiber of their being. Daddy was now there with my mom all the time. He went from abusing to living for this woman. She had hip issues and sciatica nerve pain.

He would massage her legs and her feet. He would cook for her. He would take care of the grandkids. MaMama loved to go to Atlantic City. Whenever she wanted to go, she would call me to pay for the trip and he would go with her. One time, she got sick while they were there. I got a cryptic phone call: "Grandma's sick. They're on their way home," and I found out later Daddy was right there with her, terrified of losing her, holding her the whole time as they rode home on the bus.

When I began to witness his transformation, I started having conversations with him to encapsulate every single moment. His first changes were evident when I was a student with no money, but when I gradually started making money, I began to do things for and with my parents, as much as my money would allow. I didn't have to make a lot of money for us to do things together. I would bring them to New York to stay with me and they loved it.

I sprung for August Wilson's favorite hotel in New York. They were so happy. They stayed with me in my one-bedroom apartment when I did *Intimate Apparel* by Lynn Nottage in New York at the Roundabout Theatre Company. I flew in from California for the months *Intimate Apparel* ran and I invited them to come at various times to stay with me. Their visits were simple togetherness times. I liked to take them out to eat. When I would do *Law and Order* I would invite them to come and stay with me in the hotel I was provided. They loved it.

When I would go to either the train or the bus station to pick them up, they would be waiting for me, sitting side by side. As soon as they saw me, it was as if they hadn't seen me for fifteen years. So happy. They would make me laugh. We would have the best time. I would always tell them before they left home, "Daddy, Mom, when you get off the bus, stay exactly in that spot. I will be there. I will be waiting for you or I will be right there two minutes after the bus arrives. Do not roam around looking for me. Don't do that because you're going to get lost." Then I would have them repeat it.

"When the bus get there, get off and stay exactly in that spot where the bus let off. If you not there waiting don't go looking for you," they repeated. Most times, they would be sitting there, staying in one spot, as instructed. I could tell it took an incredible effort for them to sit still.

Other times I'd find my father walking around. "Daddy, I told you not to walk around."

"I know, daughter. I know. But I'm so excited. I love New York." And he'd begin a story, like, "Do you know where Lenny is? I was in New York back in the day when I was at the racetrack, and Lenny lived right here on Forty-Second Street."

"Daddy, how long ago was that?"

"Fortysome years ago."

"Okay, Daddy, I don't know who Lenny is. I don't know if Lenny is still alive."

My mom always complained, like clockwork, "Oh, Viola, my stomach is upset. My stomach is upset 'cause of that bus ride."

"I tried to give your mama some food to settle her stomach—" MaDaddy would say, treating her like a princess.

"Okay," I would reply, "well, maybe we should get some soup."

"I don't want no damn soup," MaMama would shoot back. "I want some chicken wings. I want some hot chicken wings." I would just laugh and shake my head. A part of me began to understand the importance of time. I was trying to freeze it. It was especially driven home by how much time my career was taking up. It made me appreciate and value it as a life goal. I wanted to take in every part of their faces, hands, laughs, stories.

We'd do whatever they wanted to do. It was great experiencing my parents at this age. I was working steadily and, at the same time, saving money. Although I experienced my parents on a whole different level, the family situation was still constant drama—fifteen people living in my parents' apartment sometimes. My family issues were ever present and had metastasized into the children who were living with my parents to avoid ending up in the child welfare system.

My parents were older and their needs greater. I sent $300 to $400 home every week for my parents to get food or whatever. I didn't have it to send, but I was sending it anyway. I got a phone call about a $3,000 gas bill. This had never happened before. I only had $600 left in my account. A friend said, "If you're in a hole, who's going to help you, Viola?" I thought I could save them. I thought my money and success could save all of them. I learned the hard way that when there are underlying issues, money does nothing. In fact, money exacerbates the problem because it takes away the individual's ability to be held accountable.

A part of me felt that my mom had already been made to feel accountable for every burden that wasn't hers. I wanted to calm that internal storm of guilt and anger inside of her.

Daddy turned from our terror to our hero. Forgiveness is giving up all hope of a different past. They tell you successful therapy is when you have the big discovery that your parents did the best they could with what they were given. Even without knowing this at the time, I didn't just see the man who was violent, abusive. I saw the man my niece Tiana saw, my sister Danielle's daughter.

"Grandpa went with me to my first day of school, Auntie," she told me. "I was crying. I kept crying and crying and he said, 'It's going to be okay. It's going to be okay.' We went inside the school and I was still crying softly. Before all the parents had to leave, he whispered, 'You gotta be brave.' I nodded and said, 'Yeah.' I was about to cry again after he left. I couldn't hold back the tears. Then I looked out the window and saw him standing there. He was there looking up at the window. He stayed there for the longest time looking in the window, waving at me until I was okay."

At this point in my life, everything shot out like a rocket ship. I was getting more and more work. They all mesh together in my brain now. I had a few unsuccessful pilots. I had a few TV shows, *Century City*, *Laws of Chance*, *Fort Pitt*, and *The Traveler*, that made it on the air for two or three episodes and got canceled. I did a number of guest star roles on *Law and Order: Criminal Intent*, *Law and Order: SVU*, *Judging Amy*, the *Jesse Stone* series, *Without a Trace*, *The Practice*. They just kept coming, and it was enough to make a life change.

The biggest life change during that time was getting married. Julius asked me to marry him but it's not a great story. My ten-year-old daughter says, "Mommy, you messed up a really awesome proposal." Julius wanted to take me to Santa Monica to this beautiful restaurant. I didn't know that he planned to propose. I thought he wanted to go to Santa Monica to eat and I did not feel like going. I was still in my I-hate-LA mode and to get to Santa Monica we had to drive an hour and a half down the 405 Freeway. He kept saying, "Vee, it'll be great. Once we get there, it's going to be wonderful and beautiful. We can just love each other . . ."

"I don't wanna go!"

So he proposed in our living room. I could tell he was very nervous about something. Then he got down on one knee and said, "Will you, will you become engaged to me?" He had bought the ring. He was so nervous because he had been married before. He had raised his children on his own. To me, we might as well have been on the Eiffel Tower. It was absolutely perfect.

We decided to choose a date to get married. He said, "Vee, it can't be anybody's birthday, a holiday, nothing. It needs to be a date that we celebrate. It's only our anniversary."

"Oh, okay, let me focus." I paused a long time.

"What about June twenty-third?" he asked.

"June twenty-third, June twenty-third, June twenty-third. Wait a minute. I don't know." I kept racking my brain calendar, then I finally said, "I think that's clear.

Maybe, I don't know. I don't think that's anyone's birthday."

We got married June 23 . . . my niece Annabella's birthday.

I chose the wrong day. Damn! Every June 23 we're calling her saying happy birthday and she's calling us saying happy anniversary. I have so many nieces and nephews, and I was really good at keeping their birth-days in my head, but I messed up with that one.

A year later, we decided to get married in our first condo, in front of fifteen people. The pastor from our church married us. My family wasn't there because they were working or didn't have money to fly out, and at that time I didn't have the money to fly them all out. Plus, we decided at the last minute to just go for it. Close friends, Julius's daughter, and his two grandkids stood with us. We had a Sweet Lady Jane's triple berry cake. A beautiful concoction of white cake, whipped cream frosting, and filling with fresh berries. I had no anxiety, only pure joy. I was filled with certainty. I had done the work on myself after being in therapy for seven years. I was thirty-eight. I was ready. We went to the mall the day before, holding hands, going to the Express store to find pink linen shirts. I went to bed that night and had a nightmare.

In my nightmare, I was waiting for an elevator, a

glass elevator. There were other people around. The elevator door opened and we all got in. I pressed the thirty-eighth floor. And the elevator looked like a subway car but it was going up. I sat down, looked across, and saw this woman holding the subway strap standing up. She was holding on but looked asleep or dead. She had long braids and was dark-skinned but ashen. It was me! It was me the way I looked at twenty-eight!! I got up and tried to shake her awake but she wouldn't wake up. She was alive but . . . dead. I woke up.

I called my therapist the next day to ask about the dream. She said, "Getting married is like a dying of one's self. It is a big deal." It felt like the easiest decision in my life. At twenty-eight, I was trying to wake up. That year I graduated from Juilliard and started my career. Now, I was starting a new life. My conscious mind was taking it in, but not my subconscious. I always seemed to be carrying either the eight-year-old or the twenty-eight-year-old with me, as if I was calling on them to help me. The eight-year-old was mad for not being acknowledged and the twenty-eight-year-old was dead.

Julius and I had been together for four years. The wedding went beautifully. We had a spectacular time.

I looked at Julius afterward and said, "Doesn't feel any different."

We had another wedding ceremony in October in Rhode Island that was fantastic! Rhode Island Casino, which is not a casino, but a beautiful house built in the Gay Nineties (the 1890s), had wide, wraparound porches, huge windows, a gazebo in the back. We had a ceremony there with my entire family. The wedding guest list was supposed to be eighty-five people, but Mae Alice Davis decided to invite everyone that she saw at bus stops. She invited everybody that she thought I might have gone to school with, everybody she knew who knew me. Forty extra people, on top of the eighty-five. Laurie Rickell, my best friend in third grade, was at the wedding.

My family had never had a celebration together, a meaningful, joyous ceremony. My sisters Deloris and Dianne were married and neither had a ceremony. Deloris went to Vegas. Dianne said her vows in the courthouse. No one in the family had ever had a wedding, and most had never been to one. I wanted to gift the experience to my family. That's why I did it. I didn't have to wear a wedding dress. It was just a party, but I bought the wedding dress because I knew MaMama and Daddy would love it. It was the most unbelievable party celebration any of my family members had ever been to. A college professor of mine was an ordained minister and did the ceremony. One of my nieces said, "Auntie, I wrote a poem for you and Uncle Julius," so I said, "You can recite the poem."

My sister Deloris had a student who was an excellent singer who wanted to sing. The flowers were beautiful. We had lots of hors d'oeuvres, then an enormous, sit-down dinner, the best food you could possibly imagine, with different buffet stations, pasta station, salad station, chicken station. We had an open bar—dangerous because we've got a lot of addicts in the family. A great DJ played. The only thing we messed up with was the photographer. We (Julius) didn't want to spend money on the photographer. Someone gave us this idea that we should have disposable cameras on the tables and let our guests provide the pictures. Well, we ended up with a hodgepodge of well-intended, out-of-focus pictures of the floor, ceiling, feet, backs of heads, et cetera. We chalked this up to being a reflection of too much alcohol combined with dancing and having a good time as the focus of the evening, not picture taking.

Although I didn't have a maid of honor or bridesmaids, we had a wedding rehearsal. A few of my family walked down the aisle: my niece Annabella whose birthday is June 23, my niece Tiana, my sisters Anita, Deloris, and Dianne. My sister Danielle decided that she didn't want to walk down the aisle. Then my mom and dad, of course. Daddy walked me down the aisle. He was so happy. MaMama looked beautiful at the wedding in a suit with a skirt made of lace. When I asked at the rehearsal what she planned to wear, she said, "Viola, I got a suit from Salvation [Army]. I spent ten dollars on it."

"Oh my God, but MaMama, is it nice?"

"Real nice. Wait till you see it?"

I was crossing my fingers, thinking *Jesus, please.* Jesus answered my prayers.

At the rehearsal all MaMama had to do was walk down the aisle. Deloris was organizing it, directing: "Okay, Tiana, it's your turn. It's your turn now, Annabella," and so on. Each one walked down the aisle to "Ribbon in the Sky." When it was my mom's turn to walk down, Deloris called her and after the longest time, my mom had not reached the altar. I'm thinking, *What's going on? She's still walking? She's still walking! How could she still be walking? It's not a long aisle.* I had never seen anything like it in my life. It was as if she was walking a tight rope, real, real slow, one foot in front of the other, like she was going to topple over. That's how slowly she was walking, probably taking one step every ten seconds. Finally, I said, "Mom, what are you doing?"

"Viola, I'm trying to walk down the damn aisle."

"Mom, you're walking too slow. The song is going to be over. You got to *walk*."

"Okay," she said and we paced it with her.

Deloris cued her again, and this time she ran down the aisle! Ran!

I said, "Okay, this is really easy, Mom. It's not difficult." She eventually got the right stride and the ceremony went off without a hitch. Julius and I gave this wedding as a gift to my family. It was a gift to me, too, because I love weddings. It looked like a $50,000 event, but did not cost us even $9,000. It was in Rhode Island, which has restaurants with some of the best food imaginable.

There was a huge parallel between settling into this beautiful life with Julius and stepping into another world—on another level—that wasn't manifesting itself yet, but I knew God was preparing me for.

So much that Julius and I did made us want more. Edwina Findley, an actress friend of a friend from New York, got a play in California and stayed with us because she was trying to save her money and do all that. By then, we were living in a new house—after the condo—a bigger house with five bedrooms and five bathrooms. It was just Julius and me. My friend called and said, "She is awesome. If you guys help her, you'll be so blessed." While she was living at our house, she planted a seed in us. We already wanted to start a production company, but it was a scary proposition, but she helped us look over the edge, inspired and encouraged us to start an LLC—JuVee Productions.

Maybe the dream I had the night before my first wedding ceremony was preparing me for the stratospheric catapulting that was about to happen to my career and our life. One job after another came and I just went with it because that's what journeyman actors do. I was the actor who got five days of work here or a guest star role there or the lead in a play. I wasn't the household name but enough of one to be considered for the roles where I could make a living.

I was in NYC doing *King Hedley II* when I auditioned for a movie called *Antwone Fisher* directed by Denzel Washington. The shooting of the movie took place right after 9/11. Literally, the week after the attack I had to fly to Cleveland. The airports were empty; it felt like death. Everyone was so scared that security would take your ID, hold it to their chest as if to hide it, and try to ask you trick questions. It was a learning curve. I got to freezing cold Cleveland and shot the role of Eva Mae in a scene with Derek Luke. It ended up being two days of work because someone stole the car we were using in the scene and Denzel demanded that the set designer redress the house/apartment we were using. It looked too dirty.

I was playing a pretty severe crack addict, but in life, there's always a balance. In the movie, I play the long-lost mother of Antwone Fisher. He spends a good part of his life trying to find her to make sense out of the holes in his life. Finally, someone tells him that he knows where she is and he comes to meet her in this climactic scene. In the script she didn't have many lines, and frankly the few she did have seemed disingenuous. By the time we got ready to shoot, I cut it down to maybe two lines.

I didn't know Eva Mae personally, but I knew people like Eva Mae. She was very real to me because my sister Danielle had fallen into addiction. I saw the human being. I saw the woman who had been beaten down by life and the pain becomes so great, the only choice becomes numbing. My sister Danielle was the most loving woman, mother, sister in the world but the one person she couldn't bring herself to love was her. But like most of my career, I had a lot to convey but very little material to do it with. That one scene literally shifted my career in a big way. I received an Independent Spirit Award nomination for that role.

Soon, I was packing my bags and going to Toronto to shoot *Get Rich or Die Tryin'* with 50 Cent, Curtis Jackson. Once again, it was cold and once again, I was trying to make the most out of material that simply wasn't developed. I had no idea how to find the material that was developed. None! There're always those one or two movies that Hollywood churns out every year that are great. If you didn't get those, you got what was left. There are not enough pages to describe the potency of good source material. It's about 80 percent of the work.

Acting is a collaborative art form. The actor needs the director, writer, makeup artist, hairstylist, cinematographer, and finally the audience. You can't act in your bedroom. Most people don't understand what it is we do. That's not being condescending, it's true. Even other actors don't get it. So they watch a movie and if they like it or don't, they really don't have the aesthetic to articulate why. Therefore, everything becomes the actors' fault. If the role was smaller than they anticipated or not fully written, it becomes the actors' fault. If the direction wasn't good in a scene, it becomes the actors' fault. There's no real cognitive approach to directing the work of an artistic piece. If you are that character actor out there getting the leftovers, it's very hard to compete with the actor who's getting the filet mignon of roles. It just is.

Once again, it's a profession that is a tangled web of artists getting jobs based on bankability, clout, and not ability. There's no rhyme or reason. In Black projects, a lot of the "stars" are musicians and comedians. They're the ones in the public eye. They sell records internationally as musicians so they have crossover appeal. Or they're comedians. No shade there. I'm being honest. The African American actors out there don't or at least didn't have the quantity of material to give them clout. They're either in NYC doing theater or are nameless, faceless, trying to break in.

Then if you have a plethora of roles that are gang members, drug-addicted urban mothers, then it filters a lot of actors out. Not a lot of filmmakers are looking for trained Black actors to play drug addicts. Those actors are told that they're not Black enough. You're already dealing with a business where talent takes a back seat. But at least with white actors, talent has been able to seep through because of the sheer amount and quality of material. Martin Scorsese is not going to cast Eminem over De Niro.

I did a huge slate of what I call "best friends to white women" roles. Hollywood has a love affair with those, but they're in Black rom-coms, too. And if you're a dark-skinned actress, you'll probably be the best friend over the desired one in Black movies . . . with all the qualities of the best friend in the white movies. Once again, no shade. I worked with fabulous actresses like Diane Lane in *Nights in Rodanthe*. Julia Roberts in *Eat, Pray, Love*. Every role was a chance to problem-solve. Now, I can pick up a script and figure out a way to make it work, even if it's not fully realized. I can articulate what's wrong and articulate how to fix it and that's if they want to fix it. Or maybe they don't see a problem with it. But I force my hand with every job I get to make the role better.

I got the *Jesse Stone* movies with Tom Selleck. Any job for an actor is a good job, really, but some are really good and that was a good gig. We shot in Halifax, Nova Scotia, Canada, and it was cold. One of the marks of a good gig is when it runs like a well-oiled machine.

Tom Selleck and the rest of the producers just had it down. Plus, they paid well and that part of the world is just beautiful. It's like God just took a bunch of paint-brushes and splattered yellows, blues, oranges all over the trees. There were both ocean and mountain views surrounding the city. Ironically, I loved it because it reminded me of Rhode Island. Whenever a place reminded me of home, I felt safe and at ease. When it didn't, anxiety would rear its ugly head. Halifax is small and there's a lot of seafood.

Tom himself is a great man. I just felt like he respected

me. I never felt overworked or confused by the schedule. There was always a lot of laughter on the set and great craft services. Honestly, the food was good. I did a few of the *Jesse Stone* series of movies and people loved them. One of the last ones I did, I was flying from Vancouver where I was shooting *The Andromeda Strain*. I was on set one day when my sister called. She asked, "Viola, are you sitting down?" Oh my God!

"Did someone die, Dee."

"Yes," she said gravely.

"Oh my God! Who?"

"Dwight."

Dwight Palmisciano was the father of my sister Danielle's three children, Derek, Daryn, and Tiana. He was twenty-eight. Dwight, my sister Danielle, and Tiana were asleep at my parents' apartment. It was about one o'clock in the afternoon. Dwight was snoring really loudly and erratically. He was snoring so loud Danielle tried to wake him up to stop but he wouldn't wake up. Tiana, who was three years old at the time, woke up and started shaking him. Danielle told Tiana to go wake up Grandma and Grandpa. Tiana ran in their room and said, "Grandma, Grandpa, my daddy's neck is purple!" Then hell broke loose.

My parents ran into the room and tried to revive him. Danielle called 911 and my parents picked him up and laid him on the floor. My sister Anita lived upstairs with her girls and they came down. My dad kept saying, "Please, son, wake up! Please wake up!" Tiana just stood there petrified and wet her pants. My niece Breanna who lived upstairs was screaming. The paramedics came and tried again. He was already gone. It was an aneurysm. Everyone was catatonic. Danielle had the mammoth task of calling Dwight's mom. What made it worse is that she had lost another son just a few weeks before.

Dwight was a little bit of a wayward soul. He and Danielle loved each other very much. They actually had issues with some drugs and keeping an apartment but still he gave Danielle some grounding and protection. When he died, a part of her went right with him. The thought that stays with me, other than my niece wetting her pants, was something Danielle told me. She said she saw his body at the mortuary. She got up on the gurney and just lay with him, holding him for hours. She couldn't let him go.

A whole other layer of pain settled on our family. It just came like bullets. One more tragedy to overcome. And once again, life continues. It keeps moving. It moves through deaths, tragedies. It doesn't wait for you to recover or heal before hitting again. No one had money to bury him, except me and Julius. Literally, the priest refused to give the eulogy until he was paid. Julius was in LA at the time and I was in Nova Scotia.

My sister Deloris told me later that she was with Tiana one day and she bought her a honey bun, which is a sugary Danish, and Tiana said to her, "That's what my daddy called me, Honey Bunny."

Meanwhile, life pushes ahead bringing back an old problem. Even though I had my fibroid surgery a few years ago, they were growing back. I was forced to use a low-dosage birth control eventually to control the bleeding. At one point, I was wearing two superplus tampons and two pads and was changing them constantly. I was performing *Intimate Apparel* around this time and at one point I was walking off the stage at intermission. Out of nowhere, I left a stream of blood on the path from the stage to my dressing room and it wasn't even my time of month.

In the mist of my fibroids wreaking havoc and my career taking off, the pangs of wanting a child permeated every part of my life. Every child I saw evoked it. Every announcement about a pregnancy or an adoption fueled this growing need. Living for my career just didn't fly with me because I was slowly seeing the limitations of it. You get to a city to do a job and . . . nothing. There's loneliness, isolation, having to bond with people you normally wouldn't but you do because they're there.

I was very involved in church at this time. I was serving as an usher and going twice a week. Oasis Christian Church. It was a church that Julius had gone to years before he invited me when we started to date. He served in security. We loved it for its vibrancy and authenticity. I always felt the sermons were accessible. I got baptized in that church. On the night of my baptismal, Julius sat in the back because he was rushing from work and had just made it in. I had asked him a few days before, "Uhh . . . Julius? What am I going to do about my hair? I'm going to mess my weave up."

"Vee! Don't worry about that shit. Just put a Speedo on your head."

"Julius . . . really? A Speedo? You want me to be baptized in a Speedo?"

"Vee. God ain't looking at your Speedo! He just wants your heart."

That was it. I got baptized in a Speedo . . . in front of a lot of people. And yes, there were some loving laughs, but it was an unforgettable experience. Julius clapped and shouted and then we went out to eat. I felt born again, renewed in the same body but a shifted spirit. I was officially different. I had changed. Everyone who knew me and spent time with me would stare and exclaim, "Man, Vee! You look great and seem so happy. You have changed!" "Wow, Vee . . . Julius has changed your life." Yeah, he did, but I changed my life and Julius was the reward, my peace was the reward.

It was the sort of change that you don't notice until someone says it. It's like Rudolph running away from home because he felt unwanted and along the way he grows up. He's got antlers. That one character trait that got him ostracized, his shiny red nose, now saves Christmas and becomes his sword. Well, I had grown my antlers. I had created a life, a home. I was standing on my own two feet and could take care of myself.

Right around this time, when Julius and I were just about to get married, I got two big jobs back-to-back. I booked *Far from Heaven* directed by Todd Haynes and *Solaris* directed by Steven Soderbergh. I shot *Far from Heaven* in NYC and *Solaris* in Los Angeles. The great part of *Far from Heaven* was working with Julianne Moore and Patricia Clarkson. I love broads. I love authentic, ballsy women who are unapologetic about who they are.

Solaris, just fun. We were a very small cast that clicked: George Clooney, Natascha McElhone, and Jeremy Davies. Soderbergh is probably the most relaxed director I've ever worked with. I mean it was as if we were just meeting at a restaurant by the ocean for a sandwich and a beer. Relaxed. Because he's relaxed, you relax.

George was and is the nicest human being. At the premiere of *Far from Heaven*, Julius and I saw him and we told him that we were married. He was so happy for us and he said, "Listen, when you guys are ready, come to my villa in Italy. You can stay for free and I'll send someone to pick you up from the airport." What?

"I'm serious. I know a lot of people make promises out here but this is real. The villa is beautiful. It'll be my honeymoon gift to you." Julius and I were speechless.

We didn't know how to call him and ask. This was before me and Julius were savvy in that area. He had even told our agent to contact his assistant. When we finally called, I had done *Syriana* with him and asked between scenes about that promise of his villa. He made me choose a date and called his assistant.

Well, when Julius and I arrived in Milan, flying over the Swiss Alps, we couldn't speak. A car picked us up and when we got to the villa, I felt like I was in *The Great Gatsby*. The tall iron gates. The cobblestone pathway leading to the front door where we were greeted by his staff with umbrellas because it was raining. We tried to get our bags but they told us they would get them. We stood in the entryway of the twenty-two-room, eighteenth-century villa that had frescoes on the ceiling, marble stairs, big overstuffed chairs. We stood in front of the staff, which was a family—husband, wife, and their eleven-year-old son. They asked us what we like to eat. Me and Julius? Eating? Julius said, "That's so nice! We like fish and chicken."

I said, "I love pasta! I love ice cream and pizza . . . and eggplant!" Their response was just "Okay."

I mean . . . really. This woman was going to cook for us.

"Uhh . . . so where do you want us to sleep?" Julius asked.

"You can choose any room in the house."

What?!

"Any room?" we asked.

They said we were the only guests.

Julius and I proceeded to look at every room in the house and settled on the biggest one with the canopy bed and fireplace. It overlooked Lake Como, the church, and the Alps. The bathroom was fully stocked. There was a toilet and a bidet. The staff told us that breakfast was casual but for the rest of the meals, they would ring the bell. Well . . . me and Julius would get dressed early every morning and sit on the edge of the bed, silent, waiting for that bell to ring like Pavlov's dog and trying to look dignified running for that food.

Because let me tell you, the first meal was in a room that was built with big stones from floor to ceiling. There was an enormous wine cooler with hundreds of bottles of wine on the side. They had set the table with candlelight and bread. Then they proceeded to come in with a four-course meal that was beyond anything we could imagine. Every course was followed by a different bottle of wine that was presented for us to approve before they poured. The food was artistry. Julius and I teared up. We did. Julius kept saying, "Vee . . . how do you repay this? This is so nice. Can you believe he gave us this trip? George is . . . he's something else." I couldn't speak.

We worked out in the part of the villa called the Factory. It was a separate house that had five more bedrooms and a garage with lots of motorcycles and cars. There was a lounge area bar and a state-of-the-art gym. There was great music George left. Every day and night was a different meal experience. One night the wife made pizza in a built-in pizza oven. I lost count of how many we consumed. Not one second of any day did we feel anything less than at home. We found out that George had the smallest room in the house. We peeked in and it cemented our opinion of him being beyond compare. We took side trips to Venice, Florence, Milan. We wanted to tip the staff but George emphatically told us not to do that . . . several times.

We got back home renewed.

But what did I say about life? It never stops. We

always hope that it lands in our favor. At least, that's how stories play out onscreen. There is living life for pleasure, great moments, and living life waiting for doom and gloom. Life exists somewhere in the middle.

MaDaddy had a heart attack, a pretty massive one while I was shooting the movie *Life Is Not a Fairytale* in New Orleans. He was sitting down eating and fell over screaming my mom's name. They had rushed him to the hospital. The next day he had quadruple bypass surgery. I was so nervous. I couldn't get away but I was on that phone with family constantly, looking up everything about heart attacks, recovery from bypass surgery, life expectancy.

You become desperate when you think someone you love is dying. Realistically you're not even taking any facts in that don't support your need to keep your loved one alive. He woke up from bypass surgery the next day so happy to be alive! He kept saying, "Oh! I'm so happy to see y'all! Oh! I love you so much." I was home for a short time after he had the quadruple bypass. I wanted to see him. Shopping with my sister one day, my cell phone rang. I rarely answered that phone.

People today say, "Viola, I was calling you for two years and you never answered." I don't know why I picked up the call. It must've been God. His doctor called to tell me they saw lesions on his liver and were pretty sure it was cancer. As he was recovering, he felt extraordinary back pain. It was first believed to be liver cancer, but it was pancreatic cancer that had metastasized, spread to his liver, lungs, kidneys. It was diagnosed in May. My father, who was just in recovery from the quadruple bypass, which he got through like a boss, was dying.

Deloris and I were silent. One of the things she said was, "Viola, Daddy is going to die in that nasty apartment they live in, infested with mice, roaches." They had not wanted to live in another city. We hadn't been able to get them a new place in Central Falls because so many people lived with them. No joke!! By this time, there were fourteen people living in an eight-hundred-square-foot space. There were better apartments in Central Falls but not for fourteen people. MaDaddy was the stricter one in the house. He always said he just wanted it to be him and mom. He wanted a quieter life but he loved those kids, especially my sister Danielle's newest baby, James. He just kept saying, "Daughter, I love this baby."

We would try to get them homes, but there was too much activity in the house. Too many kids, friends, other addicts coming in and out, items being stolen. It was a minefield. I just couldn't get them a better place to live. I wanted them to come live with me but they wouldn't or couldn't leave the children. So, instead we bought beds, appliances, paid bills, food, phone bills. Their life was such chaos trying to raise all those grandchildren: kids out of control; their friends in and out all times of night. I constantly tried to furnish the apartment.

The most beautiful furniture and best appliances would get broken. I helped. My sister Deloris helped. My sister Dianne helped. But there was a lot of need, a lot of people. Now, my daddy's life was coming to an end at seventy.

Deloris was crying and spoke words that triggered healing in me. "Viola, Dad hasn't really done anything with his life."

I thought, *We have given them trips to Jamaica. I've flown them out to California, to Atlantic City.* "What were his dreams?" my sister asked, crying. "What were his hopes? He only had a fifth-grade education."

What became apparent to me as he was dying was that *we* were his dream; his children and grandchildren were his dream. For a whole generation of Black people we were the dream. We were their hope. We were the baton they were passing as they were sinking into the quicksand of racism, poverty, Jim Crow, segregation, injustice, family trauma, and dysfunction.

Deloris and I had to tell him he was dying. I had to gather my courage to tell him. We went to my parents' place and I couldn't say anything. I couldn't tell him. But he already knew. Over and over again during this time my father apologized to my mom. "Mae Alice, all that stuff I did to you back in the day, you know I'm sorry. Right?"

"I know that, Dan," she said.

And he said again, "I am sorry." He was sewing it up. Closing out all unfinished business.

They had stayed together forty-eight years.

My father did not want to go into hospice. He did not want to go to a hospital. I was trying to take care of everything, and at the same time grieving myself. I told my mom, "MaMama, if you took him to hospice he would feel more comfortable. They have everything, they can even help him with the pain."

"He don't wanna go. He don't wanna go," she said.

He lay on that daybed and screamed in pain. He was down to eighty-six pounds and it was a horrible sight to witness. It was a daybed in the middle of the teeny tiny kitchen. He couldn't nor did he want to be moved. They were trying to provide palliative care, pain management at home. He was wasting away in agony, in the crowded apartment. He was so tiny the visiting nurse could not find a vein. They had to give him liquid morphine. As he was dying, as if it couldn't get worse, someone stole his morphine. There were so many people coming in and out of the house and drug addiction is in my family. Dementia had set in. His mouth was dry. Every five minutes he would sit up and scream, "Mae Alice!"

"Dan!! I'm right here!! Tell me what you want."

But he would just sit there and she would hold him.

I came home because I wanted to be there. Because I lived three thousand miles away, I didn't realize what their day-to-day life was. I saw so much foot traffic in and out of the apartment—"friends" of people I didn't know. Daddy was covered in waste that my mom and nephew cleaned up, barely taking water, screaming in pain at times. Boxes were stacked from the floor to the ceiling because my sister Anita had moved back in. There was literally no room to sit down in a chair. That's how cramped it was.

Daddy's condition was so bad that I finally called my mom one morning and said, "He's got to go to hospice. They can manage his pain. I know he doesn't want to go, but he's got to."

"Viola, I've already, I've already called them. I already made the decision," she said. She sounded so exhausted.

"Okay. I'm on my way," I said. I drove over, with my niece who had spent the night with me. The hospice people came, carried him down into the ambulance.

We were all wailing. My father was not coherent. His eyes were open, but dead. I followed the ambulance in my car with my niece and nephew. I got to the hospice facility and MaMama was already there crying over Daddy's bed.

"Viola, the nurse told me I got to tell him to go. I can't do that. I can't tell him to go. I can't do it. I can't do it."

"It's okay, Ma. I'll tell him." I knew he was holding on because of my mom.

He was doing the Cheyne-Stokes, the labored breathing of the dying. His hand was up. In hindsight, I know he was telling me to hold his hand. He had just gotten there. I was stunned that I was witnessing the last breaths of my father. I wasn't thinking of the fights, the abuse, the cheating . . . I was thinking this is the man who participated in giving me life. This is my daddy and I love him.

"Daddy, it's okay if you go," I told him. "You don't have to be in pain anymore, all right?" He just kept breathing . . . almost fighting for every bit of life. "God loves you. Jesus loves you. They're waiting for you, Daddy. You did such a good job. We all love you so much. I'll take care of Mom. I'll take care of . . ." And I named all my nieces and nephews. "You don't have to worry about anything, Daddy. Okay?"

He arrived there at 12:05. I was by his bed at 12:10. The doctors came in to examine him and then talked to us. They were so compassionate: "It's probably going to be another day and a half and he will be gone."

He survived a quadruple bypass, only to die a few months later of cancer.

As soon as the doctors had spoken those words, the nurse came, pointed to my mom, and said, "Mrs. Davis, can you come with us, please?" I followed her and brought my niece and nephew with me. The nurse said, "Mrs. Davis, can you stand here, please?" and put a stethoscope on my dad's chest. She held my mom's hand and said, "I'm so sorry, Mrs. Davis, but he's gone." Five nurses stood behind me, my niece, and my nephew, as we each reacted in our own way. My nephew held Daddy's hand and mumbled, "Grandpa, no." My niece cried. MaMama held his hand and looking into his face repeated, "Oh, Dan. Oh, Dan. Oh, Dan."

He died at 12:31. He didn't even last a half hour in hospice. Afterward everything happened fast. You have a lifetime with someone, memories—good, bad, devastating, filled with love, every freaking kind of memory—and then you see a body. The nurse said, "Mrs. Davis, we have to know where to send the body. We need to know in the next half hour or so, because the body will start decomposing."

That's when Julius, the provider, protector kicked in. Julius had been through it before. I phoned him that my dad had passed, and he said, "Oh my God. Oh my God. I'm so sorry. I'm so sorry. Okay, I'm going to catch the first plane. This is what you have to do." He gave me step-by-step instructions. Within three months of meeting him, he had insisted I get insurance on my parents, saying, *You got to get life insurance on your parents. The way their life is, all the stress, Viola, I'm telling you, your parents can go from really good health to bad health within a very short period of time. And when it happens, it happens fast and no one has the resources. Get life insurance because when it happens, you will be devastated.* I had listened to him and got life insurance on my two parents. When Daddy died, Julius said, "Viola, call the life insurance company, tell them your father has died, where you're going to have the funeral, the address of the mortuary and they will pay for it immediately."

"It's that simple?" I asked, between sobs.

"It's that simple," he said.

Viola, who was the most shy, had the most social anxiety, used to have the smallest voice, was suddenly at the funeral home with my mom, filling out the death certificate, giving all the information, picking out the casket. My sister Deloris wrote the obituary. "I'll do that part, Viola," she said.

Then I needed to buy clothes for all the nieces and nephews. No one had any clothes to wear to the funeral. I don't mean nice clothes. I mean clothes—clean and presentable. I had a day or so to outfit ten people and inform as many people as possible that Daddy died.

The funeral was devastating, but they did a great job with Daddy. He looked beautiful. Because he was so sick, he was emaciated, but they made him look great. That sounds macabre but it helped me a lot to look down at my dad and see my dad, not the sick, dying dad, but my dad. We got a suit together. We put pictures of all the grandkids in the casket. As we closed the casket, I looked down and saw he didn't have any shoes on. I got so mad. I thought, *We gave you his stuff to dress him. Why doesn't he have on any shoes?* and then realized, *Viola, he doesn't need any shoes.*

My dad, who only had a fifth-grade education, didn't make it into history books except mine, had a turned-out homegoing. Everyone came to his funeral. We had a police escort to the grave site with I don't know how many police cars and officers in full regalia, usually designated for dignitaries. That's how much my dad meant to them. We had lived in the city since 1965. At funerals, no matter how much you think you know someone, you see a whole part of their life at the end. People sharing memories, stories that you never heard. I'm sure there were memories that would've surprised him because how many people make themselves vulnerable enough to share how you touched them? That's something that you cannot always see when they're alive.

When my dad passed, part of my heart went with him that's never coming back. I feel the same way about Julius. I feel the same way about my child, my mom, sisters. It's one heart. They are completely entwined in my spirit.

I remember seeing an episode of *Golden Girls* where Bea Arthur, who plays Dorothy, responds to a question from Rose, played by Betty White. "What do you want in your next husband?" asked Rose. And Dorothy says, "I want someone to grow old with." That's what most people don't want. They want the young. They want the cute. When you get older, you change. You change physically. You change emotionally and a whole other area of life rears its head. Your body slows down, retirement; death becomes all too real. A lot of people are not in it for the long haul. They're not in it for the changes the life journey brings—the health scares, death. I *do* want someone to grow old with. I understand those elements. I saw it with my mom when she had to sit next to Daddy's deathbed. That's marriage. That's love. That's commitment.

I found out weeks later when I had the courage to look up how to comfort the dying that they don't feel heat or cold in the end. They usually have visions of people in their life who had passed before them. They have them because they need permission to cross over. You have to validate that. You keep their lips moist and give them little sips of water if they can take it. Most importantly, the number one comfort is this . . . hold their hand.

My daddy was gone.

How can life keep going after this? Why is no one celebrating, honoring the life that was Dan Davis? All that kept playing out in my mind was, *The purpose of life is to live it.*

The purpose of life is to live it.

Chapter 17
There She Is

*"You can either leave something for people
or you can leave something in people."*

—ANNE LAMONT

Doubt, the movie based on John Patrick Shanley's parable, came out in 2008, several years after Daddy's death, and although it was only two weeks of work, it marked my transition from stage actor to film/Hollywood actor. On the stage, you reach for the Tonys. *Doubt* catapulted me to an Oscar nomination. I was forty-two years old when I got the role in *Doubt*.

When I heard that the stage play was going to be turned into a movie, I said to my agent, "I would really love to do that role. Meryl Streep. My God." I read the play and auditioned for the movie in LA, at Warner Brothers. After that, I got the call from my agent that they wanted to fly me to New York to do a screen test. It was my first actual screen test ever. I flew to New York, they put me in a hotel, I signed in, got a call sheet. Every day when you shoot TV or a movie, you get a call sheet with all the actors' names, all the crew, what the weather is going to be that day, and a list of the work for the day. Beside your name is a number that indicates your place in the cast and the time that you have to be in makeup and on set.

I got nervous about the screen test for *Doubt* when I saw the six actresses on the call sheet and our times to be on set. We were each in forty-five-minute time slots: Audra McDonald, Sanaa Lathan, Taraji P. Henson, Sophie Okonido, and Adriane Lenox who had played the role on Broadway and won the Tony for it. Some of these actresses were already in New York and some of us were flown in from LA. A car came to pick us up. We got to the set, and each of us had to put on a wig and hat. Six Mrs. Millers were walking around the set. You could hear each audition and people clapping after the audition. They all sounded wonderful.

I knew I had gotten the role because I left my audition knowing it went really well. After I went back to get my head fitted for the wig, I returned to my hotel room and fell asleep. My hotel room phone rang and it was my manager, Estelle, saying, "Viola, you got it." No words describe those moments of winning the audition lottery. The luck of the draw is what it feels like. Talent and preparation play a huge part of it, but luck also plays a huge part.

I knew this was it. If the Tony Award nomination for *Seven Guitars* and winning for *King Hedley II* were my stage coming-out, this was my coming-out movie role. This was a busting-through-everything role. This was the game-changing role—Meryl Streep, Philip Seymour Hoffman, Amy Adams, with John Patrick Shanley directing. It was absolutely set up for awards. And I love all the actors. I was so excited. I was jumping up and down.

I put the phone down and then it rang again. It was the assistant director (AD) who organizes everything. She said, "Okay, Viola, congratulations. You have a rehearsal tomorrow with Meryl Streep, Philip Seymour Hoffman, and Amy Adams, but just Meryl first." I fell apart. This is what I did. I got two yellow cans of homeopathic stress relief tablets from the health food store and downed one can in less than an hour. I was that nervous, terrified. There's a part of me that knows that she would hate me saying this. She is as humble as she is talented and she is as kind as she is absolutely,

100 percent NOT intimidating. She simply is seen as the best, and acting opposite her agitates the biggest beast that lives within every actor . . . the impostor syndrome.

The next day I got to rehearsal probably half an hour early and just sat there and stared at the front door, waiting. She came through the door and said, "Hi, Viola, I'm Meryl." I froze. She had to go to the bathroom and I said, "You know what? I have to go to the bathroom too," and followed her although I didn't really need to go. I went because she was going. I acted stupid at first, but we broke out of that.

We weren't filming yet, only rehearsing, and there was a break in rehearsal because of the Thanksgiving holiday. That was one of the best Thanksgivings because I went home to Rhode Island knowing I had that job. I took the train there and Julius flew to Rhode Island to meet me.

When I went back to New York, Meryl and I were to film in the Bronx, in a housing unit. Amy, Philip, and Meryl were one of the greatest casts I ever worked with because it was absolutely, completely void of ego. Everybody was trying to figure out the work. We had great discussions during rehearsal: what it's like to be on top with the impostor syndrome constantly chasing you and making you feel ostracized because you were the chosen one. Meryl said something wonderful that helped me let go of the impostor feeling. "Yeah, Viola, we know the truth." What she was saying is we know the truth of what it means to be in this position. It doesn't puff up your walk if you love what you do. It's a great responsibility. That's constantly overlooked and misunderstood.

If there were a poster of actors who had the impostor syndrome, always working to do better, we had poster children in that room, constantly trying to figure out the characters we were to portray, not focusing on anything, anyone else. We rolled in there, carrying the script, tearing it apart, focusing on being there 100 percent with each other, absolutely putting ourselves to task. Philip was always saying, "Oh my God, bring in Brían F. O'Byrne," who did it on Broadway and was so fantastic. Philip was fabulous because he had such respect for other actors, he pushed himself, and was always self-judgmental about his work. This was the best room to be in. When you're in a room full of great actors, you want to step up.

I couldn't figure out Mrs. Miller. The character wasn't working for me. I didn't understand her. I didn't get her, in my opinion. We were in that sacred space of the artistic process, and I could tell, the other actors would listen to me. You try to problem-solve. You try to figure it out. Nobody gives you any answers. These are actors who absolutely respect your process. Everybody's talking and, although I was the least known of the group, you would never have known it. Every one of us was on the same playing field. I was given my space and time. Everybody stepped aside. Meryl was given her own space. It was an absolute ensemble.

Still, I felt I had to go back to LA and work on the script before I shot it because I couldn't figure this woman out. What made Mrs. Miller tick?

Because of my Juilliard training, I knew my task as an actor was to figure out what was driving this character. I was using everything in my arsenal and I couldn't figure out a mom who would allow her son, who she believes is gay, to be with priests who could be molesting him. I didn't get it. I saw it as an incredibly dynamic scene, but in reality, I didn't get it. The read-throughs had been really wonderful. Meryl's was the greatest read-through I have ever heard. When we finally did a read-through with the producers, everybody was happy, but for me, for my pace, for my standard, I knew I didn't have Mrs. Miller figured out.

After the three weeks of rehearsal and before filming, I was excited to go back to LA and work on it more. I did a hundred-page bio on the character. I finally figured Mrs. Miller out when a college professor

I talked to said, "She doesn't have a choice, Viola. She's doing the only thing she knows to do." That opened up the whole Mrs. Miller character to me. She didn't have a choice.

When we shot in the Bronx, my scenes were with Meryl. Oh my God, was I nervous. I'm one of those people who finds it hard to make small talk. If you're working with only one actress that day, between scenes you just sit with them and talk. I didn't have anything to say. I just sat there, smiling.

"How are you, sweetheart?" she asked.

"Really good, Meryl. How are you?"

"I am so good."

Meryl sat reading a paper or knitting. She's a good conversationalist. Not me. I just sat. I couldn't think of anything to say. Finally, I asked, "Do you want some tea? I'm going to craft services. I'll get you some tea." That's the only thing I could come up with.

We shot the interior of the scene first. No words describe working with a great actor. You don't ever have to worry about her not passing you the ball. You don't ever have to worry about her giving it her all when she's on camera. Meryl was 100 percent there with me. The exterior part of the scene took most of the time because it kept raining. It would stop and we would do the scene again. While it rained, we would sit together.

She'd always say, "Oh, come sit with me. Let's talk. Sit with me."

Eventually, we had the best conversations. About life, about her kids, and about the work. It was perfection. After a while I could lean forward and say, "Let me ask you about this or that. Did you ever? Do you ever do this with a role?" I was now sharing the screen with Meryl Streep who I'd seen onscreen for so many years in so many different roles. There's no word to describe it. In between scenes, she'd share a chocolate with me. We ate *a lot* of chocolate.

We finished the work and it was an awesome experience. Later, I went in to do looping work, which is additional voiceover work to fix a line that is hard to hear because of background noise. When I returned home to LA, I lay on my couch for a week, eating bread, every kind of food I could imagine, thinking, *Oh my God, I look a mess.* We were in the new house during the filming of *Doubt* and Julius finally asked me: "Why are you lying around like that? Eating all that food?"

"I don't like my work in *Doubt*."

"What's wrong with it?"

"It's just not working. It just didn't look right."

"What was Meryl doing in the scene?"

"I don't know. I wasn't looking at Meryl. Meryl?

Meryl. She was great. I'm not looking at her. I was looking at me."

Julius said, "You need to get your behind up! Get your ass off that couch! I don't want to hear this anymore! Let's get in the Jacuzzi."

When the movie was about to come out, I was named one of the ten most promising artists, the ten artists to watch, and invited to the awards event at the Hollywood Film Festival, 2008. The day before the ceremony, dresses were delivered to the house for me to try on. I was so excited. But I was having cramps. I didn't know what was going on and told Julius, "I'm having cramps." I was trying on dresses to see which one I was going to wear, and nagging cramps continued. As I tried on dresses, looking in the mirror, the cramps got worse, so bad that I told Julius, "I'm going to try on dresses later on," and went upstairs to lie down.

"Do you want something to help you with the pain?"

I said, yes, Julius got me some Tylenol, and I lay down. After an hour, the cramps were worse. I didn't have my period and wondered where this pain was coming from. Pilar, my old friend from Julliard and roomie in that eight-person house in Brooklyn, called me to chat, and when I answered, she asked, "What's wrong?"

"I have really bad cramps."

By then, I was on my hands and knees. Pilar's sister

is a doctor, so she's always hyperalert. She said, "Have Julius take you to the emergency room."

"No, I don't think so. Maybe it's just my fibroids." My whole family has fibroid issues. Deloris, Dianne, Anita, my mom, all of us had fibroid issues.

"Have. Julius. Take you. To. The emergency room!"

Julius was already in the room by then and had decided to take me to the ER.

I had an abscessed fallopian tube. The doctor came in with the diagnosis and said, "We have to operate immediately." I had already had two surgeries for fibroids. I had nine fibroids surgically removed when I was about thirty years old. Later, I had another surgery where thirty-three fibroids were removed. Now it was a fallopian tube. My sisters Dianne and Deloris both almost bled to death after giving birth and each had to get a complete hysterectomy. Anita had three children and never had surgery, but she has bad periods. It felt like a generational curse. I was anemic. I constantly had issues with my reproductive organs.

I didn't want to continue to be in and out of hospitals, bleeding during my periods for extended periods of time, sometimes for a month straight. I thought of what that was doing to my life with Julius, my career. I felt I had to make a Sophie's choice, a transformative decision. I was done with the suffering. As I was about to go under, I said to the surgeon, "I'm going to tell you something right now: I'm not going through this anymore. I'm not doing this anymore. When I wake up, I don't want my uterus to be there. I want a hysterectomy."

The doctor began reciting the rhetoric—

"I'm electing to do this."

"Well, what if—"

He was a very nice doctor, but I said, "Let me tell you something, if I wake up and my uterus is still here, I'm going to kick your ass. Okay? Kick your motherfucking ass."

The doctor was terrified and said, "Oh, okay. Ms. Davis. Okay. Ms. Davis. All right."

Julius was laughing.

Later, my doctor would tell us that when they opened me up, I had many adhesions, much scar tissue, but my uterus actually looked good and they probably could have kept it intact. But keeping an intact uterus and fertility are two different beasts. As the surgical team went back and forth, he said he reminded them, "I'm telling you she is going to kick my ass!"

The next day was the ten artists to watch Hollywood Film Festival event. I missed it. I went into surgery in horrific pain from that abscess on one of my fallopian tubes, had a partial hysterectomy, and was in the hospital for eight days with an infection they drained through a tube in my stomach.

When *Doubt* came out, the accolades propelled me to a whole other lane. It was more than I could possibly have imagined.

Julius and I attended the Golden Globe Awards and the Screen Actors Guild Awards. At the Screen Actors Guild event, we didn't think *Doubt* was going to win anything, because we were nominated for all the awards that season, but we were not winning anything at that point. We thought, *This is a table where all of us got nominated, but we were not going to win anything.* When Meryl won the Screen Actors Guild Award for *Doubt*, we went nuts. And then it was like someone set us on fire.

Then came the Oscars. My first Oscar nomination in 2009. My first time feeling like the chosen one. That first Oscar nomination was extremely exciting. There are no words to express what the life journey of an actor is, the bumps in the road, the struggle, the unemployment. An Oscar nomination washes it away. In interviews, all that is skimmed over. My life was as a journeyman actor, taking the bus for three, four hours to get to the theater in the Newton, Massachusetts, church basement and working for $300 a week. Oscar nomination means you've become a success. Then people forget all that and see your life backward.

More than twenty Black women have been nominated for that award since Hattie McDaniel first won it in 1939 for *Gone with the Wind*. Whoopi Goldberg and Jennifer Hudson had won it by the time I was nominated in 2009.

Two years after my surgery and Oscar nomination, we adopted Genesis. We started the adoption process because of Lorraine Toussaint, a fantastic actress I know. She told me that she decided to adopt her child because she didn't want "series regular" to be written on her tombstone. Denzel always said, "There's no U-Haul in the back of a hearse." I wanted my life to be about something more than work.

The process of adopting Genesis was long. It lasted almost a year. Seven social workers, classes, evaluations, home inspections. One social worker ran the water in our sink and stood there for fifteen to twenty minutes with a hand under the faucet making sure the hot water didn't go past a certain temperature. We put a fence around our swimming pool, covers on all the fireplaces, child safety latches on cabinets, preparing for a baby in the house.

There are no words to describe the paperwork, hundreds of pages in which you revisit how you were raised, what your home environment was like as a child. Were you abused? What was the effect of the abuse? How do you feel about having children? How are you going to discipline? We sat for hours and talked to a social worker about all that. It's all something that every prospective parent should probably do, but when you are adopting you have to explore whether you are fit to have a child in your life.

I felt more comfortable with the social services in Rhode Island than any place else because so many of my friends were social workers and I had nieces and nephews who had been in the social services system. I was comfortable navigating that system. It took more time to adopt, but I knew what the process was. I didn't care about it being hard, in the same way that I didn't care about acting being hard. Hard was relative to me.

Growing up food insecure, washing my clothes by hand in cold water the night before I had to go to school, hanging them up and if they were still wet the next morning, wearing those wet clothes even if I'd pissed the bed—everything had been hard for me. I had mastered hard. Now I wanted joy. That joy came from adopting a child, and joy was worth more than the sacrifice.

I visited Genesis in foster care in Rhode Island and would take her for the day. We would go everywhere together. I would take her to the zoo. She always cried. I would count how long she cried and it was always the same amount of time. By the time I got to twenty-five seconds, she would stop crying and was having the best time. In foster care, you don't often have a choice, but I identified her. I met her for the first time when she was about five months old. I had to do a lot of paperwork before I could even see her. As soon as she saw me, the smile on her face was like she was inviting me to be her mommy, had accepted me. Every single visit I had with her, she fell asleep in my arms, held on to me and fell asleep.

When I was finally able to take her home to LA from Rhode Island, in 2011, it was awesome watching her running around the house, fearlessly, exhibiting a huge personality. Stacey Snider, one of the producers from *The Help*, gave a beautiful shower for me at our home, where cutie pie Genesis just held court. Genesis was and is everything to me.

While working with Kerry Washington on the *Scandal/How to Get Away with Murder* merging show, she asked me if I had read the book *The Conscious Parent*. She said, "Basically, Viola, the book is about your child coming into your life to teach YOU a lesson. They're completely different from you and act as a mirror."

I was doing August Wilson's play *Fences* when I auditioned for *The Help*. At that time, I remember people talking about Kathryn Stockett's novel and that they were going to make it into a movie. I remember picking up the book and thinking it was good, but there was a huge disconnect between what white people thought was great and what Black people thought was great. And I'm one of those people. I already knew what the backlash was going to be. I had a party at my house and a friend of ours told me that a friend of his was looking for me because he wanted me to be in *The Help*. I said, "I don't know if I want to do that." I remember thinking, *Oh, but you know what, it's going to be a big movie. Maybe I can make it work.*

I just thought, *It's going to be wonderful with great actors in it*. I'd already worked with Octavia and we were all going to live in Greenwood, Mississippi, for three months. Plus, the love and trust I had for the actors and Tate Taylor was enough for me to move forward. Every job becomes about the collaborators involved.

We flew down to Greenwood, Mississippi, and had the greatest bonding experience I've ever had. It was pretty much similar to the bonding experiences I had with August Wilson movies *Fences* and *Ma Rainey's Black Bottom*.

The Help was spectacular because we all had our

own houses or apartments in Greenwood and we would visit one another. We didn't know anyone else in the town; all we had was each other. It was like living in a small town with family members. We'd go to each other's homes to eat and drink. Tate Taylor (*The Help*'s director) wanted us all to look like Elsie women, so we were given permission to eat as much as possible. He didn't want that Hollywood look. That was all he needed to say. We ate our asses off. That first day in Greenwood, Mississippi, Emma Stone, Octavia Spencer, and I had what must have been a four- to five-hour lunch before we even started filming.

I cannot tell you how much food we ordered. I know we ordered at the very least four or five different desserts. I lost track of how many entrees we had. We never laughed so hard in our lives.

Octavia is absolutely hysterical. We were underneath the table laughing. We relaxed, laughed, ate, laughed, ordered more food, and when we said, "Okay, it's about time to leave," we ordered more food. I gained so much weight. I have fantastic memories of going out to the Crystal Grill to get a lemon pie and caramel cake. I would keep saying, "I don't eat like this. I'm a workout girl." And before I knew it, I'd eat another slice. Octavia would call me on the phone. "I'm at Crystal's getting a hamburger." All of us ate the jalapeño fried chicken on the set, the mac and cheese, the moonshine, which we drank because we were in Mississippi. There wasn't a lot to do—go to Walmart or hang out at each other's houses.

Tate is probably the best person in the business in creating a family environment. His home is always open. He leaves that door open. He cooks for you. Everybody feels like they're part of it. You're going to other people's house next, and they're cooking for you. You're cooking for them. It's naturally what happened. You feel part of a family, not just a group of actors.

New friendships were made and old ones rekindled, friendships so strong that to this day whenever I see Emma, Bryce, Jessica, Octavia, Allison, Sissy, it's absolute love and support. We were a group of women, all together, no egos, no jealousy. Being with that group of women who so easily gave up their vanity and just went for it was a huge learning curve for me. Everyone had each other's backs especially because we were in a place shooting a movie that was conjuring up a part of history when that was not happening. Right where there was separation and pain, the filming of *The Help* contributed a huge level of joy. It was a piece that demanded that we trust one another. I could not have been with better artists. Everyone was fantastic. Once again, no egos. I felt blessed to have another situation like that.

That beautiful time was juxtaposed with being in Greenwood, one of the hotbeds of the KKK, and seven miles down the road was Indianola, the birthplace of the White Citizens' Council. And Greenwood is where they found Emmett Till's body. My apartment was right there at the Tallahatchie River, the murkiest river you'd ever want to see. Ghosts of the past were still so palpable. They were another character in the film, not just the landscape of Mississippi, the history we still felt and saw.

So much poverty in the nearby town of Baptist Town compared to the rest of Greenwood. Baptist Town was the oldest Black community in Mississippi, but it hadn't had a single high school graduate in five years when we filmed *The Help* and the unemployment rate was close to 86 percent while the rest of Greenwood, Mississippi, was 16 percent. The conditions were beyond anything that I could speak about, even having grown up in poverty. Spirits called me throughout the entire filming, demanding that I honor them, the same way that young Viola demanded me to honor her.

We were housed in a fabulous apartment in Greenwood, but Julius was very nervous that something would happen to us in Mississippi while shooting. It was ghosts of history, maybe the heat, but he was so nervous about safety that he booby-trapped our front door. He set chairs underneath the doorknob. He kept a baseball bat and big piece of wood in the bedroom, so if someone broke open the door, you would hear them because of the chair underneath the door knob and we would have enough time to get up and bash somebody's head in with the bat and wood, or at least that was the plan.

Tate was great, too, because he was open to script changes, completely open to the monologue I suggested in the movie where my character talked about her son. Tate was open to it. He said, we're going to do it, Viola. And I sat with him and he's just one of those great collaborators and we wrote it.

Unfortunately, *The Help* is a movie our culture, our country was not ready for. Jack Nicholson's quote in *A Few Good Men* describes it best, "You can't handle the truth."

Another narrative took place in *The Help* that was not explored. That had absolutely nothing to do with the artists involved. It had to do with history and indictments and the fact that Aibileen was a maid. I didn't have a problem playing a maid; I don't care about someone's occupation. My misgiving was playing a character who was unexplored.

I wanted to hear how Aibileen felt about working for racist white women and about the person asking the questions—a young white woman who's coming to visit at night. Aibileen's life is on the line. Aibileen is literally almost sacrificing her life to talk to her about what it feels like to be Black in 1963, working for a white household where you can't even use the bathroom.

My other issue was when Aibileen and the others were offered money and we refused it because we were so honorable; we felt it was more important for us to tell the story than take the money. I disagree. We would have taken the money. Being honorable is fantasy. Survival and how it brings out our nature is human.

Kathryn Stockett did a wonderful job with so many aspects in the book. Aibileen was food insecure. The only food she had in her house was the preserves that her next-door neighbor gave her. If Skeeter offered her $38 and said, "I know you're putting your life on the line, but I need to know how you really feel," Aibileen is going to take the money. She's hungry. The fact that they didn't take the money, the fact that, nowhere in the course of the movie or in private, did they call any of those people a white motherfucker or anything— well, it would be how we would talk in private under those sorts of extreme circumstances.

I felt that our voices were being tethered in speaking to press. Two different, even opposing, viewpoints can be aired at the same time. I can speak my truth and so can the other side. One of my best pieces of work was in *The Help*; even the local actors who were in that scene where all the maids give their testimonies were fantastic. You can't work with better producers or actors or directors.

I loved working again with Tate in *Get on Up*. He's fantastic. Criticism of *The Help* has nothing to do with the people involved in it. It has to do with everything that has gone on, even now, with conscious/unconscious bias and microaggressions. This is the stuff we don't talk about but is threaded throughout time. I didn't know that those thoughts, feelings, and messiness weren't marketable.

I was nominated for an Oscar again in 2012, this time for best actress in *The Help*. My nomination had been for supporting actress in *Doubt*. *The Help* best actress nomination has tattooed itself in my mind because there was so much controversy coming at me after playing a maid and for being in a movie where the white gaze was so prevalent. With that nomination, I felt like I was being pitted against one of my favorites, Meryl Streep, for her role in *Iron Lady* and everyone was saying, "Let's see who wins." Very exciting for the audience. Not so much on my end.

By the time it was time for the red carpet for the *The Help* Oscars award ceremony, I had gotten shingles twice. I was that stressed out, no sleep. Not stressed out because I wanted to win, I didn't really have any feelings about that—it was stress about the pressure I felt to win.

After *The Help* Oscar nomination for female lead, I was not getting leading lady roles. I was offered five days of work on *Ender's Game*. I had ten days of work as a friend/maid in *Beautiful Creatures* and eight days of work in *Prisoners*. No one was offering me lead roles. I'm not complaining. Not at all. I was able to make a fantastic living. I'm grateful for work. I emphasize what I've already said: 95 percent of actors do not work and less than 1 percent make $50,000 or more a year. So I'm very grateful. But even after two Oscar nominations, one for best lead actress, I was not getting the same roles as my white or even some of my Black counterparts.

My career mirrored my childhood. My Blackness was as much an issue on the stage and screen as it was in my childhood. It became apparent to me that all those things that were within me still needed healing, and it also became frighteningly obvious that God was using me to be a leader in the area where I very much felt a victim.

In 2011, Julius and I formed JuVee Productions, a production company to develop film, television, and digital media. The next year, 2012, *TIME* magazine named me one of the 100 Most Influential People in the World and *Glamour* picked me as the Film Actress of the Year. Still, nobody was offering me lead roles. Except Shondaland.

I won an Emmy Award for Outstanding Lead Actress in a Drama Series for *How to Get Away with Murder* in 2014, the first African American actress to receive this award, blah, blah, blah. It's more than that. A lot more. I was forty-seven when I got *How to Get Away with Murder*.

I am a dark-skinned woman. Culturally, there is a spoken and unspoken narrative rooted in Jim Crow. It tells us that dark-skinned women are simply not desirable. All the attributes that are attached to being a woman—desirable, vulnerable, needing to be rescued—don't apply to us. In the past we've been used as chattel, fodder for inhumane experimentation, and it has evolved into invisibility. How it plays out in entertainment is that we are relegated to best friends, to strong, loudmouth, sassy lawyers, and doctors.

We are there as eye-rolling, ambiguous sidekicks. It sends a clear message that we, as a society, believe the lie that has been fed to us. A lot of Black female actors hired for certain roles, as one of my agents said, look "interchangeable" so that if you put their features on a white actress, there would be no indication that they are Black. They have to be the perfect shade of Black; not too dark to be considered ugly, but not too light that you can't tell that they are Black. I've heard these comments throughout my entire career.

As much as I hate to admit it, despite the awards, I felt cursed. I felt invisible. My healing balm came when Pete Nowalk and Shonda Rhimes offered me the role of Annalise Keating in *How to Get Away with Murder*. Everything changed.

I felt a great deal of fear. It was a leading lady role on network television. She was described as a sexual, smart, vulnerable, possibly sociopathic, highly astute, criminal defense attorney. And she had a husband, and a boyfriend. I never saw anyone on network TV who looked like me playing a role like this. It was one of those moments that I always prayed for, but suddenly it was forcing me to confront my own shortcomings. It's like the saying goes—that you have to see it to believe it. I didn't see it.

On TV and in general, womanhood is defined by how "classically" pretty you are, how dainty you are, how close to white you are. Kerry Washington was Olivia Pope, the first Black female lead actor since Diahann Carroll in Julia in 1967. I was not Kerry Washington. I know it's just a side effect of what we absorbed from systemic racism, but the bottom line is

I absolutely was not the definition of a female lead on television, especially to play a character described by all these adjectives—sexualized, sociopathic, smart.

A friend of mine was acting in a play in New York. She is Black and the cast had a lot of Black males, other Black females, and whites. It was a mixed cast. When word got out that I would play Annalise Keating, she called me. She was happy for me, but she shared the backstage conversation about my news. Many of the Black males and Black females in the cast were saying, "There's no way that show is going to work with Viola Davis in the lead. There's no way that it's going to work. She's not pretty enough. She's not feminine enough. She does not turn me on."

It is a widely held belief that dark-skinned women just don't do it for a lot of Black men. It's a mentality rooted in both racism and misogyny, that you have no value as a woman if you do not turn them on, if you are not desirable to them. It's ingrained thinking, dictated by oppression.

That eight-year-old girl in me ached in pain when my friend called. I already knew you either have to be a Black female version of a white ideal or you have to be white to play a leading lady on network television. It certainly helped that in every scene, this fictitious character named Annalise Keating found herself unapologetically standing against oppression. Still, I knew the media would say I was miscast. That beautiful moment of finding out that I got the lead role in *How to Get Away . . .* was mixed with a fucked-up moment of feeling that I didn't deserve it. Until I remembered the teachings of Sanford Meisner, who said the most important question an actor can ask is "Why?" I asked myself: *Why can't I be sexualized? Why can't I be vulnerable? Why can't I have a husband and a boyfriend? Why can't I be a leading lady?* As I continued to ask myself the question *Why?* I reached a dead end that asked me *Why not?*

An actor's work is to be an observer of life. My job is not to study other actors, because that is not studying life. As much as I can, I study people. If you're my audience, it's not my job to give you a fantasy. It is my job to give you yourself. In people there is an infinite box of different types, different situations, different behaviors. Those types contradict perceptions. They tear down preconceived notions. They are as complicated and vast as the galaxy itself. In life, I exist. We, dark-skinned women, exist. My mom had me. My mom is dark-skinned. My mom had boyfriends. My mom got married to my dad. My mom had six kids, so she obviously had sex. Someone wanted her. There are 327 million people in this country and only blond, petite, white girls are sexual?

As soon as I opened myself to the possibility of playing Annalise Keating, and using myself as the palette, I created a different character for television, and I slayed the demons within myself. At Shondaland, and on *How to Get Away with Murder*, I found my tribe. I let myself feel the fear, face the pain of my eight-year-old-ugly-girl self, but I didn't let it rule me. I used it as fuel, because, after all, you bring everything you are into a character. You bring memory, you bring triumphs, you bring pain, you bring insecurity. That is what makes a character human.

So I arrived on television in a leading actress role. Please note the word I used to describe Annalise: *sexualized*. Not *sexy*. There's a difference. I hate the word *sexy*, because sexy is a mask that you put on. It lives in women becoming a symbol of male desirability. It's not authentic. It's self-conscious. Sexualized is just another facet of you. It's a part of your self-actualization, maybe even part of your DNA. Black women who look like me are not usually allowed to be sexualized because "we don't think you're attractive."

And if we don't think you're attractive, then you aren't an innately sexual being, you don't have any anatomical sexual organs. We want to see you strong. We want to see you curse someone out. We want to see you holding a baby. Maybe you can commit a crime. We can see other values in you, but we don't see your vulnerability and we definitely don't see you as a woman. That view is perpetuated in our culture, and therefore, it metastasizes in our art. It is a lie, one that I have told in my life when I constantly apologized for my looks, by walking differently (I have very flat feet and a bunion I recently got worked on), by trying to make myself look different with wigs and lashes.

The eight-year-old girl who had never been told "You're worthy; you're beautiful" suddenly found herself as a leading lady, and a mouthpiece for all the women who looked like her. I had no weapons to slay those naysayers, to change culture itself. The obstacle blocking me was a four-hundred-year-old racist system of oppression and my own feeling of utter aloneness. My art, in this instance, was the best healing tool to resolve my past, the best weapon that I had to conquer my present, and my gift to the future.

Annalise Keating released in me the obstacles blocking me from realizing my worth and power as a woman. Before that, I created a story. Sometimes stories are straight-up lies that you make up because you want what you remember to be different. Sometimes a story is simply how YOU saw that event, how you internalized it. And sometimes the truth simply is. Simply straight-up fact. I was erasing that made-up story. I decided it was time to tell my story, as I remember it, my truth.

I said yes to the role. I answered the call to adventure, and I was on the journey and in many ways, I was on Joseph Campbell's hero's journey, redefining the world's view of Black women in America. I said a big hearty yes to this adventure. Until Annalise, I had never been complicated in movies or TV. I always tried to be more dimensional, but there wasn't enough on the page to catapult it.

In the first season of *How to Get Away with Murder*, Annalise faced off against Ophelia (Cicely Tyson's character), accusing her of failing to protect her from being molested by her uncle. It was a thrill to shoot the scene with Cicely Tyson, who turned ninety the day our scene was shot. I was working to convey all this history of sexual assault, the pain. I will never forget Miss Tyson's face when she gave her response: "It happened to all the women, that's our curse," she said with ease. "It happened to my mother. It happened to her mother." Her look revealed all the sexual assault that she'd witnessed. It was in her eyes, her demeanor. Miss Tyson showed a specific deep history that no one can teach you in school. It was exactly why I wanted to become an actor. The depth of the emotional life she was able to convey is what I have to work on.

If I were to mark the first time I fully used my voice it was in *How to Get Away with Murder*. Shonda Rhimes; Betsy Beers; my manager, Estelle; and Pete Nowalk were all on the phone making the offer. I listened to them pitch this character who was complicated: married but had a lover, could or could not be sociopathic. Her name at the time was Annalise DeWitt. I thought, *That doesn't sound like a Black woman's name*. I knew that it hadn't been written specifically for any ethnicity. It was the one time where the enormity of the job didn't restrict my voice or my needs.

I had experienced all the above in considering the role. It strengthened my character, gave me the impetus to advocate for myself. What did I advocate? "You have to allow me to take my wig off in the first season." I knew that if I asked them to write a human being, it could go either way. The TV and film business is saturated with people who think they're writing something human when it's really a gimmick. But if I took the wig off in a brutal, private moment and took off the makeup, it would force them to write for THAT woman. Taking off the wig in *HTGAWM* was my duty to honor Black women by not showing an image that is palatable to the oppressor, to people who have tarnished, punished the image of Black womanhood for so long. It said all of who we are is beautiful. Even our imperfections. With *How to Get Away with Murder*, I became an artist in the truest sense of the word.

We began filming the pilot episode in freezing cold Philadelphia in 2014. After years of playing authoritarian cops, FBI agents, ambiguous lawyers, drug addicts, it's hard to play just a woman. I hadn't been given permission. Hell, I had seldom been given that permission in life, let alone onscreen. Every image was loud and clear and emphasized how I simply don't look or sound like a woman. I'm baffled by those who are annoyed that I should even care. Of course, I care. Our level of dreaming, of self-love and acceptance, is equal to the love, support, and permission of the images around us.

Now I was Annalise DeWitt and I was not fitting into the role of Annalise DeWitt. The second big choice or ask was the change of her name. They changed it in Philadelphia to Annalise Keating. That was better but still didn't fit right. I thought that any woman trying so hard to wear the mask had probably always worn it, especially navigating a white, male-driven world. Maybe she had changed her name? My mom had changed hers. Once again, the woman I tried so hard not to be was the muse sitting on my shoulder.

My choice was that Annalise was probably Anna Mae. That choice of Anna Mae changing her name to Annalise began to shape her for me as a woman always morphing to "fit in." The extent to which she morphed to fit in was character revealing to me. Why work so hard? A dark-skinned woman operating in a primarily good-ole-white-boy world has to have day-to-day battles, but I knew from my own life that it always starts at home. What memories was she running from?

Annalise had a husband *and* a boyfriend. I'm always fascinated by sex and the impunity of sex onscreen. Especially when perpetrated by a woman. Women enjoy sex and are sexual, yet it is still one of the most unexplored terrains in my business. The engine behind our sexuality is vastly different from men. Unfortunately, as portrayed on TV and in film, female sexuality is used to tantalize. The lie that they tell actresses is that it's liberating, but the truth is that it is rarely specific and character revealing.

Here I am, as Annalise, with boyfriend, Nate Lahey, aka Billy Brown, who I would always joke with that he looked genetically modified. He was a character who I allegedly had sex with in a bar. I had to make her human. I had to somehow make this fictitious character have some semblance of realness. Most of the women I know, unfortunately, sadly, have been sexually abused. Her probable dissociative disorder could stem from that because it is prevalent in most sex abuse survivors.

Every character you play forces you to explore your

brokenness. Growing up, I experienced a frightening level of different forms of sexual abuse. It was a
basic understanding that your lot in life was to fight off
sexual predators—including babysitters and neighbors,
even before you knew the term. It was a side effect of
poverty, of parents too busy with brutal survival to
protect us 100 percent. "Ugly Black nigger" allowed
these predators to see me as not human, not a child. I
was a sexual fetish, a shameful stain that they couldn't
admit to themselves or the world. I used that for Annalise. That brokenness, mixed with her intelligence and
strength and success, felt right. Her marrying white,
sleeping Black, along with being bisexual, made her,
for me, complicated.

Some roles come along that expose your vulnerability. Annalise Keating was one of them. I had to make
peace with who I was. I was a dark-skinned woman,
close to fifty years old, in a leading role on network
television. And the chattering was already starting
about me playing this role. *Who's going to believe her
in this role? Who would believe, not just her in this
role, but anyone who even looks like her?* That's what
I heard.

I felt like I had two choices: either apologize for who
I was and try to alter how I looked to meet their stan-
dards and try to fit in to what the masses were saying;

or I could stay true to myself and make Annalise me, what I look like, what I sound like. I was at the point in my life where I chose me. That was a huge busting-out moment. I achieved on a different level than awards. I was finding me.

I'm aware of what my presence out there means to Black women. And how important it is to speak my truth. Because here's the thing you can't take away or replace: You can't replace my authentic story with a racist one. So who I am at the end of the day is absolutely in stark contrast with what society dictated I am. At the beginning of my career I didn't have much power, but now I do. Or for instance, if I presented Annalise Keating as just a strong, no-holds-barred, nonsexual, invulnerable woman who was just kick-ass in the courtroom, then that would be very inauthentic for me. Because that's not who we are as Black women. As Black women, we are complicated. We are feminine. We are sexual. We are beautiful. We're pretty. There are people out there who desire us. We are deserving. So that's why I'm very aware of what my presence means. And that's why I'm also aware of why I need to be emotionally healthy. Because that's a lot of responsibility. Because you're coming up against a four-hundred-year-old narrative.

During *How to Get Away with Murder*, Julius and

I renewed our vows. Everyone came out—my mom, sisters, Gayle King, Phylicia Rashad, Debbie Allen, and so many people Julius and I love were there, 130 people, maybe more. It was a very different wedding than the first two. I planned everything again myself. We held it at Casa Del Mar, a hotel in Santa Monica by the ocean. I had a designer, Carmen Marc Valvo, who designed beautiful dresses for me, my mom, my sisters, and Genesis.

How to Get Away with Murder was where my radical transformation took place. In the course of playing Annalise, I understood that I was no longer and never was that ugly Black nigga. The role liberated me. I said to myself: *All I've got is me. And that is enough.*

Because I had started finding me in *How to Get Away with Murder*, the making of the film *Fences* was perfect. Perfect material for the screen based on the play by August Wilson, who exhumed and exalted ordinary people. To me, the original Troy was my father Dan Davis, born in 1936, who groomed horses, had a fifth-grade education, didn't know how to read until he was fifteen years old. These characters in *Fences* were real to me, they were my life. August's material is great because he lets us bleed and he lets us talk. Rose was a fully realized character. You don't get characters like that as an actress of color. Black actresses don't often get roles where their pathology and womanhood are fully explored. We're the fourth, fifth, ninth lead. We come on and say a few powerful and sassy words and then your ass is gone and that's your only contribution. But *Fences* was a well-made narrative, with the right director to pull it all together.

Denzel is that actor's director. He knows how to use one word or make you add in one gesture that can unlock your performance. If you are confused, he knows it. He discerns when you're not in your body. He knows when a moment does not ring true and he will stop it if he doesn't believe it. He forced me to go deeper as Rose in the film by saying something very powerful, "Remember the love. . . . Don't play the pain and betrayal, play the woman fighting hard to restore the love."

In ten cycles of plays that August Wilson wrote (often referred to as his Century Cycle), he portrayed Black American life in every decade in the twentieth century. So, you get a history lesson, but you also get to sit with us as human beings and see how that time period affected us. In *Fences*, Rose is a housewife who just wants to keep her family together. She is an absolute product of the 1950s, suppressing her own dreams, even being cheated on after she gives her whole life to her family.

In the play *Fences* I never hit that final scene. Onstage, I always felt that it never worked. It's an occupational hazard: sometimes you just have emotional blocks that affect your ability to be able to fully play out a scene truthfully. In the scene, Cory comes home after being estranged from his father for ten years or more. Their relationship was always broken, Cory had always been haunted by feelings of never being loved or liked by his father. So the final scene is him coming back for his father's burial. And the scene starts with him saying, "Mom, I'm not going to Daddy's funeral."

I just never know how to make a choice in this scene and how to respond to Cory's statement and his pain. When I did it onstage, I was not a mother yet, but when we filmed *Fences* I was. In the film it was my chance to hit that final scene. The complexity of healing and forgiveness suddenly materialized for me. And I realized that your depth of understanding of yourself is equal to the depth of understanding a character. We are after all observers of life. We are after all a conduit, a channeler of people. What you haven't resolved in your life can absolutely become an obstacle in the work that you do. Denzel's advice to me to unlock the scene was to start the scene by slapping Cory. I froze. I said, "I can't do that. No way!"

Denzel pushed me, "He is a big guy. He can take it. Go ahead and slap him."

I said, "No way!" and he replied, "Do it and see where the scene goes."

I froze. Then, I slapped Cory.

Denzel egged me on, "Slap him again."

So I slapped him again. And again. Suddenly, Rose's anger with Cory's announcement that he was not attending his father's funeral mixed with both of their pain and reconciling with the resentment and fractured relationships within the family. All that culminated into forgiveness. It was so suddenly released. It started with that slap. And with each slap, as God would have it, I thought of my mom. I thought of the difficulty of motherhood. Reconciling your pain. Fulfilling your needs and at the same time sacrificing, juggling the huge task of binding the family together. Shelving your dreams and hopes. I felt her. Fully . . . and it was beautiful.

Denzel will guide you to the truth. Sometimes, lovingly brutal, he will force you to be simpler. Perhaps that is the reason that this scene worked beautifully in the film. In terms of the ensemble, except for Jovan Adepo and Saniyya Sydney, I filmed *Fences* with the same group of actors I performed with on Broadway— Mykelti Williamson, Russell Hornsby, and Stephen McKinley Henderson—the most wonderful artists I've ever worked with. Shooting in the Hill district of Pittsburgh, the birthplace of August Wilson and the setting of all his plays, the protectiveness of the community made me feel safe.

I haven't had a lot of princess moments in my life. I've never been comfortable in princess moments because I never felt like a princess. For the first time, I experienced what it feels like to know you deserve something. Not the feeling that you're the best, not at all. Rather, like your hard work over the years meant something and amalgamated into this "perfect" moment.

I had a goal. I saw it. I worked for it. I achieved it. It's not so much about getting the Oscar for *Fences* but rather for shooting a movie that gave me so much joy. It almost was like a fireworks display. Even if the Oscar had never happened, it would have still been a defining moment. It was an overflow of blessings that I could not even possibly have imagined for myself.

What I have realized since is that those moments of feeling alive are part of a continuum. You find that moment. You bask in it. Then as soon as it passes, life becomes about chasing the next moment. I now understand that life, and living it, is more about being present. I'm now aware that the not-so-happy memories lie in wait; but the hope and the joy also lie in wait.

The filming of *Fences* took six weeks. The Oscar

campaigning in award season lasted for five months. It was almost six months of an awesome ride, not even a year in my life, yet it was an incredible marker. I'm not just talking about a marker in terms of holding the award but getting to a mindset of believing that I deserved the moment of joy and feeling worthy of a real experience that had only existed in my dreams. "A perfect moment in my imperfect story," a moment in my life that I can remember feeling alive.

Everything—history and activism as well as the perfect material, cast, and director—had culminated to create that Cinderella moment when I strode to the podium to accept the Oscar. It was perfect. The entire evening was a perfect memory.

Memory is powerful. Powerful hardships as well as powerful successes make up a life fully lived . . . my life. My dearest joy is the joyful moments and memories of loving and being present in my daughter's growth and development, the special relationship and memories of pure joy just loving my husband, cherishing the life that we continue to build, and moments and memories of my life as a working actor.

There's the factual part of memory that has to do with details, timeline, but the other part of memory is abstract. How did I feel when this was happening? What did I want at that time? If the memory is bad, you try to forget it. Or you change the memory in order to survive. I am surprised that one of my most powerful memories involves me getting on my knees. It's what happens when there are no answers in this world and no access to getting the answers.

My friend Edwina asked me how I got to where I am today. How did I claw my way out of poverty? That question always baffles me. Mostly because I simply don't know. Oftentimes, honestly, I just feel I got lucky. But . . . this day, without hesitation, I told her a story of when I was nine years old. It flowed out of me as if some powerful force was pulling it out.

In the middle of the night, I witnessed my dad attempting to break my mom's legs. She ran out of the house and was hiding in a woodsy area down our dead-end street waiting for my dad to calm down. She finally tried to sneak back but he was hiding in our front yard with a thick wooden stick and began to beat her violently in her legs. She screamed like an animal. He kept whacking and beating. My sisters and I ran outside in a panic. No one came out to help. No one looked out their windows despite the close confines of the homes. I screamed. I screamed a primal, earth-shattering scream as if willing it to stop. But I couldn't stop the whacking. My sister Dianne shook me and yelled, "Stop screaming!" But I couldn't. My other sisters tried to shush me and I couldn't stop screaming. Finally, my sister Dianne yelled, "Just go in the house!" I ran in the house, still screaming.

I ran into the bathroom, where I often escaped, and slammed the door. I fell to my knees in front of the toilet and screamed, "God! If you love me, you would take me away from this place! I don't want to be here anymore! I'm going to close my eyes and count to ten. And when I open them, I better be gone or I'll know you don't exist! One. Two. Three . . ." I kept my eyes shut, really believing that God would take me. ". . . Eight . . . Nine . . . TEN!" Silence. I opened my eyes. I was still there. Alone. Aware of my aloneness. I said softly, "I knew you didn't exist."

Edwina stood staring at me. Holding her breath. I didn't know why I was being led by some invisible force to tell *this* story.

"God did take me," I said.

We stood there. Her a believer in God and his power. Me? A believer but . . . not a believer in my worthiness. But this magical alchemy of her presence and the power of that question was forcing me to acknowledge this big boulder of truth.

"He took me on his terms, Edwina," I said as if discovering it for the first time.

I supplicated like the Kanyala women in The

Gambia, screaming, laughing, singing out to God so that he can hear them. Screaming to make my heart known . . . to be saved. Everything that transpired in my life after that was a mixture of magic, hope, mentors, lovers, friendships, gifts that were like leap pads that carried me.

After that bathroom incident there was no more escaping. No escape routes. My spirit was plucked but my body was kept right in the same place because it was the only way that, when I gained vision and strength and forgiveness, I could remember what being in trauma means. I could remember what it means to be a child who is hungry. I could remember poverty, alcoholism, abuse. I could remember what it feels like to be a child who dreams and sees no physical manifestation of it. I could see it and be amazed by my power to survive it. I lived it! I was there! And that has been my biggest gift in understanding the act of serving and my biggest gift in embodying other human beings.

The question still echoes, how did I claw my way out? There is no out. Every painful memory, every mentor, every friend and foe served as a chisel, a leap pad that has shaped "ME!" The imperfect but blessed sculpture that is Viola is still growing and still being chiseled. My elixir? I'm no longer ashamed of me. I own everything that has ever happened to me.

The parts that were a source of shame are actually my warrior fuel. I see people—the way they walk, talk, laugh, and grieve, and their silence—in a way that is hyperfocused because of my past. I'm an artist because there's no separation from me and every human being that has passed through the world including my mom. I have a great deal of compassion for other people, but mostly for myself. That would not be the case if I did not reconcile that little eight-year-old girl and FIND ME.

I'm holding her now. My eight-year-old self. Holding her tight. She is squealing and reminding me, "Don't worry! I'm here to beat anybody's ass who messes with our joy! Viola, I got this."